God

A Guide for the Perplexed

ABOUT THE AUTHOR

Professor Keith Ward is a Fellow of the British Academy, and Professorial Research Fellow at Heythrop College, London. He was formerly Regius Professor of Divinity at the University of Oxford, and is one of Britain's foremost writers on comparative theology and Christian issues. Notable works written by Keith Ward and published by Oneworld include *Christianity: A Beginner's Guide*, *God Chance & Necessity*, and *God, Faith, and the New Millennium*.

God

A Guide for the Perplexed

KEITH WARD

ONEWORLD

*The author would like to express his gratitude to
Mel Thompson and Mary Starkey for their valuable and helpful
suggestions regarding this book.*

© Keith Ward 2002

First published in hardback by Oneworld in 2002
This paperback edition published in 2013

ISBN 978-1-85168-973-6
ebook ISBN: 978-1-78074-122-2

Typeset by LaserScript, Mitcham, UK
Printed and bound by CPI Group (UK) Ltd, Croydon, CR0 4YY

Oneworld Publications
10 Bloomsbury Street
London
WC1B 3SR

Stay up to date with the latest books,
special offers, and exclusive content from
Oneworld with our monthly newsletter

Sign up on our website
www.oneworld-publications.com

Contents

I

A feeling for the gods

In which the reader will discover what happened in Book One of the Iliad, *will discover many curious facts about Greek gods and goddesses, will remark a strange similarity between English Romantic poets and German theologians, will come to suspect that Descartes, though he doubted everything, did not quite doubt enough, will find Schleiermacher lying on the bosom of the infinite world, will discover what terrified Professor Otto, and why certain German professors talk to trees, will be forced to distinguish between symbolic and literal speech, and may develop a feeling for the gods.*

God, literalism and poetry

Traditional images of God seem to have lost their appeal in modern American and European culture. It is not that God's existence has been disproved – philosophers continue to debate the proofs inconclusively, and no informed and honest observer of the philosophical scene really thinks a case has been established either way, or ever will be. No, God has simply become boring and irrelevant. We no longer care for big men with white beards. We no longer feel the weight of tremendous guilt that drove the Pilgrim onto his Progress. Jesus has sunk into the pages of irrecoverable history, and it seems impossible to draw him out again in a new resurrection which might make him a powerful image of infinity for more than a tiny handful of our contemporaries.

The sad thing – and it is sad, for it is a loss of a kind of perception, the atrophy of a distinctively human way of seeing – is that there seems to be nothing to replace such images, to show us how 'to be one with the infinite in the midst of the finite and to be eternal in a moment' (Schleiermacher, *Speeches on Religion,* second speech, 1799).

Spirituality, the cultivation of exalted states of consciousness, may thrive in the borderlands of our culture, but religion, the organised official cult of worship of God, is dying. This is most obvious in Europe, where places of pilgrimage have become tourist attractions, churches have become architectural monuments, and religious rituals have become performances to be observed by anthropologists with camcorders. But in America too, while popular religion remains strong, there is a widespread intellectual revulsion against organised religion. There is a hostility to the seemingly naive biblical literalism of many Christian churches, which is met by an equal hostility on their part to many of the teachings of modern science. In the furious battles about creationism and fundamentalism, it often seems that we in our age have simply lost a sense of what religion is really about. We argue about theories and doctrines and facts which are very hard to establish, and in the process we reduce religion to a sort of argumentative and speculative science. We very often seem to lack a feeling for God or for the gods, the primal vision which lies at the roots of religion.

Why is this? I think it is partly because people have come to take the traditional images of God too literally. In an age where science is the queen of the academy, it is widely thought that the literal, the countable and weighable real, is the true, and the only form of truth. So God, if there is a God, must be the sort of being the sciences could describe – God must be a super-person, making differences to the world which we can test and verify. God must be a cause whose effects we can discover by experiment and observation. Yet that God has turned out to be superfluous to requirements. God is, to put it bluntly, redundant. No special divine effects have ever been recorded in the laboratories of science, and science explains the world very well without God. So that God, the God who ought to be another fact that we can record and document, seems to have disappeared from the modern world.

This prompts the thought that maybe what has gone wrong is the idea of God as a sort of literal extra fact. But what else could God be? To discover that, we might need to return to the roots of religious belief in human experience, and try to see how talk of God, or of the gods, arises and what it is meant to express. Is there such a thing as a feeling for the gods, which the modern emphasis on factual knowledge has somehow suppressed? It may be illuminating to look at one of the earliest literary works in Western history, Homer's *Iliad*. The subject of the epic is the Trojan war, but it is filled with references to the gods, who appear to its human characters, take part in their battles and ultimately dictate their fortunes. The *Iliad* could be read as a literal text, for which clearly fictional supernatural persons walk and talk with Greek and Trojan warriors. Indeed, the *New Shorter Oxford English Dictionary* suggests such an interpretation:

> **god** – 'a superhuman person regarded as having power over nature and human fortunes'.

But the *Iliad* is, after all, poetry, and so we may suspect that Homer (let us follow tradition in allowing there to be such a poet who is the author) is doing something else with his stories of the gods, something that may still have the power of shedding light on human experience, and counteracting the sense of irrelevance that God and the gods now so often seem to have. The gods and goddesses might not have been thought of as real persons, who lived on top of Mount Olympus, who feasted and quarrelled and indulged in plots of many sorts. After all, Mount Olympus was not too difficult to climb, and it could quickly be discovered that Zeus had no palace on top of it. Perhaps if we explore the *Iliad* as poetry, we might gain a better sense of the feelings that Homer was seeking to express in writing as he did of the gods.

A world full of gods

'Sing, goddess, of the anger of Achilles ...' So begins the *Iliad*. Here is a god, or at least a goddess, already, in the first line. The poet is not telling someone else to write the poem for him. Or is he? The goddess will sing through him. He will write the words, but they will come from a source from beyond his conscious mind, from an inspiring power, creative, expressive, truly supernatural since it is beyond the natural powers of most humans (who are not all poets, thank goodness).

Homer conjures up the goddess or her power to infuse his mind, filling it with imaginative power and beauty. That is not just some archaic, primitive fantasy. It is a wholly contemporary fantasy, too. When we sit down to write that great novel which, we are told, lies within each of us, we wait for the Muse to inspire us. Unfortunately, the Muse usually seems to be on vacation, and the great book does not get written.

> **muse** – Each of nine (occasionally more) goddesses, the daughters of Zeus and Mnemosyne (memory), regarded as the inspirers of learning and the arts, especially of poetry and music again (the *New Shorter OED*).

There is something almost supernatural about Homer, about Mozart and Bach, about Leonardo and Rembrandt. Mozart, we are told, could be a puerile prankster, but sublime music poured out of him. I sometimes look intently at pictures of J.S. Bach, as if trying to discern the genius, the difference that marks him out from other men. But however hard I look, he just looks quite ordinary, a bourgeois gentleman in a conventional wig, with a rather plebeian, fleshy, complacent face. Where is the B minor mass, the St Matthew passion, the hundreds of deeply moving chorales? Not written on his face, anyway. Amazingly, all those beautiful, passionate, inspired faces with flowing hair, high foreheads, aquiline noses and piercing eyes seem to belong to actors, who could not write a note of music. The trouble with the really great is that they look like gardeners (no offence). The aristocrats of the spirit, the gods of art, tend to have coarse features and bulbous noses. (I am thinking of Rembrandt, admittedly. You must admit he does have a rather bulbous nose.)

Well, obviously then, these flesh-and-blood individuals can't be the source of all that beauty of sound and vision, that miraculous order and heart-wrenching feeling. They are taken over, those earthy instruments, and used by the daughters of memory to spin evanescent images of the immortal world in which the gods, the truly beautiful, play.

This is the first lesson to learn about the gods. They are poetic, symbolic constructs of human imagination. The Muses, the nine goddesses, are not pretty young women who live on top of Mount Olympus with their parents, and come down to earth every now and then to write poems and sing songs. The Muses are imaginative symbols of the creative energies of wisdom and beauty which seem to inspire rare human individuals (but maybe most of us very occasionally), and which come and go, as if from beyond the control of the conscious mind.

Why nine? The number corresponds to the various different sorts of creativeness – singing, playing, dancing, etc. – that were distinguished in ancient Greece.

Why young women? Because masculinity has tended to be associated, certainly in ancient Greece, with the virtues of war – courage, heroism and aggressiveness. In the *Iliad* the young men spend all their time either killing one another or thinking of better ways to kill one another. Femininity is more associated with care, sensitivity, and the virtues of leisure and home life. The nine Muses symbolise the 'softer' creative energies of song and dance, rather than the more savage energies of storm and sea.

Why the daughters of Zeus and of memory? 'Memory' is taken in a very wide sense here, to mean the whole store of knowledge and experience that exists in a human mind. The creative energies of wisdom and art use that store of experience to fashion stories and images which give new insights into the human condition. They are 'daughters' in the

Apollo dances decorously with nine buxom Muses in this painting by the Italian artist Baldassarre Peruzzi.

sense that they spring from, or arise out of, the mind's store of experienced images and feelings. They also spring from Zeus, who is the final controlling will of all things in human life, and so they act under the general will of the ultimate creative energy underlying this human world.

So these goddesses are constructs of the human imagination? Yes – they are not 'superhuman persons', real distinct individuals who have parents, brothers and sisters. In their particular form and number, they are products of art. They are, in short, symbols and not real living persons, superhuman or otherwise.

But that does not mean they are false. They represent deep and important powers which can transform human life. The creative energies of art inspire and enthuse human beings. They possess human lives and transport them beyond the everyday. They arise from the mind's experiences (and so are daughters of Memory), and express the hidden things of human reality, the ultimate causes of human life (and so are daughters of Zeus), in indirect and mysterious ways. Any aspiring artists would be well advised to invoke the Muse, to raise their minds to superhuman insights and, hopefully, fashion immortal works of beauty.

The creative energies are not persons. But they are addressed as persons. And what that says is that the energies that set boundaries to human life, some of which can be channelled through human consciousness in moments of 'possession' or inspiration, are not simply impersonal unconscious forces. They have something akin, however remotely akin, to human will and consciousness.

This is the second lesson to learn about the gods. To see the world as 'full of gods', as the Greeks did, is to see the world as fundamentally personal in nature. Many of its active energies have or express something like purpose (will) and responsiveness to environment (consciousness). That sense has been completely lost to many in the modern world. If we see nature as the Great Machine, of which we are tiny computerised parts, then the personal aspects of nature will become invisible. Many people see the progress of modern European thought in this way. Enter the Great Villain, with a Faustian promise of complete knowledge and control of nature, and a determination to drive the gods out of the machine altogether.

Descartes and the cosmic machine

The French philosopher **René Descartes** (1596–1650) thought, therefore he was, but he was not what he thought he was. He had thought he was a living, feeling person, but what he discovered, apparently by sitting for a long time in a hot stove, was that he was essentially a purely thinking thing, whose body was a sort of optional extra.

This is a bit of a travesty, but it is true that Descartes divided reality into two sorts of things, bodies – which are spread out in space and visible to everyone – and minds – which are not in space at all and are quite invisible to everyone but their private owners and occupiers. In the mind all sorts of interesting things can happen – free will, logic and mathematics, feelings of happiness and, unfortunately, physical pain. But the body is a machine which proceeds in accordance with deterministic laws of physics, and is totally unfeeling and unconscious.

Body and mind had to be connected, and the obvious place to connect them was the brain. (Descartes suspected the pineal gland specifically, which was a bad guess, as it turned out. But the brain was right, and a much better bet than the stomach, which was where the Greeks placed their thoughts – thinking that the brain was a sort of air-conditioner.)

However – and this was the villainy – Descartes believed that only humans had minds. Other animals only had brains, with no minds in them. Animals were not conscious, and they were not free agents. They were just machines, and could be dissected and experimented on and pieced together in various ways just like watches or steam engines.

More recent philosophers have not been impressed with the idea that chimpanzees, whose DNA differs from ours by only one per cent, are just machines, while we are free and responsible agents. Surprisingly, however, many philosophers have not concluded that chimpanzees really have free will. What they have concluded is that we do not. They agree with Descartes that chimpanzees have no consciousness and free choice, but add that humans have none either. Consciousness is just a function of the physical brain, and freedom is the feeling that our brains have not yet decided what to do. Will and consciousness are driven out of the universe altogether, and replaced by the laws of physics, which make the little bits of matter out of which our brains are made act in extremely complicated but totally automatic ways.

Obviously, if human minds have been driven out of the universe, there is not much room for the gods. But the gods have been defeated, not by a human hero, but by a set of rather inefficient robots (a latter-day description of *Homo sapiens*) which suffer from the illusion that they are something special – and which will themselves probably be superseded by a more efficient set of machines which are even now on the horizon, as the supercomputer Deep Blue beats the human world chess champion resoundingly.

Now, Descartes himself believed in God, just as he believed in the immortal soul, which would go on doing allegedly interesting things like pure mathematics long after its body had rotted in the grave. But his God did not have much to do. Having designed and set up the perfect machine, God was virtually redundant. According to one of the philosophical successors of Descartes, Gottfried von Leibniz, if anyone prayed to God to ask God to change the future, God would have to say, 'My dear sir, I have already designed everything for the best. If I changed the future to suit you, it would only make things worse. So please stop praying; it is interfering with my perfect design.'

Wordsworth and Blake: the gods and poetic imagination

But all this was going to happen about two-and-a-half thousand years after the *Iliad*. In the ancient Greek world, still full of gods and unaware that it was really a machine, prayers were a very important part of military strategy. The story of the *Iliad* begins with an insult to a priest of Apollo, which has dire results for the Greek army besieging Troy.

> **Apollo** – originally the patron of shepherds: after his installation at Delphi he acquired power over archery, music and medicine. As Phoebus Apollo, he is the god of the sun (*A Dictionary of World Mythology*).

Chryses, a priest of Apollo whose daughter had been captured by the Greeks, came to King Agamemnon with a ransom for her, but King Agamemnon refused the money and sent him packing. The priest prayed to his god to avenge this insult, and, Homer relates of Apollo: 'Down he came from the peaks of Olympus with anger in his heart, his bow on his shoulders, and the enclosing quiver.' He shot his arrows at the Greek army, and they were felled by the plague. The plague did not end until the priest's daughter was returned to him, and a hecatomb (a hundred oxen) or two was sacrificed to Apollo. The Greeks offered the sacrifice. They all shared the meat (a great amount, one would think), and drank in honour of the god (also a great amount, no doubt). So they 'appeased the god with music, singing a lovely hymn and dancing ... and he listened with delight in his heart'.

Poetic imagination is hard at work here, seeing the plague which raged through the Greek camp as the arrows of the archer god. As with the Muses, it is hard to believe that Homer did really think a young man flew down from a mountain with his bow and arrow. He depicts the furious energy of the plague as the arrows of an angry god. This is not exactly creative energy. It is destructive energy, but it is certainly energy. The Greeks saw that many of the energies of the world were far from creative. Hurricane, earthquake, storm and plague – these are gigantic energies, and they course through the world, apparently indifferent to human fate.

When we get through the veil of literalisation, we see that we are not dealing with quarrels among a race of superhuman persons. We are dealing with the raw energies of the natural world, beautiful and terrifying in their power. We can see that there was really no Apollo, who enjoyed the roasted meat, the poured wine and scattered barley-grains, the songs and the dances. But Apollo stands for something real, something the modern world has lost, a sort of perception of the world that is now very difficult, but not impossible, to recapture.

For a scientific, post-Cartesian, mind, we relate to nature by poking about in it and tinkering with it. We look for the causes of disease, and try to counter them with anti-viral drugs. Very sensible, too, and few would recommend sacrificing a hundred cows to Apollo instead of taking antibiotics. Antibiotics are much more reliable, since who knows whether Apollo will like our sacrifices or not?

Still, there may be another way of relating to nature. As we might expect by now, art and imagination give the clue.

> I have felt
> A presence that disturbs me with the joy
> Of elevated thoughts; a sense sublime
> Of something far more deeply interfused,
> Whose dwelling is the light of setting suns,
> And the round ocean and the living air,

And the blue sky, and in the mind of man:
A motion and a spirit, that impels
All thinking things, all objects of all thought,
And rolls through all things.

WORDSWORTH; 'Lines composed a few miles above Tintern
Abbey', 13 July, 1798, *The Penguin Book of English Verse*, p. 262

Even after Descartes, something stirs beneath the machine. Something 'interfused', 'deep' and 'rolling'. What can it be? Is it nothing but engine oil? Or is this sense of presence a symptom of the suspicion that the machine itself is a construct of the human mind, and an especially desiccated and abstract one at that? When the god is evicted from the machine, the machine becomes god, but a particularly impersonal, heartless, disinterested god, indifferent to all purposes, intentions and values, and to all things human. The English Romantic poets rebelled against that vision.

William Blake (1757–1827) has the distinction of having painted one of the most frequently misinterpreted pictures in the history of art. Publisher after publisher has used his painting *The Ancient of Days* on the cover of books about God. The solid human figure in the sun, shattering the dark clouds of chaos with shafts of light, white hair and beard flowing, holding in his left hand a pair of compasses as if to measure out the universe that he is about to create, has become an image of God comparable to the equally human figure by Michelangelo on the ceiling of the Sistine Chapel. It is a powerful image, clearly irresistible to publishers.

Yet what Blake meant to portray in this painting was not the true and living God, but the pseudo-God of Newton, of the machine. His compasses are measuring out the universe. They represent the mechanistic approach to nature, always measuring, dissecting and putting things in their place. This is, for Blake, the Great Mathematician, the killer of life and joy, the supreme artificer and impartial surveyor of all things.

The picture publishers cannot resist – The Ancient of Days, by William Blake.

The greatest of all Scottish philosophers, David Hume (who during his life was never considered good enough to be appointed to a chair in philosophy at any Scottish university), died in 1776. In his posthumously published *Dialogues Concerning Natural Religion,* he analysed in devastating detail the arguments that were then fashionable from the evidences of design in the universe to the existence of the Great Designer in the Sky. It was precisely that designer god to whom Blake was so completely opposed. If we had come to a stage in religion where God could not be discerned within the universe, but had to be inferred from the elegant construction of an unconscious and purposeless cosmic machine, religion had already died. 'We do not want inferred friends,' remarked a once-famous Oxford philosopher. The believer does not want an inferred God, a compass-wielding God, whose existence depends on the strength and validity of the arguments that philosophers devise for proving or disproving his likely existence.

What then does the believer want? Blake the poet knew:

> To see a World in a Grain of Sand
> And a Heaven in a Wild Flower,
> Hold Infinity in the palm of your hand
> And Eternity in an hour.
>
> 'Auguries of Innocence', *Penguin Book of English Verse,*
> p. 243

In this Blake and Wordsworth are in entire agreement. The authentic religious sense is to discern infinity and eternity in the bounded and transient, to see in all particular forms of beauty a Beauty which is unlimited in perfection and everlasting in value. The sense of an interfused presence, living in the light and air and sky, and in the mind of man: the sense of such a presence, splitting, like light, into a thousand glittering shafts of individuality, each taking on the character of its own environment: the sense of a world filled with presences sublime and interfused, many and yet one, beautiful and harsh, wine-dark and rose-fingered: that is the sense of the gods, who excite human reverence and awe, dread and delight.

Conflict among the gods

Wordsworth's sense of the gods was very English. Dove Cottage, now the mecca of thousands of tourists, filling the roads in droves in their search for the solitude and tranquillity of Wordsworth's poetic visions, was once a small isolated cottage in a rain-green valley. No tornadoes or hurricanes disturb the gentle drizzle of the rain, shot through on rare occasions with a sun which does not burn or scorch. No vast deserts or bare mountains interrupt the vistas of rounded hills, leafy trees and tastefully purple moorlands. There is, it is true, a hint of danger and risk, in the rushing mountain streams and the fogs which descend on the sharp crags. It is possible to get lost or fall among the rocks, but it takes a bit of effort to do so. It is more likely that one will wander lonely as a cloud among a host of golden daffodils, feeling how beautiful and gentle nature is, how bountiful her gifts, and how very kind she is to grant such great beauty at so little cost.

Greece, too, is beautiful. Thousands of tourists, fed up with the incessant rain at Dove Cottage, book package holidays to Greece, and lie on the beaches in wine-soaked stupor: worshippers of the sun, offering up their bodies in sacrifice to Apollo the shining one, god of the sun and now, perhaps, of package holidays.

But in the days before bottled water, flush lavatories and frozen lasagne flown in from factories in Athens, the sun was an enemy as well as a friend to life. The search for water and shade was serious. And when the rains came, they beat down in torrents, with winds raging from the sea and storms threatening homes and human lives in their fury. In the Mediterranean world, nature is harsh as well as beautiful. The gods are not by any means wholly benevolent. What presence is to be discerned in the earthquake and hurricane? Not the gentle green goddess of Cumbria and the English lakes, but the thunder and lightning of Zeus, warrior god and victor over the Titans, and the burning arrows of the sun god, who so often kills that to which he has given life.

For the ancient Greeks, there was not one infinite presence 'rolling through all things'. There was a multitude of presences, some benevolent and some threatening, all unreliable, and the Greek religious sense was not that either of a Romantic English poet or of an even more comfortable international tourist. It was of something ambiguous or many-sided. The intrigues and quarrels of the gods of Olympus express the uncertainties and conflicts of the energies of the natural order, of sun and storm, fertility and death, victory and plague.

There was little or no idea of one supreme creator God, according to whose will everything happens. The creative and destructive energies of the cosmos relate to one another in an almost haphazard way. They have wills of their own. In the first book of the *Iliad*, Athene, power of war and wisdom, restrains Achilles' anger at the request of Hera, power of earth and protectress of the Greeks. Achilles, smarting under his humiliation by King Agamemnon, goes to talk to his mother, Thetis, a goddess who is the daughter of Nereus, a god of the sea. Thetis is the power of sea-mist: 'She rose up from the grey sea like a mist ... she rose through the swell of the sea at early morning, and went up to the vast sky.' She pleads with Zeus to find a way to bring honour to her son, Achilles, and he agrees to her request. Then Hera, wife of Zeus, attacks Zeus with words, accusing him of making secret plots without her knowledge. A quarrel ensues, with Zeus asserting his ultimate power over the gods. All ends harmoniously, however, as Hephaistos, power of fire and trickery, persuades all the gods to a feast, and Apollo plays the lyre as they descend into uncontrollable laughter and sleep.

At one level, this is a simple story of intrigues in the court of the gods, who interfere in human affairs at will, look down at human joys and tragedies with distant amusement, and are easily appeased by vast amounts of roast meat and wine. And of course Homer is telling a story, and he is concerned with developing the characters of the gods in various ways, and involving them in an Olympian soap opera of his own devising (soap opera: a serial story dealing with sentimental or melodramatic domestic themes, so called because they were first sponsored on American radio and television by soap manufacturers).

It is also possible that Homer was an early example of the ancient Greek scepticism about the gods that characterised the plays, about three or four hundred years later, of Sophocles and Aristophanes. To that extent he was able to write about the awe-inspiring powers worshipped devoutly in an earlier age in a very human and humorous way. Homer, together with Hesiod (author of the *Theogony,* the first attempt to give a systematic genealogy of the gods), was said to have 'given the Greeks their gods', But perhaps in fact in Homer's work the gods were already losing their ancient power.

Yet even in the first book of the *Iliad* one can discern traces of a more archaic sense of that power. When Achilles decides not to fight Agamemnon, it is Athene, wisdom, 'visible to him alone', who restrains him. That wisdom is prompted by the thought of the well-being of the Greek army in general ('the white-armed goddess Hera sent me, as she loves both of you alike'). Achilles sits by the sea as the morning sun draws the mist from the sea, to ponder his future. However unfathomable it is, all this will be 'the working of Zeus' will'. That will is hidden even from the immortals.

But the powers have their own purposes. Thetis, mother and protectress of Achilles, cares for the honour of her son. Hera, protectress of the Greeks, cares for the preservation of the Greek army from destruction. The powers that care for humans are divided: 'There was uproar among the heavenly gods.' Each spiritual power has its own devotees. Like the guardian angels of later Christianity, when their devotees come into conflict, so do they. The honour of Achilles contends against the safety of the Greek army. The gods are the projections of this conflict onto the Olympian screen.

Ultimately, however, the will of Zeus prevails, and the best thing is for the gods to make their peace with their father Zeus. Although there is little sense of one all-determining will, there is an awareness of a power which is 'far stronger than all of us'. It may listen, it may be cajoled, it may scold, and it may even sulk. But in the end, as Zeus says to Thetis, 'no word of mine can be revoked, or prove false, or fail of fulfilment, when I nod my head in assent to it'.

So, though there is often conflict among the gods, harmony is possible, when the Muses sing, Apollo plays, the wine is poured, and the gods laugh. Human destiny will play itself out, through all the conflicts of purpose and desire, until in the end, just possibly, the world may reflect, as in a mirror, the laughter of the gods.

Right at the beginning of Homer's epic we see the wisdom and honour of Achilles, the precarious situation of the Greek army, made up as it was of potentially conflicting city-states, the ultimate power of destiny, and the possibility of reconciliation by submission to that inscrutable power. All these factors are symbolised in the acts of the gods, active powers which determine the future, and which work in and through the events of history, the forces of nature, and the minds and hearts of men.

It should not be thought that this is a reduction of the gods to 'mere symbols' of natural powers and processes. The gods are symbols. But what is symbolised is not 'natural', in the sense of being purely physical, or explicable in terms of laws of physics or the other experimental sciences alone. The gods do not symbolise natural phenomena. It would be truer to say that they empower natural phenomena to symbolise other powers that lie beyond them. Nor do the gods symbolise what is 'supernatural', in the sense of being a sort of immaterial duplicate of the material, a shadow world which mimics this substantial world in a ghostly way. What then is symbolised?

There is a story of a Russian ballerina who gave a superbly moving performance at the Kirov Ballet, leaving the audience enraptured at what they knew to be a uniquely inspired occasion. Afterwards, she was asked, 'And what did it mean?' 'What did it mean?', she responded, 'What did it mean? If I could say what it meant, I would not have danced it.'

So it is with speaking of the gods. If we could say in other words what such speech meant, we would not need to use such language. We could drop the symbols, and talk of literal facts. 'Zeus is the thunder storm', we might say, or 'Thetis is the sea-mist'. But then why continue to speak of Zeus and Thetis at all? Well of course the fact is that we do not speak of them any longer. We have all become literalists about the world we live in. We know the thunder and we know the sea. But the Greek gods departed from Olympus-long ago. Where did they go? What have we lost, in ceasing to speak of them? Is the world the poorer for their departing?

Wordsworth and Blake would tell us, or many of us, that we have lost the sense of presences deeply interfused in light and ocean, air and sky, of the whole world seen in a grain of sand and infinity held in the palm of a hand. We have lost the language that makes these things possible, and we have no other words that can evoke again the vanished awareness of the sacredness of the reality in which we exist and of which we are part.

Friedrich Schleiermacher: a Romantic account of the gods

While Wordsworth was swooning sensuously in Dovedale, over in Berlin a minister of the Reformed (Calvinist) Church was writing a set of speeches aimed at the 'Cultured Despisers of Religion'.

Friedrich Schleiermacher (1768–1834), who has the singular misfortune that no English-speaking student can spell his name correctly, much less pronounce it, was doing his bit to sabotage the cosmic machine.

Calvinists sometimes have a bad name among those devoted to the arts. Did they not ban dancing, cards, theatres and other enjoyable pastimes, and make Sunday the most boring day of the week for generations of Puritans? If that is the image you have of Calvinists, Schleiermacher will come as quite a surprise – even though he became one of the most successful preachers in Berlin. He was aware that many cultured people viewed religion as a narrow sectarian affair, issuing sets of largely reactionary moral rules and unintelligible dogmas, and instilling the fear of a vengeful God or the hope for an illusory heaven into anyone it could catch in its net.

In the *Speeches* he set out to dispel that impression, and he tried to do so by going back to the roots of religion in the human psyche. He suggested that religion is not really about creeds and speculative beliefs, which are largely devised by desiccated old men who have nothing better to do. And it is not about moral rules handed down from some Mediterranean mountain, which perpetuate old tribal taboos for which everyone has forgotten the reason, if there ever was one. Religion, he said, is 'the sensibility and taste for the infinite'. It is a matter of intuition or feeling: 'Religion's essence is neither thinking nor acting but intuition and feeling' (from the *Second Speech*).

It must be admitted that this idea is a little hard to pin down. How do you intuit the infinite or the eternal or 'the whole'? What does it feel like, and how do you know it has happened? But that is the analytical philosopher speaking, ready to pour scorn on whatever cannot be precisely defined and expressed. Schleiermacher is seeking to evoke a certain sort of attitude, a way of seeing life-experience. This is not to be an analysing, labelling and defining way. Struggling for words, he says that the attitude he attempts to describe is 'to accept everything individual as a part of the whole and everything limited as a representation of the infinite'.

These days we might call that the 'holistic vision', seeing all things as parts of a totality, ceaselessly active in all its parts, but seen in an infinite number of different ways. Each person has the capacity to apprehend some part of this universal action, but each may be sensitive to some particulars as vehicles of the eternal and images of infinity, and not to others. So there may be a million different forms of religion, or 33 million 'gods', since 'in the infinite everything finite stands undisturbed alongside one another', without contradiction.

The gods will be individual, and yet they will be fractured images of one infinite totality, which is the world but is also infinitely more than the world. As one of the earliest Indian sacred scriptures, the *Rig Veda*, composed hundreds of years before the *Iliad*, puts it, 'Truth is one; the sages call it by many names.' The gods have a thousand or a million faces; but behind them all lies the unlimited energy of the whole world, expressed in endless diversity. The gods together, in all their infinite variety, image the active power of the whole, the active power of being itself, in its ever-changing and always particular forms. That is why the worshipper of Apollo does not ostracise the worshipper of Athene, and why the same sorts of powers take different names in different cultures – Zeus, Jupiter; Ares, Mars – while also possessing a particularity of their own. The gods flow into one another, merge and multiply, grow and die, as particular images fire the imagination or lose their attraction and simply become archaic and boring.

But was Schleiermacher just a little too nostalgically Romantic about the gods, just as Wordsworth and Blake in their different ways were also? Their common vision is of a wholly benign plurality of gods and their devotees, all intuiting the infinite in their own way, and evincing 'a friendly inviting tolerance' of others who intuit it differently. I think Schleiermacher's vision does capture something very important about religious feeling, about the 'feeling for the gods'. And though Wordsworth and Blake represent very different strands of Romanticism, their poetry is a penetrating expression of just such a feeling. They all represent a revolt against Cartesian mechanism, a wish for a return to a more poetic primal vision, one for which the world as experienced by humans speaks of presences and energies which can challenge, move and inspire, expressing a dimension of being which can only be apprehended by a specific form of human sensibility.

If this is right, Homer's poetry will not be a story of real persons, living on top of Mount Olympus. It will be a metaphorical personification of those powers and energies in and through which religious sensibility perceives the divine, the whole, the infinite and eternal imaged in the finite and transitory. If you read Homer that way, it may take on a more profound depth, and become itself an encouragement to cultivate again a feeling for the gods in a world from which the gods seem to have fled.

Yet we cannot assimilate ancient Greek religion too closely to German or English Romanticism. There were wars among the gods, and among their devotees. Zeus himself usurped and banished his father Kronos, who had in turn emasculated his father Ouranos. The gods who supported the Greeks were at odds with the gods who supported Troy. And some historians of the classical world suggest that the whole Olympic pantheon, or its priests and seers, replaced an earlier form of matriarchal worship of the goddess by military force.

Not only was tolerance not always so inviting, but Schleiermacher did not mention human sacrifice, temple prostitution and orgiastic fertility rites as particularly productive ways to intuit the infinite. Of course he could always say that these things were never part of 'true religion', just as he claimed metaphysics and morality were not. The trouble is that what he has left is something which has never existed, except in that short Romantic period of European history when the French and American revolutions promised, for a moment, a new dawn to humanity.

Ancient Greek religion was almost certainly much less concerned with the 'infinite whole' than was Schleiermacher. He, after all, lived after humans had become fully aware for the first time of the vast extent of the universe, after the idea of 'laws of nature' had been formulated, and after philosophers like Kant and Spinoza had developed a concept of 'the whole' as a desirable idea of Reason. The gods of Homer, though they form a sort of family, do not really form an overarching unity, such that they can be considered as aspects of one unified totality. They are much too fragmented and unsystematised for that. Yet it remains true that the individuality of the gods is a relative matter, and they all express what lies beyond their imaginatively devised forms.

Greek religion also contained elements much less benevolent than those stressed by Schleiermacher. When he says, 'Let the universe be intuited and worshipped in all ways', he is perhaps not really thinking of the sacrifice of children to the god of war, in order to achieve victory in battle. There are dark and chaotic forces among the gods, and human relationships with them vary from the frankly utilitarian ('I will obey you if you do this for me') to the mystical ('Let your wisdom live within me').

The worshippers of the gods are also surely more concerned with the causal powers of their gods than Schleiermacher allows. They really do want to rid themselves of plague, gain good crops of wheat and defeat their enemies in war. They entreat the gods to help attain their human desires and allay their human fears. This may be crude and it may be ineffective. Fertilisers may be a better way to get good crops than praying to Hera. But prayer to the gods was part of the religion of the Homeric age. It is hard to imagine that the only thing these worshippers were really concerned about was 'yielding themselves wholly to leisurely contemplation'. The gods symbolised active powers, after all, and as such they were believed to have some effects on what happened in the world. Schleiermacher, of course, knew about the laws of nature and realised that the old gods had been pensioned off long ago. But for the ancient Greeks the gods could affect human affairs if they wished. Whatever causal powers the symbols of the gods denoted, they could be influenced by human rituals and entreaties, and that was part of their importance. To that extent Schleiermacher's construal of religion as consisting in its pure form in feeling alone does not seem entirely to reflect the complexity of the human psyche, the way that humans think they can have some sort of causally effective relationship with the gods.

Even the way Schleiermacher describes the religious feeling has a decidedly late eighteenth-century ring about it. There is a rather notorious moment in the second of the *Speeches* wherein Schleiermacher compares religious intuition with sexual intercourse:

> Even as the beloved and ever-sought form fashions itself, my soul flees toward it; I embrace it, not as a shadow, but as the holy essence itself.

I lie on the bosom of the infinite world. At this moment I am its soul, for I feel all its powers and its infinite life as my own; at this moment it is my body; for I penetrate its muscles and its limbs as my own, and its innermost nerves move according to my sense and my presentiment as my own.

Speeches, p. 113

The idea of union with the infinite in an ecstatic embrace, though it may have been appealing to poets like Goethe and Wordsworth, is not, I imagine, often mentioned in Presbyterian churches these days. Rare is the Calvinist preacher who ascends the pulpit, and declaims: 'Put aside all your doctrines and creeds. They are the vain speculations of dead philosophers and divines. Put aside all your moral rules and principles. They are the product of centuries of socialisation. Concentrate just on the one truly religious thing: I adjure you to lie on the bosom of the infinite world.'

This does not seem to be what Agamemnon and Achilles, those bloodthirsty and heroic warriors, would really care for, any more than it seems to be what Presbyterians go to church to find. Nevertheless, it is not absurd to think that ancient warriors and Protestant businessmen alike could find sense in the idea of being filled with power, with strength, courage, flair and energy, which comes from beyond their own conscious minds. And they could find sense in coming to see their own lives as parts of what Schleiermacher calls 'a work of the world spirit progressing into infinity', or, in what would be perhaps a more Greek way of thinking, a participation in the play of the gods, giving deeper sense and more enduring value to the seemingly arbitrary vagaries of good and bad fortune.

In the *Iliad* human lives are taken up into the purposes of the gods – often themselves haphazard and perverse, no doubt, but at least immortal and aiming at goals that some of the gods, at least, value. They are imbued with the powers and values of the gods, the strength of Apollo, the wisdom of Athene, the wild savagery of Ares. Their brief lives are sanctified, touched by immortality, sustained by a vision of wider purposes, strengthened to face pain and disappointment, by their walking in the world in the company of the gods.

If all that is embraced by what Schleiermacher means by 'feeling', by the 'intuition of the infinite', and I think that it is, then the religious sense is not simply a rather self-indulgent leisurely contemplation. It is an attempt, in a world hardly known and understood at all, and in a society of lives brief, tenuous and almost certain to end in violence, to share in the happy life of the gods. For a little while, humans grasp at immortality, and occasionally feel its power. They do not indeed become eternal, but they see the sacred Olympian mountain from afar. They see the gods ascending and descending to touch human lives briefly with unending life. For a little while, so far as it is possible for finite beings, these humans are able to see all things temporal under the aspect of eternity, and to 'hold eternity in an hour'.

It is the strength of Schleiermacher that he has drawn attention, naturally in terms of the German Romanticism of his time, to the peculiar sort of apprehension or intuition which gives rise to talk of gods. He draws attention to the way in which finite things can come to speak of something beyond themselves, of a transcendent depth which fills them with significance beyond their transient individuality, and which can draw the mind and heart into a felt unity with that source of significance and power. The Romantics catch something important about the gods. But there is also something that they miss. That is the element of terror and dread which is also part of the human response to the gods – or part of that way of apprehending the powers and energies of experienced reality which gives rise to images of the gods.

Rudolf Otto: the sense of the numinous

Rudolf Otto (1869–1937) lived in darker times than Schleiermacher. The heady optimism that followed the French and American revolutions, which saw Europe rise to cultural pre-eminence in the world, collapsed during Otto's lifetime into the carnage of the First World War. Great art, it turned out, was compatible with moral obtuseness, and the pointless deaths of eight-hundred thousand French and German soldiers at Verdun was contemporary with performances of the extravagantly Romantic music of Richard Wagner and Richard Strauss. Beneath the Enlightenment appeals to Reason, deeper and more disturbing passions waited to be unleashed, in the mud of the trenches and to the sound of the screams of shells and men.

Otto cannot be blamed for this, But, reflecting his own times, he was more aware than Schleiermacher of the non-rational and often destructive powers that live in the human soul. His great work, *The Idea of the Holy,* published in 1917, and therefore completed during the Great War, locates the heart of religion in that non-rational realm. Like Schleiermacher, Otto looked for, and thought he had discovered, the essence of religious feeling. Oddly enough, he found a different feeling from that of Schleiermacher. To name this feeling he adapted (or thought he had invented) the word 'numinous', giving it the special meaning of standing for the object of the special and distinctive non-rational element of feeling or intuition in religion.

Whereas the Romantics found religious feeling in the sense of a basically benevolent Infinity, Otto describes the numinous in terms of the 'uncanny', the 'weird' and what arouses in us 'grisly horror and shuddering'. He depicts the birth of the gods in the arousal of this feeling in human prehistory. The sense of the numinous he describes as the sense of a reality *mysterium tremendum et fascinans* (such ideas always sound more significant in Latin).

The feeling is one of 'submergence into nothingness before an overpowering, absolute might'. It contains an element of mystery, because it is rationally incomprehensible, extraordinary and beyond any concepts. Naturally, since it is beyond concepts, there is nothing much one can say about it. But it is a sense of being confronted by something 'wholly other', quite outside normal experience, completely alien, incommensurable with thought. It is not a puzzle, which we might one day understand. It is a mystery, something thought just cannot get any grip on. And it encounters us in some sort of experience – we might say, it is apprehended but not comprehended and not even comprehensible. Otto simply challenges us to think of such an experience in our own lives, and if we cannot, he says that we may as well stop reading his book.

That might seem a good way of ensuring that the book remained unread, but in fact it quickly became one of the classical writings on religion – one of a handful of books you should read if you want to understand thoughtful discourse about the strange phenomenon of religious belief. At least it moves away from thinking that meeting the gods is like meeting a particularly handsome young man or woman in the street. Although Otto thinks most people have some inkling of this sort of experience, in its full form he holds that it is confined to a few rare individuals, 'diviners' or seers, whose lives are transformed by such an encounter with ultimate mystery.

How would they be transformed? I suppose it is rather like suddenly sensing that all of one's life up to that point has been a sort of dream, something poised between reality and unreality, something without the sort of solid reality one thought it had. All the things that seemed so important to us – career, the esteem of others, even the love of family – are diminished and become insignificant. Plato put it very elegantly in his dialogue *The Republic,* to which we shall return later. Having for a moment emerged from the cave of illusions, we can never again return to our former lives in the same way. We will never be able to say what we have seen, but we will carry with us the unshakeable conviction that things are not what they seem, and that our rational little lives are lived out on the edge of infinite mystery.

That is not enough for the religious sense of the numinous. So far, it might lead mostly to our possessing a permanently puzzled expression, but not much else. There is more to come. The numinous experience is not only *mysterium,* it is also *tremendum.* It contains an element of peculiar dread, of 'terror fraught with an inward shuddering'. This sounds rather like the experience you might have on watching a horror film, similar to how you feel when the unlovable baby alien bursts out of a human body in *Alien*. It is something that makes your hair stand on end.

We can just see the young couple approaching the isolated house on the hill, hearing a strange shuffling noise, looking at one another and saying, 'There's something not quite right here, darling.' We do not expect them to say, 'I think I am having a religious experience.' Still, it is no accident that such stories are commonly called 'ghost stories', that they tend to be told at Halloween, when the dead walk the earth, and that they often involve the return of dead people or of demons from Hell.

We call them demons, but in Greek the word *daimon* refers to a minor god or attendant spirit or genius. For the Greeks all the gods were capable of displaying dreadful power and malignant or dangerous aspects. Thus Apollo in his daimonic aspect brings plague on the Greek army, though in his beneficent aspect he embodies the light-bringing power of the rising sun. Zeus is the great father of all the gods, but in Book Seven of the *Iliad* it is related that when he planned evil, 'thundering fearfully, terror took its pale grip' on the Greek soldiers.

There is not only the sense of terror. The terror is connected with a sense of overwhelming power and energy. The gods are not just ghosts. They are stupendous energies which are not so much malign as indifferent to concerns of human well-being or morality. They are the energies of the cosmos, or more properly energies which express their natures in and through the cosmos. They are beneficent energies of new life and startling beauty, but also fearsome energies of death and time.

All the gods have this double aspect, and nowhere is it more evident in religious literature than in the great revelation in chapter 11 of the Indian classic the *Bhagavad Gita*, the 'Song of the Lord' (which may have been composed as early as 300 BCE). Krishna, who is in this text the supreme god, disguised as the charioteer of the warrior Arjuna, reveals his true form to Arjuna, giving him the 'mystic eye' which alone can see that form. What Arjuna sees is a blazing and all-encompassing, unlimited unity of a million names and forms. Within that limitless infinity are countless gaping mouths with many teeth, in which all beings are sooner or later engulfed: 'I see all people rushing swiftly into your mouths, as moths dash to destruction in a blazing fire.' Gods and warriors, peasants and kings are swallowed up, 'some with heads crushed between those terrifying teeth'. Arjuna sees this vision, his hair standing erect and full of dread (just as Professor Otto expects), and, trembling, asks who this is, whom he had all too familiarly addressed as his charioteer. Krishna, the Lord of the Universe, replies: 'I am Death, the destroyer of worlds' – the words which the American physicist Robert Oppenheimer uttered as the first atomic bomb exploded over the New Mexico desert on 16 July 1945.

Death and Time destroy all things, and the primal religious vision does not flinch from the thought that the same gods who create also destroy. For the Greeks, it does not pay to be too familiar with the gods, and it is wise to feel terror before their destructive power. It is wise to approach them with great respect, and a hecatomb of oxen is a small price to pay for the friendship of Apollo. For all people, the occurrence of disease, disaster and death is something that has to be faced. The Greeks were not unreasonable in seeing these things as due to the malevolence of gods who were in conflict among themselves, but who might be brought under the authority of a higher god whose purposes might win out in the end. Respect and fear are parts of a proper attitude to the gods.

So it seems that the sense of the numinous adds to the feeling of perpetual puzzlement one of paralysing terror. For Otto, however, the account is still not complete. There must yet be added the sense of the *fascinans,* an intoxicating rapture which transports the mind into an altered, heightened frame of consciousness, before which ordinary experience pales into relative insignificance. In other words, the total sense of the holy is the sense of a reality at once wholly beyond rational comprehension or description, which fills one with awe and dread, yet at the same time evokes fascination and irresistible desire. If you feel puzzled, paralysed and simultaneously intoxicated, you have the sense of the numinous, the holy.

This is a much more precisely drawn picture of religious feeling than those of Schleiermacher or Wordsworth. One may well feel that it is too precisely drawn, and that it would be extremely difficult to decide whether one was having this precise experience, thus never being quite sure if one was really religious or not. Otto's claim that this is the one source of all religious feeling is probably much too bold. Religion is more diverse than that. There are, as William James put it in his classic book, *The Varieties of Religious Experience,* many varieties of religious experience and many ways of encountering the gods. Otto has not found the one essential core of religion. But he has very effectively described some of that range of feelings in human beings that give rise to a sense of the sacred.

We can probably recognise the feeling that sometimes occurs that we are in the presence of something stupendous which it is impossible to put into words. There is a knowledge which cannot be articulated, an apprehension which eludes conceptual thought, a sense of 'presence' which all our images and symbols only dimly express, before which we can only in the end be silent, speechless. We may also recognise the awe that fills the mind before the vast immensities of space, and the catastrophic power of planetary earthquakes and stellar supernovae. We may feel our helplessness before famine, plagues and inevitable death, as they rage through our human world. And we may sometimes sense the intoxication of beauty, almost too intense to bear, as we suddenly, in a miraculous moment, discern the world in all its intricate order and subtle intensity.

Such moments of 'divination' open up depths to reality that are not normally seen or sensed. It may be that when we truly have that sense of astonished silence, of fearful awe and of ecstatic rapture, then we come near to sensing what it was that the Greek gods expressed. The trouble is that even in Homer the gods can lose their power to evoke such a sensibility, and instead become merely quarrelsome and irritating superhuman persons, who entertain or divert, but never inspire and transform us.

How do the gods inspire? In two ways: by deepening our vision of reality, and by heightening our creative powers. The gods may grant us, or may evoke in us, the perception of an infinity which lies beyond yet in and through all things, in the face of which we are made speechless, before which our lives shiver into nothingness, and yet in whose light we see eternal significance transfiguring the world. And the gods may give to us a little of their own immortality, transcending for a while the normal limits of our mundane humanity.

Can Zeus and Hera, Athene and Ares, Thetis and Apollo, do this? For their devotees they can. Attitudes to the gods vary as widely as human interests and abilities vary. For some, the gods will be powers who can be appeased or cajoled by rituals and sacrifices. For others, there will be demons which cause disease and spirits which bring good luck; there will be charms and talismans to ward off evil, and signs of the future in the livers of dead goats. Rituals of human sacrifice and sexual degradation reflect the perceived cruelty and amorality of the chaotic powers of nature, and the desperation of those who seek to propitiate them. But also there will be those whose chosen god expresses an aspect of the world that resonates with their own history and personality, but which points beyond its symbolised form to the hidden mystery of the numinous.

Beyond the forms of the gods lies the formless, and from this all forms spring. Human imagination tries to grasp and portray this, but the portraits all bear the imprints of their human creators, and idolatry lies in taking the form for the reality. Yet those imagined forms, taken in their true self-transcending significance, can enable time to be transfigured by eternity, and the human apprehension of this sublunary world to be transfigured by a vision of the personal, manifested in a thousand names and forms, but always eluding the human passion for precise definition and description.

The sense of the gods is the vision of the personal in a thousand forms. The gods, the immortals, express that sense of eternity touching time of which Schleiermacher wrote, the sense of infinite mystery, dreadful power and ecstatic delight which Otto defined as the numinous. But to their insights one must add one more element, the element that leads, or misleads, the coiners of dictionary definitions to call the gods 'supernatural persons'.

When, instead of seeing simply a misty morning by the sea, we see Thetis rising through the swell of the sea at early morning, going up to the vast sky and to the presence of Zeus, the gatherer of clouds, then we discern in the morning sea-mist a disclosure of unbounded infinity and mystery, power and beauty, but we also see something more.

Martin Buber: life as meeting

Martin Buber (1878–1965), a Jewish writer born in Vienna, lectured in Germany until he was deprived of his university chair by the National Socialists in 1933. In 1923, just six years after *The Idea of the Holy* was published, he wrote a small poetic work called *I and Thou*.

The word 'thou' in English has a rather peculiar history. In the sixteenth century, when the English *Book of Common Prayer* was first pieced together, it was the second-person singular personal pronoun. Just as in German and French, and many other languages today, it was used to signify an especially close and intimate relationship with the person to whom you were speaking. For formal occasions, or to people one did not know well, 'you' was appropriate. But for members of family and close friends, the correct word to use was 'thou'.

Then something very odd happened to the word. It simply ceased to be used in common speech. Everybody became 'you'. Once it ceased to be used, it became a very archaic-sounding word, and before long people thought that 'thou' was a special word only to be used for God –

God being presumably very archaic – connoting very special reverence and respect. So, whereas the writers of the first Elizabethan prayer book had wanted people to address God in a very intimate, almost informal way, most people who love the prayer book now seem to think that it is important to address God as 'thou', because only that gives God appropriate respect. Ironically, those who insist on addressing God as 'thou' are doing the very opposite of what the compilers of the prayer book wanted.

Whatever the vagaries of the English language, Buber used 'thou' (the German 'du', of course) to try to capture the sense of personal address that was, he thought, peculiar to religious insight.

He begins by saying, 'To man the world is twofold, in accordance with the twofold nature of the primary words which he speaks.' These primary words are 'I–it' and 'I–thou'.

If we adopt the attitude of 'I–it' to our world, then we hold ourselves apart from it, as individuals who may inspect and utilise it. We partition it into sets of objects, which lie open to our inspection, available for our use, and to which our relationship is essentially dispassionate and unengaged – except for specific purposes we may have in mind from time to time.

But 'the primary word I–thou can only be spoken with the whole being', and 'when "Thou" is spoken there is no thing. "Thou" has no bounds.' In speaking that word, in taking up that attitude, the speaker 'takes his stand in relation'. There is a total commitment of the whole person. Indeed, one becomes a whole person only when one speaks the word 'thou'; 'through the "thou" a man becomes "I"'.

To speak that word is to enter into a relationship, a relationship in which we are addressed, and in which we hear and respond, with the whole being. That relationship is not to a thing, but to what addresses us in and through that thing, whether the thing is another person or the sea-mist or even a tree. 'Whenever the sentence, "I see the tree" is so uttered that it no longer tells of a relation between the man – I – and the tree – Thou – but establishes the perception of the tree as object by the human consciousness, the barrier between subject and object has been set up.' Before that splitting of consciousness into subject and object, there is the primal unity of relation, of address and response, of 'meeting' – and 'all real living is meeting'.

We cannot say whether that 'Thou' is one or many. It is unbounded – 'in each "Thou" we address the eternal "thou"'. But it takes form in the things we apprehend in this special way, and so it has countless names and forms. The world is full of gods, and each god signifies a living and continually renewed relational event. In a moment of theophany, 'the "thou" confronts me. I step into direct relation with it.' In such moments the gods are born, moments of meeting, in which 'there is the whole fulness of real mutual action', there is 'an inexpressible confirmation of meaning', a meaning not in some other world, but in this very world of ours.

To those who have lost all feeling for the gods, the thought of a German professor talking to a tree is a supreme absurdity. And yet this is not about talking to a tree, and it is not about talking to some supernatural person or dryad who may live, invisibly, in the tree. It is a specific way of being in the world, of apprehending it, as a relational event or a series of relational events, as a form of meeting which is personal and yet so much more and so deeply other. If that sense of meeting is added to the sense of infinity, of mystery, dread and beauty, which sometimes, and often by surprise, comes upon us, then there exists the feeling for the gods, already fading but still present in Homer's *Iliad*.

If one is to speak sensitively about God, this is the place to begin, not with abstract definitions or endless arguments, but with the sense of the sublime, the infinite, the numinous, the feeling for the gods.

Epilogue: the testimony of a secularist

In 1890 the Cambridge anthropologist James Frazer published the first edition of *The Golden Bough*, one of the great classics of comparative religion. He looked forward to the triumph of science and, correlatively, he thought, the death of religion, and his book was largely a vast compendium of what he regarded as superstitions and false beliefs. But he could not resist a literary flourish, and the final paragraph of his twelve-volume work is this:

> Once more we take the road to Nemi. It is evening, and as we climb the long slope of the Appian Way up to the Alban Hills, we look back and see the sky aflame with sunset, its golden glory resting like the aureole of a dying saint over Rome and touching with a crest of fire the dome of St Peter's. The sight once seen can never be forgotten, but we turn from it and pursue our way darkling along the mountain side, till we come to Nemi and look down on the lake in its deep hollow, now fast disappearing in the evening shadows. The place has changed but little since Diana received the homage of her worshippers in the sacred grove. The temple of the sylvan goddess, indeed, has vanished and the King of the Wood no longer stands sentinel over the Golden Bough. But Nemi's woods are still green, and as the sunset fades above them in the west, there comes to us, borne on the swell of the wind, the sound of the church bells of Aricia ringing the Angelus, *Ave Maria!* Sweet and solemn they chime out from the distant town and die lingeringly away across the wide Campagnan marshes. *Le roi est mort, vive le roi! Ave Maria!*
>
> p. 856

Even the apostle of secularism was not, it is clear, immune from a feeling for the gods.

Find out more . . .

For information on mythological gods generally, see Arthur Cotterell, *Dictionary of World Mythology* (Oxford, Oxford University Press, 1986).

Homer, *The Iliad* (trans. Martin Hammond, Harmondsworth, Penguin, 1987). I have quoted from the first book.

Friedrich Schleiermacher, *On Religion: Speeches to its Cultured Despisers* (trans. Richard Crouter, Cambridge, Cambridge University Press, 1988 [1799]).

The second speech is the one I have quoted from. There are many translations; this good one also has a useful introduction.

René Descartes, *Meditations on the First Philosophy*, in *Discourse on Method* (trans. Arthur Wollaston, Harmondsworth, Penguin, 1960 [1641]), pp. 100 ff. This gives a short and readable account of Descartes' views on God, mind and body.

Rudolf Otto, *The Idea of the Holy* (trans. John Harvey, Harmondsworth, Penguin, 1959 [1917]). This is essential reading for anyone interested in religious experience.

Although I have not explicitly talked about it, another classic in this area is William James's, *The Varieties of Religious Experience* (London, Collins, 1902).

A Jewish writer who has been tremendously influential on many Christian theologians is Martin Buber, in a little book which is really a poem: *I and Thou* (trans. Ronald Gregor Smith, Edinburgh, T. and T. Clark, 1958 [1923]).

2

Beyond the gods

In which the reader will be invited to ruminate on what a prophet is, will discover that Satan was not all bad, and that nobody really knows the name of God. They will be introduced to the Rambam, and will find out how little Thomas Aquinas knew about God, though Maimonides knew even less. They will also find out how pseudo Dionysius was, and will read a great many words explaining at length that nothing much can be said about God.

Prophets and seers

A feeling for the gods is best evoked by poetry, and it would be a mistake to take such poetry too literally. Yet religion is not fiction, and claims to truth are made in religion, even if in indirect and evocative ways. In the history of religious thought, such claims are primarily founded on the lives and teachings of the prophets, people who have a special sensitivity to the realm of the sacred or divine.

> **prophet** – A person who speaks for God or a god ... also, a person who predicts or foretells future events (*Shorter OED*, again).

There are prophets in the *Iliad*, and indeed the word 'prophet' is itself a Greek word. They are also called augurs (a religious official who

The prophet Isaiah sits on the ceiling of the Sistine Chapel looking rather pained, perhaps on being told that Michelangelo has drawn a picture of God a little further along.

interpreted omens derived from the behaviour of birds, the appearance of entrails, etc., and gave advice in accordance with them) and seers (a person of supposed supernatural insight, able to see visions).

According to the first book of the *Iliad,* Achilles consulted a seer or diviner, one skilled in reading the signs of the future, or in interpreting dreams, to enquire why Apollo was angry. The seer Kalchas, 'who knew what is, and what will be, and what was before', stood up and declared that the god's anger could be appeased only by the return of the abducted daughter of the priest of Apollo by Agamemnon, and by a sacred sacrifice. In other words, the Greeks were suffering because of an insult to a god, a wrong done which had to be remedied, and the sacrifice would seal their intention to right that wrong.

Seers are sensitive to sacred presences. They feel the savage and ecstatic powers expressed in nature, in destiny and in the human mind. Seeing into the depths of the mind, discerning the signs of the times, sensing the rhythms of the natural world, they faintly foresee the seeds of the future in the present, and from what they foresee they recommend actions which will be either auspicious or ill-advised.

The modern mind sees nature as a machine, in which human spirits, even if they truly exist, exist alone. The ancient Greeks saw nature as a vast dynamic interplay of living spirits, with humans as parts of a vast hierarchy of spirits, each with something analogous to consciousness and will. The seer enters this hidden world, of which nature and history are outward appearances and expressions, and seeks to establish relationships which make for human well-being, and to bring back powers of wisdom and healing which may alleviate human sorrow.

The gods are not only felt. They act. They send signs – Zeus sends lightning on the right as a sign of good fortune, or on the left, which is bad. The gods send dreams, appear in visions, and bring hidden things to consciousness. They give power to heal and send plagues and diseases so that prophets have something to heal. Prophets are the intermediaries of the gods, reading their signs, seeing their visionary appearances, hearing their words, and mediating their power.

In ancient Greece prophets would be routinely consulted by rulers, and while they might say things rulers did not like – Agamemnon did not like what Kalchas said – they could also influence affairs of state considerably. Of course there are prophets and prophets. Most prophets were pretty bad at their job. Many (some would say all!) were subject to delusions and personal fantasies. Some were downright frauds. Only a few got their prophecies right, and saw deeply into the trends of history and the depths of human hearts.

The prophets of Israel and monotheism

Over at the eastern end of the Mediterranean, the twelve nomadic tribes who cobbled together the dual petty kingdoms of Israel and Judah had their due quota of prophets, like most tribal societies at that time. Their prophets, just like those of other similar societies, interpreted signs and omens from the gods; they were diviners of the future. They apparently had something called Urim and Thummim (perhaps two stones) with the aid of which they determined the will of the gods (cf. 1 Samuel 14:41). Nobody knows precisely what Urim and Thummim were, or how they were used, but this method of divination seems slightly less messy than poking about in the entrails of goats. Perhaps the stones were thrown, and the one that came down face up determined a 'yes' or 'no' answer to a question.

The prophets slept in sacred groves, hoping for dreams or visions which would reveal to them the hidden mysteries of the gods. Joseph was very successful in interpreting dreams, and he beat the native Egyptian prophets in a variety of dream-interpreting competitions. Visions were almost commonplace, and a representative example is given in the account of how Abraham saw and spoke with his god and two divine attendants, who promised him that he would have a son (Genesis 18).

The prophets sang and danced, seeking some form of ecstatic possession by the gods which might give guidance in times of stress.

They could be possessed by the gods. 1 Samuel chapter 10, verses 5–7 gives one, no doubt typical, account: 'You will meet a band of prophets coming down from the high place with harp, tambourine, flute and lyre before them, prophesying. Then the spirit of the Lord will come mightily upon you, and you shall prophesy with them and be turned into another man.' This particularly noisy group of prophets were seeking the help of music to attract the spirit of the god, which possessed them and turned them into different persons – vehicles of the god.

Finally, the prophets cultivated psychic abilities which gave them powers over the natural world and over the demons that cause disease. The prophet Elijah was particularly good at miracles. He could produce food out of thin air, could bring dead people back to life (1 Kings 17:8–24), call down fire from heaven (1 Kings 18 and 2 Kings 1), and, to cap it all, he ended his earthly life by ascending into the sky in a chariot of fire, and was seen no more (2 Kings 2:11). That must have been a very hard act to follow.

All in all, these prophets of ancient Israel were very much like the prophets mentioned in the *Iliad*, and known in many ancient societies. They were interpreters of signs, they experienced sacred visions, they were sometimes possessed by the gods, and they often cultivated supernatural powers.

Yet something happened in ancient Israel that had never happened in ancient Greece. The prophets' own experiences of the gods drove them to a point at which the gods themselves were transcended and left behind. It is probable this did not fully happen until about 550 BCE, when the Jews were exiled in Babylon after their defeat by the Babylonian empire. Then a collection of oracles and poems was written down and now forms chapters 40–55 of the book of the prophet Isaiah, in the Bible. There are usually thought to have been no less than three Isaiahs, or collections of prophetic writings, which eventually got put together in the book of Isaiah, and this is usually known as the second one (more grandiosely, 'Deutero-Isaiah').

The views expressed there are, however, the culmination of a long tradition, which began in the twelfth or thirteenth century BCE, and which is associated particularly with Moses, the prophet from thirteenth-century Egypt. The second Isaiah is one of the great poets of the ancient world, whose poetry compares well with that of the *Iliad,* and in his hands the Jewish idea of their god develops in a dramatic way.

Just as Homer called on the Muse to inspire him, so this Isaiah is inspired by a god, who speaks to him and tells him what to say. But this god makes much greater claims than any of the gods of Homer. He declares unequivocally: 'The Lord is the everlasting god, the creator of the ends of the earth.'

Zeus was not a god like that. He had a wife and parents, and though he was the most powerful god, he was not the first. His father was a Titan, Kronos, and if you tried to go further back than that, you got to the primal powers of Earth and Heaven, and even before that, to the primal Chaos or Abyss from which all the gods originated. But there was no creator, and all the active powers of nature, destiny and mind had just evolved from more primal, less rational and personal powers. The world came to be as a result of a titanic struggle for life and power, as gods mutated, generated, adapted, clashed with and succeeded one another.

By contrast, the god of Moses and Isaiah, the god of the prophets, had no parents. This god was not born of Earth or of Chaos. God made the earth: 'he stretches out the heavens like a curtain', and calls the stars by name. God is the parent of all things, and called all things into being by a word of power. So Isaiah places at the beginning of all things a mighty being of knowledge and power, of will and consciousness. God's power is so great that it has no equal: 'Before me no god was formed, nor shall there be any after me ... I am the first and I am the last; besides me there is no god.'

The claim is that there is in fact only one god, who called everything else, all the heavenly host (who are now demoted to being angels of one sort or another), all the stars, the sky, earth and sea, and all living things, into existence by decree.

It was not the first time this idea had been tried. In 1363 BCE Akhenaten of Egypt had instituted the worship of Aten, the one god, but it was a total failure. The people, and especially the priests, threatened with a drastic loss of revenue, preferred their old familiar gods. Not long before second Isaiah, Zoroaster had introduced the worship of one god, Ahura Mazda, to Persia. In Greece, where Homer's *Iliad* was then being put into written form, Xenophanes mocked the antics of the Greek pantheon of gods, but was not interested in offering any positive alternative. It was only among the Israelites that the idea of **monotheism**, of one creator god, really caught on.

Who was this Israelite god, and what was his name? The curious fact is that nobody knows. There are many names for God in the Hebrew Bible, and perhaps originally they referred to different gods. But there is one main name – JHVH. In written Hebrew there are no printed vowels, so you have to guess what might go in between those four letters. They are called the **Tetragrammaton** (the 'four letters'), and after about 300 BCE the name was never pronounced, as it was felt to be too sacred to say. Instead, the circumlocution 'Adonai', the Hebrew word for 'Lord', was used. In the middle ages people tried putting the vowels from 'Adonai' between the consonants 'JHVH'. The result was 'Jahovaih', or 'Jehovah', a totally invented word which no respectable Jew would ever have thought of pronouncing. We may be sure that, whatever the name of this god was, it was not Jehovah. Most scholars think it might have been 'Jahweh', which is at least a Hebrew-sounding word. That, therefore is the name I will use here, though it is only a guess.

One account of how this name came to be used is found in the Old Testament book of Exodus, chapter 3. The prophet Moses (the name is *Mosheh* in Hebrew, though it is originally an Egyptian name) saw a vision of a god who appeared in the flame of a burning bush, and claimed to be the family god of Abraham and his descendants Isaac and Jacob. Moses heard the voice of this god promising to liberate Abraham's descendants from slavery in Egypt. He was given the power to perform various miracles – his staff could turn into a snake, his hand could become leprous and whole again at will, and he could turn water into blood. And he was given power to predict ten great plagues which were to afflict the Egyptians. In short, Moses became a paid-up prophet in double-quick time.

When he asked this god for a name, he received the remark 'I am who I am', which sounds remarkably like 'Mind your own business'. This god then said, 'Say this to the people of Israel, 'JHVH has sent me . . .'. 'JHVH' could well be the third person singular of the Hebrew verb 'HaYaH', which is the verb 'to be'. So it would say, 'He (or 'It') is', or 'He (it) will be', or possibly even, inserting a slightly different vowel, 'He (it) causes to be'. And there is a sense – represented by the Jewish refusal to pronounce the name – that the name of god, which discloses the inner nature of god, is beyond human knowledge. The god of Abraham, Isaac and Jacob is the unknown and unknowable god.

It should never be thought that the Jewish idea of god is that god is something like a human being. The most distinctive thing about the Jewish Temple, which stood in Jerusalem, is that the inner sanctuary, where an image of the god usually stood in temples, was empty; it had no carved image in it. There had been at one time, in that small dark room which only the High Priest entered, and then only once a year, a small wooden chest, overlaid with gold, with two angelic figures holding it. There was no image of God, and in fact a prohibition on making any likeness of God was one of the famous ten commandments which Moses was supposed to have received directly from God.

As the second Isaiah said, 'To whom then will you liken God, or what likeness compare with him?' Christian artists have drawn God all over the place. God glares down, among many other places, from the ceiling of the Sistine Chapel, in the heart of the Vatican. Jews (and Muslims) tend to be shocked by this. It is absolutely forbidden to make any representation of God. God is not like anything. When Moses asked the name of God, he was in effect asking what God was like, what the divine inner nature was. The reply, definitive for all subsequent

Jewish thought, was that God is without form, illimitable, ungraspable and utterly inconceivable.

Beyond the gods, the personalised aspects of the natural and human world which do so much to determine human destiny, lies not just one god much grander than all the others, but something infinitely more mysterious and inconceivable – the Beyond, the Unsayable.

Basil, Gregory Palamas and Maimonides: the apophatic way

Did the Greeks believe in such a Beyond? There are obscure hints in the *Iliad* of a power beyond the gods, which even they cannot overturn, the power of fate. But it remains a dark and shadowy reality, far from any relationship with humans or with the gods themselves. The gods to whom humans related in prayer and sacrifice play out their own parts on a wider-than-human, an immortal, stage, but the writer of those parts remains unspoken, undescribed.

From a Jewish point of view, those who worship the gods are trying to sense the presences underlying the beautiful and sublime elements of the finite world. But the great Hebrew prophets urge us to go beyond those presences, to the formless, the unspoken silence, of which ultimately nothing can be said.

Nevertheless the god of Moses is not simply the vacuous, though it is beyond all finite forms. When that god says, 'I am', it is not simply saying, 'Mind your own business'. It is saying, 'Beyond all beings there is that which gives rise to all beings. Its existence is so full that the mind, which thinks by setting down definitions and boundaries, cannot envisage it. It is unrestricted being, whose power is endless, whose beauty is infinite. It is not less than the best that you can think. It is infinitely more, and it is quite other than anything you can ever think.'

This distinction between the most elevated ideas we have of God and the true inner nature of God is very clearly made in the Eastern Orthodox tradition of Christianity, and has remained central to it ever since. **Basil the Great** (*c.* 330–79) wrote: 'In regard to the names which we apply to God, these reveal his energies which descend towards us yet do not draw us closer to his essence, which is inaccessible.' This distinction between the 'essence' (*ousia*) of God, which always remains unknowable, even to the angels, and his 'energies' (*energeia*), by which God makes himself known, was definitively made for Orthodox theologians by **Gregory Palamas** (1296–1359), who reiterated that 'the divine nature is communicable not in itself but through its energy'. Orthodox thinkers usually draw attention not only to the vision of the burning bush, but also to Moses' ascent of Mount Sinai, when he entered at the mountain top into 'thick darkness', which was all that could finally be known of the presence of God. Beyond the gods, and all finite forms of the divine, there is the darkness which conceals God for ever, and puts all human thoughts and images in question.

While it may seem that the Hebrew Bible is filled with anthropomorphic images of God, riding on the clouds or walking with the patriarchs, all such images are relativised, if not contradicted, by both the Christian Orthodox and the Jewish tradition. In Judaism, the clearest account of this is given by one of the greatest Jewish thinkers of all time.

Moses Maimonides (1135–1204), known to Jewish writers as 'Rambam' (a word coined from the initial letters of: **R**abbi **M**oses **b**en **M**aimon), was born in Cordoba, in Spain, and later lived and died in Old Cairo. In 1190 he wrote a book, *Guide for the Perplexed* (the title of which I have copied), which attempted to put together the biblical revelation about God with the thought of Aristotle. The title of the book is rather ironic, because if you were not perplexed when you began to read it, you certainly would be by the time you finished it. Some people think it should have been called, 'Guide for those who want to be even more Perplexed than they already are'. To this day scholars dispute about whether Maimonides was writing the definitive exposition of Jewish thought, or subtly undermining Jewish faith altogether.

The dispute arises because people have never agreed on whether Aristotle can really be harmonised with the prophetic revelation. Fortunately we do not need to get involved in that dispute. What Maimonides says about God is very much based, not on Aristotle, but on Moses' prophetic insight that the name (and therefore the nature) of God is beyond description, and that no product of the human imagination can be adequate to God's reality.

So he writes, 'There is no similarity in any way whatsoever between him [God] and his creatures ... the difference between them ... is absolute' (*The Guide for the Perplexed,* p. 49). The absolute difference between God and anything else is basic for Jewish prophetic thought. It means that none of the symbols and images of God in the Bible can be literally applied to God.

'God', writes Maimonides, 'has no positive attributes ... the negative attributes of God are the true attributes' (p. 81). So we cannot know what God truly is, but only what God is not. You can go through everything in the world, and say, 'God is not that'. You can go through everything you can imagine, and say, 'God is not that'. 'By each additional negative attribute you advance towards knowledge of God', writes Maimonides (p. 84). God is not a rock, not a tree, not an animal, not a person, not ignorant, not wise, not evil, not good, not many, not one ... This is called the **apophatic way** (from the Greek word for 'denial'): approaching the infinite by denying everything finite.

But this begins to sound shocking. If God is not wise, good or even one, what on earth are we talking about? For Maimonides, the point is that we are not just denying. We are denying in a special sort of way. 'Whatever you affirm is only a perfection in relation to us', he says (p. 84). To ascribe to God properties that seem good to us would be to demean God. We have to realise that God is infinitely more than we can imagine. But of course we have to realise that God is not less, and maybe here Maimonides does rather overstate his point. But he adds that 'all perfections must really exist in God', though not in any way we can imagine them. If you are given a choice between saying that God is stupid and that God is wise, you must choose wisdom. But you must add that God is not wise in the way that we are wise – as Isaiah says, 'My thoughts are not your thoughts … says the Lord … for as the heavens are higher than the earth, so are my ways higher than your ways' (Isaiah, 55:8).

That is how our knowledge of God advances – by realising that the source of all beings is infinitely greater in every respect than anything we can think of, and that indeed that being is beyond our highest thoughts. This is the final decisive 'no' to any attempt to think of God as a supernatural person. 'When we say that that essence which we call "God" is a substance with many properties … we apply that name to an object which does not at all exist' (p. 89). The whole universe has a cause, and we can think of that cause as a creator – a being with immense knowledge and power. But we must always realise that we have not really begun to understand it.

Why, then, do we speak of God as if God was a person, or at least a personal being with such properties as knowledge and power? Because the unknowable reality which we call 'God' relates to us in ways that we can only represent to ourselves by using symbols – symbols of a father, a rock, a judge, a shepherd or a warrior.

How do we know these symbols are appropriate to something that is completely unknowable? The Hebrew prophets suggest that the illimitable being takes on a finite name and form in order to communicate with us, and though that form is absolutely different from what God really is, we can accept it as best suited to our feeble minds, because the form comes to us in an overwhelming and completely convincing experience.

That is the experience of the prophet, grasped by the overpowering manifestation of the infinite emptying and limiting itself to a finite form in order to relate to human lives. Prophets are rare because most of us could not cope with such a disclosure of reality. God says to the prophet Moses, 'You cannot see my face; for man shall not see me and live' (Exodus 33:20). Yet Moses is said to speak with God 'face to face'

God as imagined by a Brazilian artist. Beyond the image is the unknowable reality.

(Exodus 33:11). This may seem like a contradiction. But it may express in a paradoxical way a deeper truth. The true face of God, the essential being, is hidden in the cloud of glory. But God speaks to Moses with the face of an angel, his finite transient form. After such encounters the face of Moses shone with an unearthly light, so terrifying to others that he covered his face with a veil.

There is a wonderful statue of Moses by Michelangelo, sculpted in about 1515, and now in the church of St Peter in Chains, in Rome. Moses quite clearly has two little horns growing out of his head, and this reflects a fairly widespread belief that when Moses met God he grew horns, though nobody quite knew why. The answer is that it was all due to a mistranslation of the Hebrew for 'rays of light', or the halo of light that seemed to surround Moses' face in the Hebrew Bible. We are now in the happy position of being able to restore Moses' halo and dispense with the horns, though it would be a pity to spoil Michelangelo's sculpture – no doubt some people will always think Moses had horns.

Horns or no horns, what God reveals to the prophet is the final mystery and absolute difference of the divine. Beyond human life, beyond the universe, beyond the gods, beyond the furthest realms of imagination and thought, there is the cloud of unknowing, which condescends to us in the form of an angel of fire. At this point, the prophet is no longer discerning one of a multitude of energies and powers, creative and destructive, conflicting, quarrelling and scheming. The prophet is overwhelmed by that which is beyond all energies and powers, in face of which they fade into oblivion: 'I am the Lord, and there is no other. I form light and create darkness, I make weal and create woe, I am the Lord, who do all these things' (Isaiah 45:7). With Moses the twilight of the gods had begun.

Many scholars think that a full monotheism has been read back into the story of Moses, and that the earlier tradition was still of Jahweh, the god of one particular group of nomadic tribes, the Hebrews. Nevertheless, that god over time developed characteristics that none of the Greek gods had, and that even Akhenaten's ill-fated attempt at monotheism had missed. Jahweh was not just the greatest of the gods, the superhuman heroes who were themselves ultimately in the grip of dark and inscrutable destiny. Jahweh, the god who is what God wills to be, whose face can never be seen and whose nature can never be comprehended, is the fathomless ocean of being from whom all worlds and gods and men originate, beyond whom there is no other, and beside whom there is no second.

Thomas Aquinas: the simplicity of God

Just as Maimonides at the end of the twelfth century placed the idea of the unknowable God at the centre of Jewish philosophical thought about God, so Thomas Aquinas (1225–74), writing in the thirteenth century, did the same for Christianity. Aquinas has almost become the official philosopher of the Roman Catholic Church. In 1879 Pope Leo XIII enjoined the study of Aquinas on all theological students. True, they do not have to believe everything he said, but what Aquinas said still forms the basis of much Catholic thinking about God. The Protestant Reformers did not challenge what he said about God – possibly they were too busy nailing up Theses about other things, or organising new churches. So it could reasonably be said that Aquinas' thoughts about God define what can be called the classical Christian view.

This is rather remarkable, because almost no Christians I have ever met have heard of this view. Many of them are shocked when they hear it, and simply do not believe anyone could ever have said such things.

It is hard to say just why this is. Partly it may be that pictures of God as an old man with a beard, like the one on the ceiling of the Sistine Chapel, have entered deeply into people's imaginations. Partly it is because people in modern culture have been so influenced by science that they think unless something is literally true it is not true at all. Then when they read the Bible, and find that God weeps, likes the smell of a good sacrifice, argues with Abraham, and sits on a throne in the sky, they think all these things must be literally true. The popular Christian god is not too different from Zeus, who lives on Mount Olympus and comes down to look at what is going on in Athens every few days.

That is the trouble with much popular religion: it is so crude and literal. This is not a matter of high-browed intellectuals knowing better than the common herd. It is a failure of imagination, a loss of the sense of poetry, a crass materialisation of the imagery of mythology. And that can happen to intellectuals just as much as to people of good common sense. So if you read modern books about mythology, what you get is just a set of weird stories about what Pallas Athene did to Hera, and then what happened next. The whole thing is deprived of religious sense. We just cannot see why people should ever have believed such stories, or what importance they could have had. The mystery of religion is turned into science fiction. Or perhaps that unduly denigrates science fiction, which sometimes does try, with some success, to re-evoke the sense of mystery in modern minds.

If there is one thing you have to say about Aquinas, it is that he did not take statements about God literally. His greatest work, the *Summa Theologiae,* or 'a comprehensive reference book on theology', states, 'We cannot know what God is, but only what he is not' (part 1a, question 3). Since this is near the beginning of a sixty-volume work (in the Blackfriars Latin–English edition) on theology, it might seem that he could have saved himself a great deal of work by just stopping right there. If you say, 'God is not like anything you can think of', there does not seem to be much to add.

But theology does not work like that. What is going on here is like a clearing of the ground: 'Get rid of all those old images. Forget the Sistine Chapel. Don't think that God is like what you read in the Bible.' That is the message, and that is what many Christians find so shocking, and many non-Christians find incomprehensible.

Aquinas is not, of course, saying that all these images are useless. He is saying that they are precisely images, and it is essential to take them as such. If we are trying to get at what God really is, we must move beyond all images. Aquinas puts this, rather misleadingly to modern ears, by saying that God is 'simple'. Nowadays we might interpret this as meaning, either that God is stupid, or that God is very easy to understand. That would be the opposite of what Aquinas means.

He means that God is not composite. That is, God is not made up of parts, is not divisible, and we cannot even distinguish different elements in the divine being. This may seem rather peculiar, coming from a Christian theologian who thinks that God is 'three persons in one substance', and so must be threefold in some sense. But it is what he says, so it is probably a good idea to ignore the Trinity (about which Aquinas later had much to say) for the moment. I will come back to it briefly in the final chapter. It is obvious, though, that whatever Aquinas thinks the Trinity is, it cannot be three different parts in God, much less three different individuals somehow existing inside God – another shock to many Christians. The Trinity, too, is an image which does not, in any form in which we can understand it, tell us what God truly and really is. The divine reality remains hidden, even in revelation, which discloses 'unfathomable mystery', and not literal truth, easy to understand.

If God is simple, there is nothing we can say about God which can be interpreted straightforwardly, as though it was easy for us to understand it. That is not really a remark about God so much as it is a remark about the nature of human language. Our language essentially divides the world up into parts and categories of things. If I say, 'This fruit is orange in colour', I am picking out a class of things – fruit – a class of colours, of which orange is one, and saying that there is an object which possesses the properties of being a fruit and being orange. I am dividing the world up into objects and lists of properties which objects may or may not possess – and I am also distinguishing the orange fruit from myself, the observer.

All such divisions and descriptions are to some extent conventional, and they presuppose that the world is a complex, composite reality which our language may be more or less good at dividing up in helpful ways. We might put it like this: all descriptions abstract and divide.

They abstract items from the totality of the experienced world, and divide them up into lists of properties in which we are interested.

That is all very well for the material world. But what Aquinas is saying is that such a process just cannot work with God. Any abstraction and division we make will falsify the being of God. Our language just does not fit God; it is quite inadequate to the task of describing God. Saying that God is simple is another way of saying that we cannot ever get an adequate description of God.

But why not? Because the God who is the origin and basis of the whole universe, and perhaps of many other universes, too, is just far greater than any human mind can comprehend. To attempt to describe such a God in human concepts would belittle God. God is an unbounded fullness of being, not limited in any way by anything else, and everything that exists is just a faint refracted image of the divine reality. Even the gods, even the manifestation of God as a creative mind, are limitations of the infinite fullness of the one reality from which all finite things derive their being. We might say that all other things receive their being as a gift. Only God has being as a possession, as the essential divine quality. God is the self-possessed, the self-existent. God is, as Aquinas says, '*Esse suum subsistens*', pure unlimited being subsistent in and for itself.

The five ways of demonstrating God

Aquinas tries to spell this out in what have become known as the 'five ways' for demonstrating God (*Summa Theologiae* 1a, question 2, article 3). These have given philosophers endless fun, as they seek to defend the five arguments for proving that there must be a God, or pick holes in them. Most unbiased observers of the philosophical scene would probably say that the result is a draw, as it nearly always is in these very basic philosophical debates. Some Catholic philosophers, following the Church's teaching that the existence of God can be demonstrated by reason, say that God's existence can indeed be demonstrated. Unfortunately, nobody has done it yet. The arguments get increasingly clever, but they never seem quite conclusive. If we depended on arguments alone, one could believe in God on Mondays and Wednesdays, not believe in God on Tuesdays and Thursdays, and remain undecided on Fridays and Saturdays. On Sundays one could play backgammon, as the eighteenth-century Scottish philosopher David Hume suggested, and forget the whole thing.

There is a different, and possibly more helpful, way of looking at these 'five ways of demonstrating God'. We could see them as exercises in meditation, attempting to generate a sense of what talk about God is trying inadequately to point to. Then they might go like this: Think of how all the things in the world constantly change. Spring changes to summer, youth to age, happiness to sadness, pleasure to pain. Everything seems to be in a state of constant change. Nothing is really permanent. Even I, the one who observes all these things, change, so that I am not really the same as I was ten years ago, much less fifty years ago. Who was that, we might think, looking back at an old photograph of ourselves? Was that really me, or was it just somebody who developed into me, but was really quite different? So, meditating on the changes of all we experience, even of the one who experiences, we might come to a sense of the transience, the fortuitousness, the fleeting nature of everything we experience.

Then we might have the sense that these changes are not just haphazard, or purely random. They seem to occur in an ordered way. People do not turn into carrots, and pigs do not fly. There seems to be some sort of cause of change, some reason why things change in the way they do, something that makes them change. Thinking on the transience of all experienced things, we might have the sense of an underlying reality which causes change, but is not itself part of the process that we experience. Beyond the changing and the transient, there is the changeless and the enduring. There is that which produces change, but is not itself changed. We might even have the sense that we can touch, however briefly, this unchanging source of the changing world, what T.S. Eliot called 'the still point of the turning world'. If we do – and nobody can guarantee that we will – then we have the sense of the boundless God, just beyond our grasp and yet sensed in that deep state of mindfulness when change fades into stillness. That is 'the first way of demonstrating God' – not a proof that God exists for anyone, whatever their state of mind is, but a way of bringing the mind to a particular state of apprehension, by meditating on change until the changeless breaks through into consciousness, and all differences are resolved into harmony.

The other four ways are similar in form. In the second way, we meditate on birth and death, on things coming into being and passing away, on the way in which all being is poised over the abyss of nothingness. And then, it may be, we sense what is beyond coming into being and passing away, that which always is, and so is beyond origination and decay.

In the third way, we meditate on the way in which all things could so easily be other than they are, the way in which all the beings we experience seem to be fortuitous, almost accidental. And we might break through to an experience of that which is essentially what it is, which just has to be the way it is, which must be, and owes its being to nothing other than itself.

In the fourth way, we meditate on the many sorts and grades of good and beautiful things that exist in the world. Thinking of beauty and goodness of many sorts, we may come to sense that which is beyond all particular beauties, but which is beauty itself, the one perfect source of which all particular beauties are faded reflections.

And in the fifth way, we meditate on the way in which there seems to be an orderedness and intelligibility in nature, so that things move according to elegant ordered processes. Thinking thus, we may come to sense beyond the natural order that which gives order and purpose, something akin to an intelligible realm from which all order issues, but which is beyond all experienced orderings.

These are not, then, dispassionate arguments. They are directions for the mind in meditation. They may not work. There is no guarantee that they will. But, if used regularly and faithfully, they may produce in the mind that sense of the 'beyond' which underlies the transience, origination and decay, precariousness, fragmentary beauty and partially apparent intelligibility of the experienced world, and puts the mind in touch with an unchanging, unoriginated, indestructible, unfragmented, wholly intelligible beauty which is the hidden ground of being and its ultimate power. This is beyond the feeling for the gods, which are the particular presences and powers manifest in the world. It is the feeling for that which is beyond the gods, beyond all particular presences and forms, for the ultimate mystery and power of being itself.

This has rarely been better put than by Plato, in his dialogue *The Symposium*, written in fourth-century BCE Athens. The dialogue is a celebration of love, by which he means desire for, delight in and respect for some object of human contemplation. He speaks of the many ways in which one might find love, in contemplating beautiful bodies or faces, or the stars and the sky, or music and art. There are many forms and ways of love. But in the end, he says,

> This is the right way of being initiated into the mysteries of love, to begin with examples of beauty in this world and use them as steps to ascend continually to absolute beauty as one's final aim. This above all others is the region where a truly human life should be spent, in the contemplation of absolute beauty. They will see it as absolute, existing alone with itself, unique, eternal; and all other beautiful things as partaking of it, in such a way that, while they come into being and pass away, it neither undergoes any increase or diminution nor suffers any change. One who contemplates absolute beauty and is in constant union with it will be able to bring forth not mere reflected images of goodness but true goodness, because one will be in contact not with a reflection but with the truth. And having brought forth and nurtured true goodness one will have the privilege of being beloved of God, and becoming, if ever a human being can, immortal oneself. For this reason, it is the duty of every human being to honour love.
>
> *Symposium*, p. 93

Here Plato is at one with the prophetic vision which sees God as a mysterious reality hidden in what a fourteenth-century anonymous English writer calls 'the cloud of unknowing', which can be pierced, if at all, only by 'the dart of longing love', a love which longs for knowledge of and union with absolute Beauty.

Here the prophet is transformed from a magician and fortune-teller, who may be possessed by spirits and who interprets dreams, into a mind and heart transfixed and transformed by a reality before which all words fail, and all images fade into insignificance. If such a prophet has supernatural power, it is the power of a fuller and more abundant life. If he is possessed, it is by a wisdom that searches the heart and lays bare the soul. If he has visions, they are of a reality which defies description and transforms the being of the one who sees. If he discerns signs of the sacred, they are the manifestations of eternity in the transient processes of time. It is only such a prophet who can discern such a God. Such a prophet, so the tradition affirms, was Moses.

Pseudo-Dionysius the Areopagite

I cannot resist bringing in a name that even beats that of Friedrich Schleiermacher for its sheer obscurity. Not only is it an obscure name, but nobody knows whose name it was in the first place. Dionysius was an early sixth-century writer, possibly from Syria. But he was very early confused with the Dionysius mentioned in the book of Acts (chapter 17), who was a member of the Areopagus (probably at that time a court for controlling religion and morals in Athens), and who became a Christian in response to Paul's preaching. Because of that alleged apostolic connection, his writings came to have great authority in the medieval church, and are often referred to with respect by Aquinas.

Dionysius was then further confused with St Denys, the third-century patron saint of France. That is when he became 'pseudo' as well as an Areopagite, but it did not do him any harm. His importance is that he is in many ways a link between Plato and Moses which later thinkers in Judaism, Christianity and Islam all exploited (it might be a pseudo-link, like Dionysius himself, but once made it was never forgotten). He connected the Hebrew tradition of the unknowableness of the divine name (and therefore of the divine nature) with the Platonic tradition of the utter transcendence of 'the Good' or 'the One', from which all other things derive their being. It was a powerful combination, which defined European and Near Eastern ways of thinking about God for over a thousand years.

Dionysius went so far with negative ways of speaking of God that he even denied that God existed: 'It is the universal cause of existence while itself existing not, for it is beyond all being' (from his book *On the Divine Names*). This might seem like nonsense. It would certainly cause a stir if a preacher went up into the pulpit and said, 'According to our greatest authorities, God is not like anything of which you can think. In fact, I can tell you that God does not even exist. Let us pray.'

But of course the point is to say that God does not exist in the same way that anything we can imagine exists. God is 'Nothing', not-a-thing, but that Nothing is not a sheer vacuum. It is that in which all distinctions fade away, but in which they are rooted. 'All attributes may be affirmed at once of God,' says Dionysius. And again: 'From its Oneness it becomes manifold while yet remaining within itself.' To affirm everything at once is just about the same thing as denying anything in particular. To say that something becomes many while remaining unchanged defies the rules of logic. What is going on here?

The point is, I think, to shake the mind out of its normal patterns of plodding reasoning into an intuition of what wholly transcends intellectual understanding of the human sort. The bondage of language must be shattered. And then what? Of course, no one can say! There is that which cannot be said, but we can perhaps show the way to it. In that sense, it can be shown, but not described. The final words of the prophet have to cancel themselves out, and leave the mind in a new world, a world that fifteenth-century Cardinal Nicholas of Cusa described as one of 'learned ignorance', a world as far from sheer lack of information as one could possibly get.

The really important point is to see how deeply the idea of the ultimate unknowability of God is rooted in the major traditions of thinking about God. These are not the writings of radical theologians bent on destroying their own beliefs. They lie at the heart of orthodoxy, in Judaism, Christianity, Islam and many other traditions too.

For example, one of the greatest thinkers of Islam, the eleventh-century teacher **al-Ghazali**, writes that the essential nature of God 'transcends all that is comprehensible'. It is 'transcendent of and separate from every characterisation', so that the instructed 'avoid denoting him by attributes altogether' (in his book *The Niche for Lights*, sections 3,3 and 3,4). And in the Indian traditions, the eighth-century teacher **Sankara** writes of *Brahman* (the ultimately real) that 'his omnipotence, omniscience and so on all depend on lack of knowledge; in reality none of these qualities belong to the self' (*The Vedanta Sutras*, in Max Muller (ed.), *Sacred Books of the East*, vol. 34, p. 329). What Sankara calls *nirguna Brahman*, *Brahman* without qualities, lies beyond *saguna Brahman*, *Brahman* with qualities. Thus in many orthodox religious traditions, it is insisted that the essential nature of God is unknowable.

Why is this fact so often unknown or forgotten? Perhaps because for so many people agnosticism sits very uneasily with faith. Faith, they think, means being certain of your beliefs, and the odder and more unlikely the beliefs are the more faith you need to have. So the person of greatest faith would be the one who really believed that the moon was made of cheese, despite all evidence to the contrary.

But is that what faith really is? It might rather be that faith is a sort of insight into the nature of reality, an insight which does not increase ordinary factual knowledge, but sets all our knowledge and experience in a new perspective, *'sub specie aeternitatis'*, in the light of eternity. True faith might actually decrease our 'religious' certainties, as we realise how little we know or can say about God, and how much depends on the wordless experience that all religious doctrines only dimly and inadequately point towards.

Christians and Jews have argued endlessly and disgracefully among themselves and with each other for generations. But what if a Christian sat down and said, 'Well, actually I do not know much about God, and everything I do say is so inadequate as to be virtually false'? Then a Jew might say, 'It's funny you should say that. I do not know much about God either'. How could they then have an argument? If they did have an argument, the winner might be the one who proved that he knew less about God than his opponent. What a change it would make if religious arguments were like that: a rather refreshing change, too.

The doctrine of analogy

But of course religious people do have to say something about God. Even if all our language about God has to be in terms of images and metaphors, some of them must be less misleading than others. If I say God is a lump of green plasticine, I suppose somebody might find that a very moving image. But most people would find it rather less emotionally powerful than saying that God is a shepherd who cares for his sheep, or a husband who loves his bride. Different religious doctrines are largely about the images of God which are felt by different groups of people to be most appropriate.

This usually comes down to following different prophets or religious teachers, who claim to have some experience of God which inspires them to use a certain sort of imagery. When the second Isaiah says. 'Your maker is your husband' (Isaiah 54:5), he is not saying that God is a male who has gone through a wedding ceremony. He is saying that the Israelites are not just slaves of God, bound to submit to the divine will in fear. They are in a much closer and more loving relation than that, something like the relation a wife should be in with her husband. There is an analogy between the relation of husband and wife and the relation of God and created persons, or at least some created persons.

God cannot really get married, and is not even a person, much less masculine in gender. But if you think of God as a loving husband, it will put you in the most appropriate and fulfilling relation to God – or so the prophet Isaiah says, anyway. And many generations of Jews and Christians have found that to be true in their own experience. Thinking of yourself as married to a totally faithful and loving person is good for your self-esteem, your sense of security, and your general happiness. Moreover, when you do think like that, you may well tend to have experiences of God's love or compassion or presence which reinforce the image you took on trust from the prophet to begin with. At any rate, enough people do have such reinforcing experiences to make that religious tradition an enduring and powerful one.

There is of course a danger that you might just adopt that way of talking because it provides comfort and security. That is what critics of religion say – faith is just a crutch for emotionally insecure people. There are two things to be said to that. First, there is nothing wrong with emotional security, and anything that helps us to have it deserves at least a second look. Second, these images of shepherds and husbands did not evolve because they give emotional security. They arose from an overwhelming prophetic experience, in moments of inspiration, and it is simply good luck that they are also emotionally satisfying (some of the time, anyway).

The basic images and analogies of religion are not invented by philosophers: they are spoken by prophets, and the rest of us have to get on interpreting them as well as we can. The general interpretation given by Aquinas is usually called the 'doctrine of analogy', and it is this: 'So far as the perfections signified are concerned the words are used literally of God ... but so far as the way of signifying these perfections is concerned the words are used inappropriately' (in the *Summa Theologiae*, 1a, 13, 3).

Aquinas' suggestion is that it is literally true that God is good and wise and, if not actually a husband, does relate to us as a really good husband should. On the other hand, these things are not true of God in the sense that we understand them. To put it crudely, we are right to use these words, but we do not know what they mean. Or a bit less crudely, Aquinas writes: 'Such words do say what God is . . . but fail to represent adequately what he is.'

Putting this in the terms I have been using, it is by thinking about all sorts of good things that we approach knowledge of God. But we must never think that God is good just in the way that any of those things are. They trace a route towards God, but they do not provide a hard-and-fast definition, and they should never mislead us into thinking that at last we have comprehended God.

Many people misunderstand this doctrine of analogy. They think it means that God really is something like people or partners or things we can imagine, whereas in fact what it is saying is that God is nothing like anything we can imagine. The analogy points to a radical difference. But it says that, though God is not like what we think, it is correct for us to *speak* of God as father or husband. It is the best we can do – so the prophets tell us – and if sensitively used such talk can lead us towards the profound silence which is the heart of knowledge of God, in the great classical traditions.

As Aquinas said when he came near to the completion of his great *Summa,* on 6 December 1273, when it is widely held that he himself had such an experience of God as he said Mass, 'All that I have written seems like straw to me.' And after that he wrote no more.

Three mystics

All of us can, to some extent, follow the way of analogy towards a state of consciousness where all words fail. But it is in the fourteenth to sixteenth centuries that three great writers in the Christian tradition sought to depict what such an experience is like when, for the few who are called to it, it becomes the central goal of the human search. They are often called 'mystics', though that word can be misleading because it has such a wide meaning and is used at different times to stand for so many different things. However, if a mystic is a person who stresses the importance of direct knowledge of, or even some sort of union with, God, which is beyond direct description, it captures quite well the thought that God is ultimately incomprehensible, but yet can in some way be apprehended by the human mind.

The anonymous English author of *The Cloud of Unknowing* writes: 'The higher part of contemplation, insofar as it is possible to possess it here below, consists entirely in this darkness and in this cloud of unknowing, with a loving impulse and a dark gazing into the simple being of God himself alone' (p. 137).

In sixteenth-century Spain, Teresa of Avila writes in a very positive way about loving God in a rich emotional way. But in the end, she too points to the ultimate silence of the contemplative vision of the divine: 'The Lord joins the soul to himself. But he does so by making it blind and deaf ... it does not understand anything, for all the faculties are lost' (this quotation is taken from Harvey Egan, *An Anthology of Christian Mysticism*, p. 445).

And John of the Cross, who knew Teresa well at Avila, writes of a time when 'God begins to communicate himself through pure spirit by an act of simple contemplation, in which there is no discursive succession of thought' (from the same anthology, p. 456).

These writers do not suggest that the search for such an experience is for everybody. But it is very important for everybody clearly to know that the knowledge of God is beyond ordinary human thought and understanding, and there is no reason why most people should not be able to attain some experience of this sort, however fragmentary. The practice of contemplation is what many people would now call 'meditation', stilling the mind so that it simply is, and is open to that power of being which does not come in emotional visions or the occurrence of uplifting sensations. For in that way the mind opens itself to that which is most fully real, which is the power of all being, beyond all change and decay. In the process, the mind itself is purged or purified of a longing for purely sensual or material things and possessions, and

Listening to silent music: St John of the Cross and St Teresa of Avila.

can achieve a deep inner calm and security. The mind becomes one with the power of being, and thus, as the twentieth-century theologian Paul Tillich put it, can attain the 'courage to be', to affirm being, in face of all anxiety and fearfulness about the future or about the passing away of all things.

Sometimes people think of the prophets as quite opposed to the 'mystics', as though they are quite different sorts of people. Sometimes people think mystics only exist somewhere in the East, while prophets are fiery characters with very crude ideas of God. In fact the prophets were well aware of the mystery of the divine being, and they speak of the way in which the human mind and the ultimate power of being can be one, as if in loving union ('marriage') or as covered in the cloud of glory which hides God's 'face' ('union'). That is an important part of the prophetic message, which takes us beyond the gods to that which simply is, without a name that can be spoken or an image that can be formed, but which may be known in a paradoxical and indescribable way by love. St John of the Cross in his poems often speaks of the soul's relation to God in terms of passionate romantic love. But beyond all these complex and moving images, there lies something else, a 'silent music, sounding solitude', a word that can never be spoken:

> The higher he ascends
> the less he understands
> because the cloud is dark
> which lit up the night,
> whoever knows this
> remains always in unknowing
> transcending all knowledge ...
> And if you should want to know:
> the highest knowledge lies
> in the loftiest sense
> of the essence of God:
> this is a work of his mercy,
> to leave one without

understanding,

transcending all knowledge.

'Stanzas Concerning an Ecstasy Experienced in
High Contemplation', stanzas 5 and 8 in
Collected Works of St John of the Cross

Find out more ...

A good introduction to scholarly views of the Old Testament is Bernhard
Anderson, *The Living World of the Old Testament* (Englewood Cliffs,
Prentice-Hall, 1975).

Moses Maimonides wrote the original, and classic, *Guide for the Perplexed* (trans.
M. Friedlander (London, Routledge & Kegan Paul, 1904).

The most important Roman Catholic philosopher is Thomas Aquinas, author of
the *Summa Theologiae* (ed. Thomas Gilby, Blackfriars, in conjunction with
London, Eyre & Spottiswoode and New York, McGraw-Hill, 1963–). The
most relevant part to read is part 1a, questions 2–11, on the existence and
nature of God. The main headings at least are worth noting carefully.

Plato's dialogue on the nature of love is the *Symposium* (trans. Walter Hamilton,
Harmondsworth, Penguin, 1951).

A key text on the apophatic way is Dionysius, *On the Divine Names* (trans. C.E.
Rolt, London, SPCK, 1977).

3

The love that moves the sun

In which the reader will discover that there are 603 more commandments than one might have thought, but will not discover why Jews do not eat pork. The reader will be invited to consider that Jesus was an Orthodox Jew, and that Calvin did not want to keep Sunday special, will find a suggestion about why God made people, and about how metaphysics was invented by mistake. The reader will then find that Kant was not quite such an out-and-out Rationalist as some people think, and will see how this Enlightenment philosopher thought that faith was still necessary to reach the parts that Reason could not.

The 613 commandments

Part of the Hebrew prophetic tradition was an emphasis on the mysterious unknowability, the total otherness of God. But an equally important part of that tradition was the insistence that God is more, not less, perfect than the most perfect thing we can imagine. As the one perfect source of our very existence, God commands our absolute and uncompromising obedience. The God of the Hebrews may be a God whose inner nature is unknown, but is a God whose commands are compelling. God may be beyond human comprehension, but insists that worshippers should be wholly committed to the pursuit of justice and mercy. It is precisely this vision of God as morally compelling that is the distinctive contribution of the prophets of ancient Judah and Israel to the world's understanding of the divine.

After liberating Israel from Egypt, Moses climbed Mount Sinai and disappeared into a cloud for forty days. There he met Jahweh, who presented him with a list of 'statutes and ordinances', which the Israelites were commanded to obey. This was a very large list. There are generally reckoned to be, not ten, but six hundred and thirteen commandments – though obviously you can count the total in slightly different ways. All these were written down – by Jahweh himself, we are told – and in addition there were many other commandments that Moses had to commit to memory, and that were not written down until much later. These form the *Halakhah,* which might be loosely translated as 'the way' of Israel. They were largely codified into the Mishnah in the second century CE, part of which received a definitive commentary in the fifth-century CE Babylonian Talmud, which then became the main text of Rabbinical Judaism.

All that may sound very confusing, and it is much easier just to say that God gave Moses the Ten Commandments, and that was that. But we have to remember that this is a great oversimplification, even though the Ten Commandments (called the 'Ten Words' in the Bible) are of special importance. What God really gave Moses was the Torah, which gives lots of statutes and ordinances, along with the history of the Patriarchs of Israel, and many stories, allegories and wise sayings. In the Hebrew Bible or Old Testament, the first five books, from Genesis to Deuteronomy, are often called the 'written Torah', and it is clear that it is not just a list of laws. It is the whole revelation or teaching (the word *torah* is Hebrew for 'teaching') of God to Moses. It includes records of the various acts of God, who calls, liberates, rewards and punishes Israel, and records of Israel's very varying responses to those acts, as well as the rules by which Israel was to live.

The point is that God does not just issue lists of laws in a vacuum, as though saying, 'Do this because I say so, and don't ask questions.'

Admittedly it can sometimes sound like that. God says such things as, 'Thou shalt not eat lobsters.' And the Israelites no doubt replied, 'Lobsters? Chance would be a fine thing. Lobsters in the middle of the desert? You must be joking!' And God said, 'Thou shalt not eat kids cooked in their mothers' milk.' The Israelites responded, 'Who would ever have thought of that? Now you come to mention it, I'm quite tempted to give it a try. What could possibly be wrong with it?' 'Also, thou shalt not eat pigs.' 'What? No sausages? Would you mind explaining that?' 'One thing I forgot to mention, thou shalt not question the Lord your God.' And that puts an end to that conversation.

Orthodox Jews do not try to seek an explanation for the laws. They come from God, and that is that. Nevertheless, they are not arbitrary. The laws set the boundaries of a way of life in relation to God that Israel was called to follow. Those things are forbidden which might compromise that way of life and that relationship. Now how eating pork sausages could do that might well be obscure. But that prohibition has become an integral part of the whole set of laws that define Jewish life, part of what makes one a religious Jew, and so it is accepted along with the rest of the territory.

Pigs and other animals

If you want to know why pigs are forbidden, the best guess is to look at anthropological work with tribal societies which deals with prohibitions that seem similar. An earlier generation thought that pork was forbidden because it tends to breed disease in hot climates, and that this was just an early public hygiene regulation. But anthropological work in tribal societies throughout the world casts doubt on this. In Polynesia, things **taboo** or 'tapu' are banned, because of their relation to 'mana', or the power that comes from kinship with the gods. Mana is a dangerous power and needs to be contained by strict regulations. Thus the tribal chiefs, their spears and homes, also the bones and tombs of the dead, and anything connected with the worship of the gods, is taboo.

A remnant of this attitude can be found in some churches, for example, where lay people, especially women, are sometimes not allowed into the sanctuary where the sacrifice of the Mass is offered. The sanctuary is a sacred place; it is taboo. Taboos protect the sacred powers and prevent them from breaking out and destroying the people.

All this might imply that pigs were originally sacred, or associated with the gods in some way. Perhaps their fertility was seen as a sign of divine power, and so they were set apart, tabooed. That is one guess. Another is that pigs, animals which, as the Bible puts it, do not both chew the cud and have cloven hooves, were seen as somehow improper animals. Many things seen as mixing categories of things are forbidden – mixing linen with wool, and ploughing with an ox and an ass, for example. Perhaps pigs were seen as ambiguous animals, falling between two categories, and therefore potential centres of divine destructive power, where it might 'leak' into the world. (This sort of explanation is suggested by the anthropologist Mary Douglas in her book *Purity and Danger* – also the name of an excellent ice-cream you can buy in an Oxford ice-cream parlour founded by two of her former students.)

The truth is, nobody knows why eating pork is forbidden in the Torah. The origin of such a taboo lies in the far past, beyond recorded time. Over many generations the taboo passed into the list of clean – *kosher* – and unclean foods, on the wrong side. Now it is accepted simply because it is there. It is a tradition of the people, it defines what it is to be a religious Jew, and observing the rules is a way of showing loyalty to God. To disobey would be to compromise the relationship with God, simply because it would be wilfully disobeying God. 'I do it not because I can work out that it is sensible, but just because God said it, and I love to do what God commands', is, after all, a very good religious reason.

Or is it? I suppose it all depends on what sort of God you have in mind. It is not a very good reason if you have a god like Zeus, who regards humans with a certain dispassionate disdain. It is a very bad reason if you have a god like Ares, the 'hater of men'. But it might be a good reason if there is a god who cherishes you and has the power to do you good. Jahweh was believed to have chosen Israel, as a husband chooses a wife, to have liberated them from slavery in Egypt, and to have promised them that they would become a great and flourishing people. Such a god would not command things for no reason, and we might be sure that doing what that God commands would work out for good.

The two great commandments

The commands of God in the Torah are of many kinds. There are rituals in which a priest mixes holy water, flour and earth and makes a woman drink it to see if she has committed adultery, which looks pretty much like straightforward magic. There are laws for purifying discharges from various parts of the body. There are laws forbidding eating animals that do not chew the cud but have hooves. All in all, it looks to an anthropologist very much as though a whole set of ancient taboos and rituals have become embedded in tradition and set into the Torah. Any Jew would say that most of those laws have long since passed into disuse, but they sometimes form the basis of more recent rabbinic decisions. For instance, the modern prohibition on mixing dishes or ovens that have been used for meat and milk foods derives in a rather roundabout way from the prohibition on eating a kid cooked in its mother's milk (not in itself a great temptation in Golders Green or Manhattan!). And the prohibition of switching on an electric light on Saturdays which some Jews obey derives from the rule against lighting a fire on the Sabbath.

It would be a big mistake to think that Jews, even the most Orthodox, take the commandments literally. The rules are more like a set of precedents which rabbis can adapt to changing circumstances, declare obsolete, or re-interpret – but never ignore. Jewish law is a body of principles for living in a covenant relationship with God, and while tradition is of very great importance for the Orthodox – and rather more flexible for Reformed, Conservative or Liberal – Jews it is never simply the written words that define exactly what is to be done in a particular situation. Ironically, although some Christians accuse Jews of being 'legalistic', it is often the Christians who are more legalistic about the written texts than Jewish rabbis, who see the statutes and ordinances as bases for rigorous discussion, frequent disagreement and ever-expanding debate about what God requires.

It may seem as though many of these ordinances are trivial rules, and in themselves they are. For an observant Jew, however, they are all part of the way of obedience to God, which is a way of expressing love and reverence for God, and marking of the whole of one's life as consciously related to God. The real heart of the Torah does not lie in those rules. It is summed up in what some rabbis – and Jesus – called 'the two great commandments', to love God with all one's heart, soul and strength (Deuteronomy 6), and to love one's neighbour as oneself (Leviticus 19).

These might seem very odd commandments, for how can you be ordered to love God or other people? Well, the Hebrews did not think of love as just an emotional feeling; it is a very practical thing. You love other people by caring for them, by giving freely to them and by helping them in trouble. You love God by appreciating, cherishing and taking care of the world God has created, and by co-operating in the divine work of creating new and wonderful things. The Torah spells out some of the ways in which such practical love can be expressed.

There were law codes, given by the gods, before the Torah. Hammurabi, creator of the first Babylonian empire in about 1792 BCE – just as Abraham was leaving Ur – created a great law code, said to be commanded by the sun god. In it there were laws of justice and punishment, very like some of the Hebrew laws. But what the Hebrew view had that Hammurabi did not was the sense that God was the creator of all things, and required reverence and thankfulness for the good things of creation, and responsible action to care especially for those who did not have a full share of those good things, the poor and needy. Jahweh was not a god who changed his mind, had moods and sulks, and needed to receive sacrifices from his worshippers. Jahweh was a god who made all things, and commanded humans to care for them and for one another. At least, that was what Jahweh had developed into by the time of the second Isaiah, and you can see the beginnings of this in the Ten Commandments given through Moses.

The Ten Commandments

These can be found in the book of Exodus, chapter 20. Some people think the Ten Commandments are a set of universal moral rules, which everybody should obey. But they are not. They are addressed to the Jews, the descendants of Abraham through Isaac. Jahweh begins by reminding them that a divine act of liberation has freed them from slavery in Egypt, so they belong to God. Jahweh forbids them to worship any other gods or to make images of natural objects and worship them. Jahweh is a 'jealous god'. That is, Jahweh claims the exclusive loyalty of the people who have been liberated. For them to worship any other god would be like adultery, it would break the special relationship that Jahweh has set up with Abraham's descendants. So these first two commandments are specifically for Jews.

Then Jahweh forbids any use of the divine name for evil or magical purposes. Jahweh is not to be used to help win petty arguments or get revenge on enemies, as many gods were used. And Jahweh commands that every seventh day is to be a day of rest from work, when not even fires can be lit. Again, these are not universal rules for the whole world. They exist precisely to set apart the people of Israel as different from other people, as chosen for a special covenant-relation with God.

In many Christian churches of the Reformation, the Ten Commandments were written up on the wall on either side of the main altar. The first four commandments were usually on the left-hand side of the altar, and the last six on the right. But in fact the ones on the left, the 'first table of the law', the ones just described, were addressed only to

Jews, to remind them to worship only Jahweh, their liberator, and to keep the laws of Jahweh – laws which Christians gave up long ago.

There is nothing really wrong with reinterpreting ancient laws from a Christian point of view, as long as you know what you are doing. Christians consider themselves to be a 'new Israel', also liberated by God, not from Egypt but from the slavery of sin. The first four commandments are then given a rather different, less social and more personal interpretation, allowing Christians to make images of Jesus, to relax the Sabbath rules a good deal, and even to change their holy day from Saturday to Sunday – in other words, to take the laws in the opposite sense from that in which they were originally intended. That is all right – people can adapt the rules if they consider it necessary. What is surprising is that some Christians think they are taking the commandments literally, when in fact they are changing the meaning quite considerably from the plain sense of the text. Christians can certainly use the Ten Commandments if they wish. But these commandments were originally, and in their original interpretation still are, intended for the Jews, for a people who see themselves as chosen by Jahweh, and not for absolutely everyone. They are the ground rules for keeping that special relationship with God going.

The final six commandments are of more universal scope – not committing murder or adultery, not stealing or making false accusations, not desiring other people's goods, and respecting your parents are fairly good ground rules for any healthy society. But if you take them literally they are rather minimal. You can keep all of them simply by sitting still and minding your own business. More to the point, you can keep all of them in a society which is hugely unequal, which has slavery, violence and harshly punitive laws (just like ancient Israel, really). You could be a millionaire with hundreds of slaves and dozens of wives, calmly watching the rest of the world descend into chaos while, like Nero, you practised your violin-playing. But you could still say, 'I have not committed murder or adultery, stolen or made false accusations, or desired anybody else's goods – I don't need to, thanks, I have more than enough of my own.' You might think you were a perfectly moral individual – but there would surely be something wrong.

A lot more is required of humans than that they keep these minimal rules of morality. We need to go outside the Ten Commandments to the rest of the Torah to discover what that is. When you do so, the pointers are pretty clear. Humans are obligated to serve and obey God, their creator. That is the first and most important human duty. But how is that to be done? There is a temptation to confine the service of God to special 'religious' ceremonies. If you perform the sacrifices correctly, God will be pleased and may do what you wish.

This temptation existed in Israel, as well as in every human religious community. So sometimes Jahweh is spoken of as a rather frightening tribal god who promises good to Israel and harm to her enemies, in return for correctly executed sacrifices (just like the gods of the *Iliad*). But by the eighth century BCE, Amos, Micah, the first of the Isaiahs, and Hosea, the first of the prophets of Israel whose teachings are preserved in the Old Testament, were protesting against this temptation in the strongest terms: 'I hate, I despise your feasts, and I take no delight in your solemn assemblies. Even though you offer me your burnt offerings and cereal offerings, I will not accept them, and the peace offerings of your fatted beasts I will not look upon. Take away from me the voice of your songs; to the melody of your harps I will not listen. But let justice roll down like waters, and righteousness like an everflowing stream.' Thus Amos (5:21–4), speaking in the name of God, rejects all views of religion as a matter of rituals for obtaining private benefits. Micah voices similar thoughts: 'What does the Lord require of you but to do justice, and to love kindness, and to walk humbly with your God?' (6:8). And Isaiah writes, 'I have had enough of burnt offerings of rams ... cease to do evil, learn to do good; seek justice, correct oppression, defend the fatherless, plead for the widow' (1:11–17).

God, whatever God used to be, is now no longer a spirit of place or family lineage, pleased by the flattery of gifts. God is the only creator of the whole earth, whose will is that the world should flourish, and that humans, made in the image of God, should find their vocation in enabling all good things to flourish. True religion is not, then, the ritually correct offering of slaughtered animals, but obedience to the will of God, which is for the flourishing of the earth, for justice and kindness and care for those who suffer.

This in any case expresses the most basic meaning of sacrifice: that you freely give to the gods part – perhaps the best part – of what they have given to you, but which you have increased by your own effort, to show what you have done (that you have 'worked well'), and to express gratitude for the gods' basic provision of the necessities of life, and for their protection and help. Of course, such gifts to the gods have other meanings, too. They may become bribes, to get a god to answer some request – at the beginning of the *Iliad*, the old priest prays to Apollo, 'If ever . . . I have burnt for you fat-wrapped thigh-bones of bulls and goats, grant this my prayer.' They may become compensation, to get a god to overlook some failing or appeasement for some fault – 'he may be willing to accept the smoke of lambs and goats without blemish, and drive the plague away from us'. They may become ways of sharing in the happy life of the gods in a feast, where good roast beef and wine can be consumed with a good conscience – 'they appeased the god with music . . . and he listened with delight in his heart'. But the main meaning, as with all gifts to a superior, is to honour and express loyalty, to give thanks for good things received, and to hope for continuing help and support. Humans co-operate in bringing about the purposes of the gods, but they always remain servants, instruments of those purposes.

The Hebrew prophets made a great leap in religious insight when they taught that the right way to honour the gods is not with sacrifices of bulls and goats, made to a petulant and limited god, for the sake of some desired good for oneself and one's friends. The right way to honour the gods is with the sacrifice of at least part of one's own life and happiness, offered to the one limitless creator, for the sake of all created beings. 'The sacrifice acceptable to God is a broken spirit; a broken and contrite heart, O God, thou wilt not despise' (51:17).

The right way to honour the gods? Fortunately not. Mural depicting Abraham offering Isaac up for sacrifice.

That is the import of the Torah, and the criterion by which all its statutes and ordinances are to be interpreted. In view of all this, the 'two great commandments' of the Torah provide the clearest way of sorting out how to interpret all the many sorts of laws, from many different times and circumstances, for current practice. The second one in particular, 'love your neighbour as yourself', is a commandment which will quite quickly rule out all sorts of laws which were once considered acceptable, when you think about it. For example, slavery and cruel punishments can no longer be defended, when you really seek to work out what you would like done to you if you were in somebody else's shoes. Women cannot be regarded as inferior to men, and when one reflects that animals, too, are our neighbours on the earth, quite a few widely accepted human practices may need to be amended – including the slaughter of animals for sacrifice! This is a rule with teeth. Of course it implies that you should love yourself – there wouldn't be much point in telling you to love your neighbour as yourself, if you actually hate yourself and intend to commit suicide. It implies that you should seek a truly good life for yourself and for other people in just the same way. At this point the 613 rules of the Torah point to a truly universal morality.

Jesus and the Law

But if that is true, is the Torah irrelevant, simply superseded by a universal human morality? Christians sometimes seem to think that Jesus taught that the Torah, which they call 'the Law', was abolished, and they tend to quote the Sermon on the Mount (found in the gospel of Matthew, chapters 5–7, and in a rather different version – where it takes place on a plain – in the gospel of Luke, chapter 6) to this effect. Jesus says, 'You have heard it said', and continues, 'But I say to you', which could sound like a contradiction of the Law. But when you look at it more closely, you see that Jesus was not contradicting the Law at all. He was comparing some rather literalistic traditional interpretations of the Law with a much deeper interpretation, which talks about inner motives as well as outward observances. But he is still talking about the Law. Indeed, the beginning of the sermon should have made that perfectly clear. Jesus says, 'Think not that I have come to abolish the law and the prophets ... not an iota, not a dot, will pass from the law until all is accomplished' (5:17, 18). That sounds fairly legalistic. It certainly does not say, 'Do not worry what the law says, do what I say instead.'

The fact that Jesus was an observant Jew who taught that the Law should be obeyed, but in a deep and inward sense, is confirmed by two key pieces of evidence in the New Testament. First, the apostle Peter, who surely knew very well what Jesus taught, always insisted on keeping the Law, and was shocked by a vision that he had on three occasions which seemed to imply that he should even speak to Gentiles. Second, at a general meeting at Jerusalem, recorded in the book of Acts, chapter 15, there was a heated debate on whether new disciples should keep the Law. There would have been no debate if Jesus had already said they need not bother. And the result of the debate was a compromise – new converts did not have to be circumcised (which saved the men from a rather painful ordeal, given that it was all done with a flint knife, and without anaesthetic), but they still had to eat kosher food. Obviously, giving up the Torah was a gradual and unexpected process, brought about largely by the fact that the new movement was rapidly becoming almost wholly Gentile.

Since this is all so clear in the New Testament, how is it that so many people think Jesus gave up the Law? I suspect it is a bit of anti-Jewish prejudice, which goes along with the ridiculous claim that Jews are legalists, whereas Christians are concerned about the innermost motives of human action. Christians can be very legalistic about the application of their own moral rules, and Jews can very readily read the Torah, as Jesus the Jew probably did, as concerned with inward motives as well as with outward acts.

The fact is that Jesus did care about the Torah, about the statutes and ordinances given by God through the prophet Moses. But he interpreted them in the light of a universal and rigorous application of the principle of 'loving your neighbour as yourself', an application which itself derived from a view of God's love as universal and unlimited. So Jesus taught that anger, lust, infidelity, dishonesty, vindictiveness and hatred are inner motives of the human heart which are all completely opposed to the universal love of God for all creation (that is the teaching of the Sermon on the Mount, Matthew 5:21–48). To love God truly is to admire and wish to be like God, and that requires rooting out all those motives from the heart. It requires that you should love your neighbour, not just as you love yourself, but as God loves you.

All this was meant as an interpretation of the Torah. But it does seem that you could adopt these principles without keeping the precise rules of the Torah. When the early Christian churches found that they were almost entirely Gentile, they were thus able to renounce the 613 rules of *Torah* – which were, after all, for Jews – while claiming to remain true to the ethical teachings of Jesus. They did not think of themselves, however, as having a totally secular morality. Rather, following the example of the Sermon on the Mount, they tried to give an inward and spiritual meaning to the revealed laws of God.

Calvin and the commandments

This is an attitude that has continued throughout Christian history. A very good example of it is found in the work of the French Reformed theologian **John Calvin** (1509–64), in his major work, usually called in English the *Institutes of the Christian Religion*. Calvin has sometimes been taken to be recovering the original meaning of the Gospels, getting back to the purity of Jesus' teaching, and away from the superstitions and corruptions of Church tradition. Perhaps he thought of himself in that way (at least on Tuesdays and Thursdays – but on Mondays and Wednesdays I suspect that he knew better).

He certainly did want to reform the corruptions of the sixteenth-century Church as he found it. But when he came to write about the Ten Commandments (in book 2, chapter 8 of the *Institutes*) he in fact gave them a new and powerful interpretation. What he did was to discard outright any literalistic interpretation, which just accepts the plain meanings of the words as they stand (Protestants are mistaken when they think that is what either they or Calvin actually do). Instead, he asserted that 'there is always more in the requirements and prohibitions of the Law than is expressed in words'. For example, 'If God forbids,' he wrote, 'He commands the opposite.'

So the commandment, 'Thou shalt not kill' really means 'we are to aid our neighbour's life by every means in our power'. We have to get behind the words to the underlying principle, which is one of respect for human life, made in the image of God. Now the obvious question is, how did Calvin know what that underlying principle is? Calvin's answer would be that he knows Jesus taught obedience to the Law (he was quite aware of that), and that Jesus, in the Sermon on the Mount, teaches that the Law must be given just the sort of radical interpretation Calvin has in mind. When Jesus takes the commandment 'Do not kill', he says that it implies 'Do not be angry'. (It is generally thought that Matthew was so bothered by this that he added the phrase, 'without a cause', which is only in some extant manuscripts.) That, Calvin thinks, implies that God commands the opposite, which is something like love (is that the opposite of anger?). So the commandment, 'Do not kill', is really equivalent to the commandment 'Love your neighbour as yourself'. If anyone was bothered – and they should be – by the fact that love nowhere occurs in the Ten Commandments, Calvin has the best answer. The underlying principle of all the commandments is love, and they explicitly spell out some of the most obvious opposites of love, which are to be avoided at all costs.

Calvin deals with all the commandments in this way. The first four express the spiritual teachings that God alone is to be adored, trusted, implored and thanked, that we should not think we can represent God adequately in our imaginations, that we should not use religion for purposes of ambition or advancement, and that we should constantly remember the presence of God with us.

His treatment of the Sabbath commandment is particularly interesting. Those who call themselves Calvinists are often chiefly distinguished by their strict observance of Sunday as the Lord's day, on which no work of any sort may be done, and no frivolous entertainments, such as playing cards or watching television, may be indulged in. Many children brought up in Calvinist homes may remember Sundays with something like dread, as days of total boredom, when they had to sit in their best clothes all day listening to edifying sermons and singing dreary psalms.

But hear what Calvin himself has to say on the subject: 'Christians should have nothing to do with a superstitious observance of days.' There should perhaps be one day a week when the servants are given time off, and there should be some time in the week set aside for public worship. But the chief principle of the Sabbath commandment is this: 'we must rest entirely, that God may work in us' – and not on one day of the week, but all the time! Such a 'perpetual resting from our works' is a purely inward and spiritual principle which is well expressed in one of the mottoes of Alcoholics Anonymous: 'Let go and let God'. It has nothing to do with sitting in your best clothes all day doing nothing, and everything to do with resigning everything to God, in everything you do.

We can now easily guess how Calvin will treat the remaining commandments. 'Honour your father and mother' becomes 'we are commanded to pay reverence, obedience and gratitude to those who are above us'. It is a general principle of order and due respect in society. 'Do not commit adultery' becomes 'be pure in thought, word and deed'. We are to respect others as having the dignity of persons, not just as objects of sensory pleasure, and therefore just as instruments for our desires. 'Do not steal' is rendered as 'give to every person their due'. 'Do not bear false witness' is 'defend the name and property of your neighbour'. And 'Do not covet' means that the whole soul must be pervaded by love of neighbour.

So Calvin makes the transition from a set of minimal tribal rules to a universal and highly demanding ethic of respect for, and empathy with, others. I think Calvin is probably right that Jesus taught just such a love of one's neighbour as the essence of Torah. But of course Jesus was still teaching as an orthodox Jew, and was not implying that the ceremonial Law should be given up. Orthodox Jews could agree that such an interpretation is what is implied by the Two Great Commandments, and that they are a good key to interpreting the other commandments.

Calvin is recovering an old insight, but he is putting it in a new way. For what Calvin does is to reject the literal interpretation altogether, to renounce the 'ceremonial Law'. Then he makes the commandments so difficult that it is literally impossible to obey them. The Ten Commandments, which started out looking very easy indeed to obey, are racked up until they are beyond the reach of any reasonably ordinary human being. Who can love absolutely everybody else as much as they love themselves? A few moments thought will show that it is impossible. What might have looked like a set of rather easy social rules is now interpreted as a set of impossible commands requiring a complete transformation of the human heart. This is not a secular morality; the trouble is that it now seems to be an impossible one.

Faith and works

That is what Calvin means by his rather odd-sounding comment that any talk of good works without faith in God is 'empty and frivolous in the sight of God'. It may sound as if he is saying that morality without religion is a waste of time. What he really means is that it is so difficult to be truly moral, truly to do what God requires, that anyone who claims to be morally good is either a hypocrite or has no idea of what morality is. The demands of morality (which are the demands of God, for Calvin) are absolute, but we can never meet them. Therefore we must rely wholly on the mercy of God if we are to have any hope of God's promise that the righteous will live with God for ever. It is well known that Calvin believed that relying on God's mercy meant accepting the sacrificial death of Jesus in our place. It is equally well known that he thought those who did not accept Jesus as their Saviour would be damned for ever (since they would thereby have rejected God's mercy).

This can be, and sometimes is, a rather depressing and exclusive view, condemning everyone to eternal punishment except those who happen to have heard of Jesus and joined the right church. It has given rise to what some rather unkindly call the 'Predestination Syndrome', which is the terror that some unfortunate souls apparently feel that they are predestined to be damned, whatever they do. After all, good works will never save you, and how can you make yourself have faith, and how do you know if you ever really have enough faith?

That is indeed a pretty depressing situation, and it is one of the ironies of human thought that a view like Calvin's, which tries to make everything depend on a wholly merciful God, can end up by filling people with the terror of eternal damnation. Maybe the doctrine of eternal hellfire is one of the moral blind spots of Calvin's thought. After all, if 'You shall not kill' is an absolute moral rule, it is a pretty good bet that you should not torture people in flames for ever, whatever they have done – at least if what goes for human beings goes for God, too.

Of course Calvin's view does not have to end up there at all. He could quite easily say (and some of his followers, like the twentieth-century Swiss theologian Karl Barth, have said) that God's law is absolute, human failure is inevitable, but God's mercy is unlimited, so all will be saved as long as they do not explicitly and finally reject God's free offer of eternal life.

Calvin himself did not get to that point. The main reason for this is that he had a highly retributive view of justice – that is, he thought that the good should be rewarded and the evil punished, in proportion to their good or bad deeds. Since none of us ever manages to live up to the moral law, we all deserve continuing punishment, which will never stop because we can never put things right. Even while we are serving the sentence for one lot of misdoings, we are misdoing lots of other things, and so the punishments just go on accumulating. That is a pretty miserable outlook. Only divine mercy offers a way out, and it must be admitted that Calvin had a rather limited (but, on his terms, just) view of the extent of divine mercy (if it is mercy, it is after all completely up to God who gets it, and nobody has a right to it). It might well seem a deeper view of divine mercy, and one more consistent with Calvin's own insights into the width of God's mercy, to say that it has no limits, and that God will make up what we lack if we are truly open to his Spirit.

Theistic morality as fulfilling God's purpose

For Calvin religion is largely about divine judgment and mercy, about the impossibility of fulfilling the moral law, and the absolute need for divine forgiveness. Moral commitment is an essential part of being religious, but morality itself does not depend on religious faith. As far as the content of the moral law is concerned, divine revelation is not needed. The 613 rules of the Torah are first reduced to the Ten Commandments, and then to the one principle of 'love your neighbour'. And surely that principle is independent of religion? According to the psychologist Piaget, children work out a rule of basic fairness rather like this by the age of seven, whether they are religious or not. What is called 'the Golden Rule' – do as you would be done by – seems pretty universal. It doesn't quite go as far as saying you should seek the good life for everyone (since you might like to be left alone by everyone else, and so you would choose to leave them alone, too). But it comes quite near to it, and it occurs naturally to thoughtful people everywhere, whatever they think about God. So there does not seem to be any particular need for God to command rules like that. Anybody who is concerned enough to consider how people should relate to one another in ways that they could publicly justify would quickly work something like that out. God might have commanded it with thunder and lightning and clouds of smoke, but really need not have bothered.

Some people would go further and say this mixing up of God with morality was a great mistake. Gods like Zeus can be prayed to, asked for favours, honoured, cursed and feared. We can make vows to them and offer sacrifices. But morality is something else, and what goes on in temples and religious rituals should not get mixed up in that. Indeed, most of the gods were found distinctly wanting in the morality department by many ancient Greek writers. Maybe, then, morality should be divorced from religion completely.

This thought is reinforced by the problems that have sometimes arisen about the relation between some ancient 'revealed' laws, and the general ethical principles of modern secular states. Some religious believers of all traditions have occasionally wished to ban such things as theatres, books and dancing, or have opposed the institution of democratic government, on the grounds that they conflict with revealed moral principles. It seems to many people very ironic that revelation should be seen as the foundation of human morality, when in fact, according to some interpretations, revelation may come into conflict with secular morality at many points.

Of course, like Calvin, you can always reinterpret the Ten Commandments, and this is just what Jews and Christians have consistently done, and what Muslims also do with their rather similar laws, in the *Shari'a*. But once you start to do that, there is no way of telling where to stop. Why don't you just jettison the whole thing, and start again? What is the point of having any religious laws at all? Maybe you can keep things like the food laws as a sign of your particular religious commitment, to Judaism or to Islam. But where the rigid application of ancient laws seems to be in conflict with common morality (like the rule to exterminate the Amalekites, which taken literally might lead you to go around the world looking for any remaining Amalekites), they might just have to be dropped.

On the other hand, it is not such a good idea to divorce religion from morality. Morality may exist without religion, but religion should not exist without morality. Consider the question: do the gods care about how human beings live? In the *Iliad,* the gods seem to care mostly about whether they are getting their due number of sacrifices. The gods will punish those who dishonour them, and they may, if they feel like it, reward those who please them. But there is a very loose connection between honouring the gods and living well. You are lucky if honouring the gods pays off, because they might have plans which are going to bring you to grief whatever happens – and they usually do, as almost all the characters in the *Iliad* find out.

The god of Moses and Isaiah, however, cares more about what people do. For a start, there is only one god who made everything, including human beings. If God made them for some purpose, presumably God wants them to fulfil that purpose. So the believer in God has a good reason for being moral – morality sets out the purposes of your creator, who has made it your duty to pursue them. This implies that you can get the content of morality by finding out what God's purposes are, what God made you for.

The main question then is: what did God make you for? In early Sumerian myths, the gods made humans to take on the hard work of tilling the fields so that they could feed the gods. This sounds rather crude, as if the gods needed food that only humans could provide. However, it is unlikely that the ancient Sumerians lacked the intelligence to notice that the gods never really ate the food they placed on the altars. It is clear that the offering of food in sacrifice was basically a symbolic act, not a literal feeding. The 'work' humans had to do was to till the fields, to make the earth productive, to care for the environment and render it fruitful for life. 'Feeding the gods' is a way of saying that the gods give humans the responsibility for caring for the earth and making it fruitful. Then, out of that abundance, produced by human effort, some of the fruits – in the form of corn or cattle – would be offered to the gods, as a token of thankfulness and loyalty, but also as a sign that the proper human work of making the earth fruitful had been carried out.

The ancient Hebrews agreed with the Sumerians that the gods made humans to cultivate the earth and make it fruitful. But there might be another reason for making humans, and it is one that became very important in ancient Israel. While God might not need food, and might not need human help in achieving the divine purposes, perhaps there is a sense in which God needs, or at least desires, companionship or personal relationship.

Why do human beings have children? Sometimes by accident, of course. But many actually choose to have these noisy, troublesome, irritating entities. We don't have children so that they can be our slaves, or to bring us food. We have them very largely because they help us to express an important part of our natures, which is the ability to care for

87

and enjoy the personalities of others. We care about them, the way they grow, their interests and difficulties, their pleasures and pains, and the complicated ways in which they interact with us. We express our love in helping other little persons to grow and develop in their own way, while sharing their own lives freely with us and letting us help them to become themselves.

Maybe, then, the Hebrew prophets reasoned, we are not so much the slaves of the gods as the children of the one God. We are beings who enable God to express love in helping us, watching us develop our own natures, and taking pleasure in the good experiences we have in our little lives.

This certainly fits what God said to Moses in the burning bush. God said, 'I have seen your affliction and heard your cry, in Egypt.... I will free you and lead you to a land flowing with milk and honey' (Exodus 3:7, 8). God is rather like a father seeing children in distress, and promising to help them to more enjoyable lives, if they will follow good parental advice. Why did God make us? Because God wanted children. So what are we for? Well, we are not for anything, in one sense. We are not tools or slaves. But in another sense we are meant to be children of God, who will develop our own unique characters and grow in companionship with one another and with God. That is why God cares about what we do – because, like any good parent, God wants us to be ourselves, to grow and flourish and live well as human persons. Being moral, therefore, is a matter of obeying God, and finding our proper fulfilment in helping to realise the divine purposes. Naturally, fairness and neighbourly love are essential parts of such a morality. But there is more to it, and the most important part of the good life is to grow in relationship with God, to feel and know and be filled to overflowing with the love of God.

Kant, the categorical imperative and faith

That may all sound very fine, if you are in the right mood. But it is exactly what sends some people into paroxysms of rage. 'We do not want to be children,' they cry. 'We want to be adults, making our own decisions. Let us get out of the nursery, and into the grown-up world, where we have left behind the gods for ever.'

This is the cue for **Immanuel Kant** (1724–1804), the Prussian philosopher who once said that there is nothing more revolting than the sight of a man on his knees, praying to God. Of course Kant neglected the fact that Jews and some Christians stand up to pray, but it was what he saw as the cringing before some higher authority that he could not stomach (even though he wrote a pretty cringing dedication to the Prussian Minister of State, Baron von Zedlitz, on the occasion of the second edition of the *Critique of Pure Reason*). Oddly and surely irrationally, he did not mind cringing before men. It was cringing before God, the absolute power and authority, that he objected to.

Kant is perhaps best known for having allegedly disproved all the arguments for God. But he also said, 'I have found it necessary to deny knowledge, in order to make room for faith' (First *Critique*, preface to the second edition). Kant's great aim was to set metaphysics on a firm foundation – though oddly some people seem to think he set out to destroy metaphysics altogether, which is the very opposite of what he wanted.

The word 'metaphysics' is worth a short digression. It comes from the Greek *Ta Meta ta Phusika*, which means the works after the book on Physics. Now 'the Physics' was a collection of Aristotle's writings on nature. When the editors of his works came across a bundle of lecture notes on various topics, including some remarks about a possible supreme being, they decided to put it after the book on Physics: *Ta Meta ta Phusika*. And that is how metaphysics was invented. It was not originally a subject at all, but just a collection of lecture notes by students who might well have been asleep for much of the time. However, in the curious history of human thought, where there is a word there has to be a subject. So a subject duly came into being, and now the *Shorter Oxford English Dictionary* gives its first definition of the term.

> **metaphysics** – 'the branch of philosophy dealing with the first principles of things', including such concepts as space, time, substance and so on.

Kant, however, who loved mangling language and giving words new meanings that nobody else had ever thought of, used the word 'metaphysics' in a way most people today would never think of. He used it to mean 'a body of necessary and universal truths, not derived from experience'. It would not be surprising if there were no such truths. But Kant thought there were, and his later, so-called Critical, philosophy, sets out to establish what they are.

His general approach was to insist that there were such necessary truths, both in physics and in morality, but that they had to be confined to the realm of experience. Where God was concerned, this meant that, since God is beyond experience, there can be no universal and necessary truths about God – and, since all human knowledge requires experience, that there can be no knowledge of God at all. But it is possible to have faith in God – to make a postulate, as it were, that God exists. Indeed, he argued that we necessarily have to postulate God, in order to have a truly rational approach both to science and to morality, even though we can have no knowledge of God at all. Many philosophers find it very odd to postulate something we can know nothing about, but we need to note Kant's very restrictive use of the idea of 'knowledge'. He means that we cannot experience God. But we can, and must, use the idea of God to make sense of our experience.

Since Kant ruled out all experience of God, he had little time for revelation, which involves some sort of experience of God as revealer. So he was adamant that morality cannot depend on revelation in any sense. His great contribution to ethics was (unless it was, as some think, a huge mistake) to argue that there are necessary and universal moral truths, and that they are innate in the human mind, not given by some external authority, not even by God. He even invented a method for discovering them (for we need not be conscious of what is innate). This was to use

Immanuel Kant looking for the Categorical Imperative: a drawing of Kant by Hagemann.

what he called the 'Categorical Imperative'. It is really a sophisticated way of applying the Golden Rule.

What you do is to ask, 'What could I legislate as a universal principle of action for all human persons, whatever situation they happen to be in?' I obviously have to find something that they could all agree to, and so I am looking for universal principles that everyone could, and would, agree to, presumably if they were as rational as I am. This method gives me an Imperative, for it comes up with the rule, 'Do this.' And it is categorical, because it does not give any other reason for doing it, other than that it is a principle all rational agents could agree to act on. There is only one categorical imperative, though Kant gives various formulations of it. One variant is 'Act only on a principle all rational agents could act on.' But there are lots of particular moral rules that come out of it. In general, Kant thought that these rules fall under the two major principles of seeking the happiness of others, and the fulfilment of your own intellectual capacities.

There are all sorts of technical difficulties with Kant's suggestion. For example, is there really any set of principles that absolutely everyone could agree to? And why should one pay any attention to a purely hypothetical principle that everyone *could* agree to *if* they were rational, when in fact most people are not fully rational, and never will agree? But Kant makes the point that it is possible to work out a rational morality without any appeal to religion or revelation. Even if such a secular morality does not resolve all our moral dilemmas, appeal to revelation will not help matters, but will only introduce more diversity, of a particularly unresolvable kind – since religious believers are not usually ready to make many compromises.

If you ask Kant the question, 'Why should I follow these moral rules?', his reply is that you can simply see they are right, and you should follow them just because they are right, and for no other reason. If you ask, 'Why should I be moral?', you are already depraved and corrupt. That is a fairly quick way to bring any argument to an end, and it might seem just a little too quick. If I want to know whether morality is important, is of ultimate importance, is what makes me truly human, perhaps my question is a genuine and perplexing one. It certainly seems that Kant had a specific picture of human nature working underneath his Categorical Imperative. It was a picture that depicted humans as rational beings, inherently superior to nature and sense-experience, able and indeed obligated to subordinate nature to the demands of reason, and finding their fulfilment in heroic devotion to reason, whatever the cost. For Kant, humans are primarily and above all else moral and rational agents. They possess autonomy, the ability to will and decide their own courses of action, to act on principles they themselves legislate, and precisely in that lies their inherent dignity and superiority to nature. This is a grandiose vision, though it may remind one a little uncomfortably of Satan's ringing cry in Milton's *Paradise Lost*: 'Better to reign in Hell than serve in Heaven!'

Kant's picture is, however, more blurred than this may suggest. He is often regarded as the great Rationalist, committed to the Enlightenment view of humans as rational agents, freed from the shackles of religion and superstition, gradually advancing to perfection through education – especially, it seems, in Prussia (Kant was Prussian). Yet he is the philosopher who announced that Reason, pressed to its limits, lands up in inevitable contradictions (which he, maintaining his reputation for never using an easy word where a hard one is possible, typically called 'Antinomies'). He held that reality in itself is completely unknowable by human beings. And he held that we must live largely by faith, since knowledge is quite unable to deal with ultimate reality. Kant was certainly a Rationalist in holding that there are innate concepts in the human mind which precede any particular experiences. But he was certainly not a Rationalist of the sort who holds that the mind is able of itself to understand ultimate reality. So he was a rather strange sort of Rationalist, on the verge of turning into a Romantic!

In morality, too, matters are not as clear as they may at first seem. One of the statements most frequently attributed to Kant is the aphorism 'Ought implies can'. That is, if it is your duty to do something, it must be possible for you to do it. However, not only did he never say this (another Prussian philosopher did, but I leave that as a research project for the curious), but he really held, like Calvin, that it is not possible for people ever completely to do their duty. In one of his lesser known works, *Religion Within the Limits of Reason Alone*, written in 1793 after his three great *Critiques*, he writes that there is a radical disposition to evil in human nature, which means that no one can ever fulfil his duty (original sin lives on!). Again echoing Calvin, he goes on to say that only divine grace can remedy this situation. But his horror of enthusiasm in religion means that, unlike Calvin, he completely denies the possibility of any actual experience of grace. You just have to hope it is there, but you will never experience it. The absolute demand, the moral failure and the gift of grace are all there, but the advantage is that you never have to go to church, which is usually rather boring, and involves disgusting things like kneeling down to pray. The disadvantage is that you never have any experience of God at all.

Still, this is not a wholly secular morality after all. In Kant's Second *Critique*, of Practical Reason, having demolished (he says) all possible arguments for God, he proceeds to invent another one. This has puzzled readers so much that it has been said that Kant did it only to console his manservant Lampe, who was depressed by not being able to prove the existence of God any more. What Kant says is that, while the existence and knowledge of morality does not depend on God, commitment to an absolute morality can only be rationally justified if you think that in some way you will one day receive the happiness you deserve for trying so hard to do your duty. Since this does not seem to happen in this life, there must be an afterlife, where people can reap happiness in accordance with their virtue (or, of course, misery in accordance with their vice). And that means there must be a God who can make sure everything works out properly. Immortality and God become postulates of reason, after all, and Lampe can be happy once more.

The trouble is that the whole argument sounds very fishy. If I find my human dignity in doing what is right for its own sake, why spoil it all by saying that I can only reasonably do what is right if I expect to be rewarded for it? However, Kant is very widely misunderstood at just this point. He tries to locate his view of morality between two opposing views which he rejects (He does this in his *Lectures on Ethics*). One he calls 'Epicurean', which is that you should do what is right in order to be happy. The other he calls 'Stoical', which is that you should just do what is right, whatever the outcome. Many people seem to think that Kant's own morality was Stoical, but he explicitly rejects this idea. What he wants is to make happiness important, and yet to make moral action an independent condition of being worthy of happiness, not just a means to happiness. I must do what is right because it is right, but in committing myself to moral action, I am, if I am rational, committing myself to something like a moral order in the universe. I am committing myself to the real possibility that goodness can triumph, that being moral is not a futile gesture in a meaningless cosmos.

In fact, Kant retains all the main components of a religious approach to morality. These are that there is an absolute obligatoriness about morality which means it is not simply a matter of long-term prudence or natural sympathy (which may vary from person to person). There is a human inability to do what is right, which leaves one in need of some sort of supplement or forgiveness for moral deficiency. And there is a moral goal which can be realised, where goodness triumphs and evil gets its comeuppance.

What he lacks is any idea of experience of a loving God, which might lead you to do what is right because you love God, rather than out of heroic free choice. He lacks any experience of divine grace, which might enable you to share in a divine love which remedies your own inability to love. And he lacks the thought that the moral goal will lie in personal awareness of a God who is no abstract postulate of Reason, but one who raises the child who has learned the ways of love to the status of a beloved friend or marriage partner. Morality may consist largely of rules for moral infants, and most of us are, when all is said and done, moral infants. But its ultimate goal is a fulfilled relationship of mutual love for those who have been guided to maturity through their unique experience of life.

Autonomy is not, in the end, the ultimate human value, which is rather, as the theologian Paul Tillich called it, 'theonomy', the capacity to live in mutuality and relationship with the source of the power to be and to love unlimitedly. In the Jewish tradition, the ultimate end of life is to be 'married' to God, and the Jewish doctrine of marriage is that within it two persons become one. The theistic goal is not just obtaining happiness in proportion to virtue, which sounds a little too prudential and quasi-mathematical for Kant's own better insights. The theistic goal is becoming like God, becoming one with God. But then Kant never married, and the notion of the 'love of God' never occurs in his voluminous writings. He may not have been a consistently secular moralist, but he was losing touch with the sorts of experience that give rise to theistic morality.

God as creative freedom, affective knowledge and illimitable love

It is quite possible to have a secular morality, and for people to do what is right without having any religious beliefs. It is quite possible to work out the basic content of moral beliefs by asking what 'love of neighbour' requires, without explicit reference to religion. But there is a distinctively theistic moral viewpoint, and it is above all in the Hebrew Bible (the Old Testament, as Christians call it) that we can see it developing over the centuries. At the time of Moses, perhaps in the thirteenth century BCE, Jahweh is the god of Abraham, Isaac and Jacob, a family deity who promises good to their friends and harm to their enemies, and whose laws are a combination of sublime moral insights and ancient tribal taboos. Regrettably, a great deal of religion has remained at that level. The gods support the ambitions of one social or ethnic group, and inspire hatred of all who stand in the way of those ambitions. The gods are no better than the ideals of those who worship them, and where those ideals are limited by egoism, nationalism or general moral myopia, the preferred gods will be limited in the same way.

Nevertheless, continued reflection on God, as the embodiment of the moral ideal, has the power to undermine such limited visions. In ancient Israel and Judah, by the eighth century BCE, a remarkable series of prophets arose who preached that Jahweh is the only creator of heaven and earth, who cares for the whole of creation, and whose laws require absolute justice and mercy. This god is still a severely retributive god, whose justice punishes the sins of the fathers to the third and fourth generation. Yet God shows steadfast love to thousands of those who love God (Exodus 20), and does not turn away the penitent and contrite. This is a god to fear, if you do what is wrong. But such a god gives to morality a centrality and importance, as the commands of the creator, which turns religion from a matter of ritual ceremony to the practice of the transformation of the heart to love the good.

The third stage in this development occurred in about the sixth century BCE, when the second Isaiah wrote from exile in Babylon. Now some of the fuller implications of the revelation of God in the experience of the prophets of Israel are brought out.

There are three major features of the character of God which Isaiah brings into focus. First, God is the creator, bringing the world into being in joyful freedom. So worshippers should make it their aim to be like God, realising as far as is possible in the lives of human beings that creative freedom for bringing about good things which is the source of all life.

Second, God is one who hears the cries of the people and feels their pain: 'Can a woman forget her sucking child, that she should have no compassion on the son of her womb? Even these may forget, yet I will not forget you' (Isaiah 49:15). God has affective knowledge, a feeling for and with creatures, in all their pain, and in their happiness too. So worshippers should seek to feel and know the pain and happiness of all creatures, which will inevitably lead to their seeking to alleviate pain and rejoice in the many forms of happiness the world affords. It will lead to lives of true compassion and shared joy.

Third, God is one whose love is illimitable. God's care for creation knows no bounds, and God wills to share the divine goodness with others: 'Your Maker is your husband ... the Lord has called you like a wife forsaken and grieved in spirit ... for a brief moment I forsook you, but with great compassion I will gather you' (Isaiah 54:5–8). God wills to share the divine life with creatures, as a husband shares his life with his wife. So worshippers should seek to live together as those who are to share their troubles and joys, who are committed to one another indissolubly, and who find their own greatest fulfilment in bringing happiness to others.

Creative freedom, affective knowledge and illimitable love: these are the qualities of God, as discerned by one of the greatest prophets of Israel. These are the qualities human beings should seek to cultivate in themselves, as beings made in the image and likeness of God. And these are not qualities we might simply strive to cultivate in ourselves, or to imitate, as if copying some external object. They are, being the qualities of God, already infused in all things and in the hearts of men and women, waiting to be brought to light. Goodness is not simply to be brought about by us; it is actual and existent, dynamic and forceful. It is, to borrow Calvin's interpretation of the Sabbath, when we rest from the works of the self, and let God work in us, that we are changed by what we dimly see.

The religious way might be unsympathetically interpreted as a matter of obeying non-rational tribal taboos and offering sacrifices to propitiate or flatter the gods. But in the major Hebrew prophets those rules, the statutes and ordinances of the Torah, are ways of relating all human life to the vision of perfect goodness. It is in response to that vision that religion is proclaimed as the absolute requirement to love others as you love yourself. True sacrifice is the offering of self so that God can realise the power of creativity, compassion and friendship in and through your life. God is the one who commands love, who forgives our inability to love, who places the divine love within us, and who will ensure that love is stronger than death.

Morality may exist without religion, and if you find religion to be only a dream, it must do so. But the sort of religion the Hebrew prophets taught gives to morality an absoluteness, a compassion, a power and a hope which is simply not available to secular morality. Belief in God has one of its firmest roots in the sense of the absoluteness of morality, the need for forgiveness, and the hope for the triumph of good, which is the legacy of the prophets of ancient Israel to the world.

That sense of absoluteness is founded on the experience of a love that is as commanding as it is unlimited, which is as forgiving as it is commanding, and as fulfilling as it is forgiving. That divine love is the final, but tragically often unperceived, object of every selfless desire, and it is the power that transforms the attentive self into a willing instrument of love. At the heart of theistic morality there is that one thing Kant failed to see, which gives life and power to his moral outlook, the vision of the active, forgiving, fulfilling love of God which draws all things to itself by their deepest, if often unacknowledged, desire.

When Dante Alighieri wrote his great poem, *The Divine Comedy*, in Florence in about 1300, he ended with these words, describing the final vision he has of God. They speak of an interior turning, by which the soul is changed into that which it contemplates, a moving by love. That, perhaps, is the heart of theistic morality, and it elegantly expresses the Hebrew prophetic vision of the nature of God, in so far as God can ever be understood by us:

> My mind, held in complete suspense,
> Gazed fixedly, motionless and intent,
> And always as if touched by fire ...
> In that light a man becomes such
> That it is impossible he should turn away
> Ever to look upon any other thing.
> Because the good, which is the object of the will,
> Is there in its entirety ...
> My sight was growing stronger
> As I looked; and that which is One
> Worked on me as I watched and changed me ...

My desire and my will
Were being turned together like a wheel,
By the love which moves the sun and other stars.

Find out more . . .

A good account of religious taboos by an anthropologist is Mary Douglas, *Purity and Danger* (London, Routledge & Kegan Paul, 1966).

The treatment of the Ten Commandments is found in John Calvin, *Institutes of the Christian Religion* (trans. Henry Beveridge, Grand Rapids, Mich., Eerdmans, 1989 [1536]), book 2, chapter 8.

There are many translations of Immanuel Kant's *Critique of Pure Reason* (first published 1781). A good abridged edition is translated by Norman Kemp Smith (London, Macmillan, 1952). See also his *Metaphysic of Morals* (trans. Mary Gregor, New York, Harper Torchbooks, 1964 [1797]). His *Fundamental Principles of the Metaphysic of Ethics* (*Grundlegung*; trans. T.K. Abbott, London, Longman, 1959 [1785]) is the book most people read on Kant's ethics. His late writing on religion is found in *Religion Within the Limits of Reason Alone* (trans. T.M. Greene and H.H. Hudson, New York, Harper Torchbooks, 1960 [1793]).

I have written an account of Kant's views on ethics and religion, as they developed throughout his life, in *The Development of Kant's View of Ethics* (Oxford, Basil Blackwell, 1972). This gives a much fuller account than is appropriate here.

There are many translations and editions of Dante Alighieri's *Divine Comedy* (1307–18). The translation of the final stanza of 'Paradise' is my own.

4

The God of the philosophers

In which the reader will discover why Plato was a metaphysical speleologist, why stupid people will turn into fish, and why Aristotle's god does as little as possible (i.e. nothing). They will also find out what God was doing before creating the universe, and why people can be held responsible for things they cannot help. They will be shown how God can make something out of nothing, and be told the most elegant definition of God ever invented — which is almost, but not quite, correct — and the most annoying proof of God ever invented (by the same man) — which almost, but not quite, works.

God and Job

On 23 November 1654, the French theologian and mathematician Blaise Pascal had an experience so vivid and intense that he carried a written record of it sewn into his clothing, which was only discovered when he died. The core of that experience he puts in these words: 'Fire. The God of Abraham, the God of Isaac, the God of Jacob, and not of the philosophers and men of science.'

He was perhaps contrasting a vivid experience of a personal and dynamic presence with the inferred God of Descartes, who had to be brought in to ensure that our sense-perceptions were not deceiving us.

Pascal's point was that belief in God is founded on human experiences, especially those of gifted (or deluded) people – the prophets – of an overpowering, challenging, fearful and fiery presence. In the Bible there is very little that can be called philosophy. There are the 'Wisdom' writings, and wise proverbs, and agonising about innocent suffering in the book of Job. But the story of Jahweh walking in the garden, asking Adam where he is (and should Jahweh not know that already, since he is supposed to know everything?), is more typical than any attempt to propound a systematic doctrine of God, or to appeal to God to explain just why things happen.

The Old Testament God does not explain anything. That God perplexes, confuses, enrages and, if you are lucky, consoles. But any suggestion that God explains the mysteries of life is utterly confounded by the book of Job, which clearly regards all such 'explanations' as given by the enemies of God, the 'friends' of Job who keep offering various plausible explanations of why he is suffering. Job rejects all these explanations, and the writer obviously regards any attempt to explain as futile.

In the end Job is confronted by a vision of God 'out of the whirlwind', which simply reduces him to terrified silence. 'I had heard of thee by the hearing of the ear,' he says. 'But now my eye sees thee; therefore I despise myself, and repent' (Job 42:5). There is no explanation, no answer: only the whirlwind, and a vision of the unfathomable power of God; only the realisation of human nothingness, and utter abandonment to the mercy of God.

Nevertheless, much reflective thought has gone into the book of Job. The final experience of Job is of an all-creating God, who asks, 'Where were you when I laid the foundation of the earth?' There may be no answer to the question of why God did things as God did. But there is a belief that there is a God who has power over all things, so that Job does not say, 'I do not know what sort of thing you are at all.' He says, 'I know that thou canst do all things' (Job 42:1). Here, in fact, is one of the very few doctrinal statements in the Old Testament – the statement that God is omnipotent, capable of doing all things. But how do you know that, except by reflection on the nature of the gods? And how do you know exactly what it means, except by using reason as best as you can to unfold its implications and presuppositions?

So belief in God might not be founded on reason, as though it is a hypothesis to explain why the universe is the way it is. But reason has to get to work on those human experiences that give rise to belief in God, to try to sort out which experiences are reliable and trustworthy. Then it has to try to see what idea of God (or of some other religiously experienced reality) is implicit in such experiences. And it has to try to see how such ideas relate to other knowledge of the world, derived from other forms of human experience. This is quite a lot of work for reason to do, even if it comes with a health warning that the ways of God are ultimately beyond human understanding.

Plato and the gods

The trouble with the gods of Greece, of Egypt, of Rome and of Sumeria is that no one ever managed to get them sorted into any sort of rational order at all. The eighth-century BCE Greek poet Hesiod did write a *Theogony*, which tried to systematise the gods in some sort of coherent way. But all he came up with is a rather boring set of genealogies, relating the gods to each other by various schemes of marriage and parenthood. These family histories carry no conviction at all, and give the irresistible impression that they have just been constructed arbitrarily to get the annoyingly large number of gods into some sort of intelligible relationship.

Plato (429–347 BCE) was an Athenian philosopher who wrote many dialogues, usually with Socrates as the main disputant. What relation this 'Socrates' had with the real historical figure who died in 399 BCE, and whose pupil Plato had been, is unclear. It is probably true that, thanks to Plato, Socrates won more arguments after he was dead than he ever did when he was alive. Most people think it very likely that he also

Plato, who looks as if he is just about to ban all licentious and interesting stories about the gods. A Luna marble head from the first century CE.

became much more dogmatic after his death. To be fair, however, he refuted his own theories just about as often as he refuted those of other people, and so he is rightly regarded as the father of critical philosophy.

Socrates first typically asks people what they think some term, such as 'justice' or 'piety', means. Then he shows that they cannot possibly mean what they say, and that they are in fact totally confused about what they do mean. Finally he tells them what they really would mean if only they understood themselves better – but everyone knows that in the next dialogue or so, he will show that even what they would mean if they understood what they said is so confused that it would be better if they meant something else. It is perhaps not surprising that Socrates made many Athenians very angry, and that they accused him of 'impiety' – whatever that means.

So it happened that when Plato came on the scene, he could do very little with the gods of Homer and Hesiod. To him they had the status of fables and legends, and so many of their goings-on were immoral or just plain silly that, in *The Republic*, he favoured censorship of the stories of the gods, leaving only those that could be examples of good and noble character (quite possibly, none of the gods of the *Iliad* would be left!). The trouble with this, as he points out, is that we should only be left with storytellers 'of the more austere and less attractive type, who will reproduce only the manner of a person of high character'. Both religion and soap operas would soon lose all attraction if this advice was followed. Religion might be more elevating; but it would be even more boring than it already is.

Socrates, whose thought Plato claims to express in his dialogues, was ordered to die by taking poison after his condemnation by the state of Athens for corrupting the youth. He had, it was alleged, thrown doubt on the existence of the gods. He was widely taken to be anti-religious, in the terms of his day. Yet no one could say that Socrates and Plato were not concerned with broadly religious themes – themes of the ultimately spiritual nature of the Universe, and of human immortality in relation to a supreme and ultimate Spirit. They just could not find any way of relating those themes to the riotous assembly of gods in Greek popular religious life.

So Plato invented his own idea of God, without relating it in any way to the religious practices of Athens. If any god is truly a god of the philosophers, Plato's god is. Even so, it is not as far removed from the voice from the whirlwind as you might at first think. And it was destined to influence Christian ideas of God – and Jewish and Muslim ideas, too, to a large extent – in a fundamental way. Indeed, it was only when Plato's ideas were joined onto the ideas of early Christianity that they really made a connection with living religious practice. The voice from the whirlwind and the voice from the Academy (the school of philosophy Plato set up in Athens) would together shape religious ideas in Europe and the Middle East for over a thousand years.

Plato was certainly a philosopher, the first fully fledged member of the species. He was even a linguistic analyst, spending much of his time analysing concepts. Yet he was not merely an intellectual. He was in many ways more like what might be called a 'mystic'. In the famous 'allegory of the cave', from his dialogue *The Republic*, he imagines people as prisoners so chained in a cave that they see only the shadows of puppets cast onto the walls of the cave by the light of a fire behind them. They see only the shadows of artificial objects, and in an artificial light. If, Plato says, they are unchained and led from the cave, they will see, first the puppets, then the persons who carried them, then the fire and the cave itself. Last of all, as they walk out of the cave, they may learn to look at the sun itself, 'not as it appears . . . but as it is in itself in its own domain'. To be freed from the cave of appearances, and learn to see the sun as it is in itself, is the goal of that wisdom which Plato teaches.

Here is another conception of the religious life, not that of offering sacrifices to the gods to get them to deviate from the path of strict justice – which is a form, Plato says, of egoistic injustice – but that of learning to turn away from this changing world, until the eye 'can bear to contemplate reality and that supreme splendour which we have called the Good'.

What is this Good? Plato says, 'This which gives to the objects of knowledge their truth and to him who knows them his power of knowing, is the Form or essential nature of Goodness. It is the cause of knowledge and truth.' It is beyond truth and knowledge, even 'beyond being, surpassing it in dignity and power'. It is the ultimate object of true knowledge, and is far removed from the world of visible things and sense-experience, which is the realm of appearance and belief.

The vision of the Good

Plato's view is almost the exact opposite of that taken by most people in the modern world. Now people often think of religion as a realm of belief, whereas knowledge is given by sense-experience and observation. But he thought that knowledge is an intellectual intuition of the essences or true natures of things, and above all of the Good from which all such essences derive, whereas sense-experience gives no more than beliefs or opinions about mere appearances. We have turned Plato upside down, and that is partly why religion seems so odd in the modern world, or at least this Platonic version of it, which has been so influential on Christianity. Such a religious vision belongs to a way of seeing things that many of us can no longer share, that is the reverse image of our own.

For Plato, philosophy, the love of wisdom, is a matter of turning from appearances towards the vision of goodness itself. Is this so far from the fire and the whirlwind? The metaphor of vision is common to the stories of Abraham, Job and the cave. When Abraham sees God, he walks away from the greatest culture in the world at that time. When Job sees God, his questions come to seem like useless babbling. When the liberated prisoner sees the sun, all that he thought he knew becomes foolishness. In each case, there is something seen which radically questions everything that had been previously thought of as knowledge. In each case, the visionary seems foolish when he returns to try to speak of what he has seen to those still imprisoned in the world of appearance. But for them that world has changed forever, and the world of change and time falls into unreality when faced with the vision of eternity.

Sometimes Plato is spoken of as the father of 'dualism', as a hater of the world of the senses and of the body, and as someone who recommended trying to escape from matter altogether to a better, purely spiritual world. The body becomes bad, and the spiritual quest is to pretend it is not even there. Those who see Plato in such a light are perhaps forgetting two other famous dialogues, the *Symposium* and the *Timaeus*. The whole *Symposium* is a celebration of homosexual love (I admit that when I read the beautiful passage from the *Symposium*, which I quoted in chapter 2, in the Cathedral at Oxford, which I often do, I do not emphasise this fact). While Plato certainly speaks of the vision of 'Beauty itself', he also regards beautiful things (and he is partly speaking of beautiful young men) as images or expressions of that Beauty, not as somehow completely opposed to it. When he says that one should move from the contemplation of beautiful things to the contemplation of Beauty itself, he is surely not saying that one should move from the material to what is opposed to it. He is saying that one should move from the image to the reality. But the image is precisely an image, not a contradiction, of reality, and as such it may have its proper, if relative, value.

Similarly, in the *Timaeus*, which was almost the only work of Plato known in the early Middle Ages (through a Latin translation by Chalcidius), Plato speaks of the material world, and particularly of the time in which it exists, and which is its chief characteristic, as 'the moving image of eternity'. The 'Demiurge', or world-shaper, formed this world out of pre-existing matter, using the pattern of the eternal Forms or Essences. So everything in the material world participates in, and is patterned on, the spiritual world of real Essences. The world is not something evil, as though it was the product of some evil god. It is good, because it is shaped by a god who is attentive to the eternal Essences, and because it is a real image in material form of a spiritual reality of supreme goodness. We should move from the image to the reality, but the image can truly speak of the reality for those who are still partly imprisoned by sensuality and ignorance.

It is true that Plato uses a Greek pun when he speaks of the human body (*soma*) as the tomb (*sema*) of the soul. That may give the impression that the soul is trapped in the body as some sort of punishment. This impression may grow stronger when we read some of the things he says about the destiny of various human souls. Plato believed in reincarnation. He thought that souls exist without beginning or end, and take various animal, human and divine forms in countless lives. There are as many souls as there are stars, and each soul is originally allotted to a star. They fall to earth from the realm of the stars, because of desire and passion, so that earthly life is a sort of punishment, though it is also an arena in which souls can learn to love justice and take the upward way to receive the prize of justice, and return home to their native star and live an appropriately happy life, after the journey of many lives which they have chosen by their desires and deeds.

Some of Plato's more reactionary thoughts come to the surface when he sketches a few details of the soul's journey. Men who live cowardly or immoral lives, he says in the *Timaeus*, are reborn as women. Those who are 'silly enough to think that visible evidence is all the foundation astronomy needs' will be reborn as birds. And really stupid people – presumably any female astronomers would be particularly unfortunate – are reborn as fish, since they are unfit to breathe pure clean air.

When reading such passages, it is as well to remember that at the time people in most of Europe were running around in paint and animal skins. One cannot expect an aristocratic fifth-century BCE Athenian like Plato to have opinions that we would regard as truly democratic. In fact, he thought democracy was the worst sort of government, the rule of the mob, to be avoided at all costs. So perhaps we might expect to find a similar rather elitist and conservative attitude to religion in his work, and we do. He thought, for instance, that the Guardians, those who know the Good, should rule all other classes of society, and exercise careful control over the arts and sciences. As Sir Karl Popper has pointed out with great force, Plato is not a friend of an 'open society', and the sort of government he favoured might today be regarded as repressive ideological tyranny.

In this respect, the religion of the Hebrews is very different from Platonism, since Hebrew religion celebrates hard physical work over abstract theorising, and visions of fire appearing to shepherds and herdsmen rather than visions of intellectual essences appearing to a group of elite mathematical gymnasts (the preparation for the vision of the Good largely consists of a course of gymnastics and mathematics). The Hebrew prophetic tradition is a useful counterweight to the Platonic idea of religion as the preserve of the Academy.

The sort of thing Plato was doing, however, was sooner or later necessary for religious thought. Abraham had been confronted by a tribal god, and his experience was unrelated to any wider concerns of what other gods might be doing, or what the world in general might be like. Job (as represented by its unknown author) saw God as the creator of the whole earth. But he still had little idea of or concern with what that creator might have in mind for the whole universe, or with what that wider universe might really be like. The purposes of God remained a complete mystery. Sooner or later believers in God had to address the question: what purpose, if any, did God have in creation, and how do visions of God relate to our wider knowledge of created being? The Academy might be in danger of neglecting the fire and the whirlwind, but, as Plato said, 'The unexamined life is not worth living', and this is as true in religion as it is elsewhere.

Appearance and reality

When Plato examined the gods of Athens, he found them wanting in intelligibility. There was no explanation of why they were there, or of what their role in the universe was. More to the point, they often seemed to encourage a narrow self-interest (my gods exist to help me), and to discourage true goodness (a big sacrifice, a hecatomb, will do instead of being just). He did not deny them, but in his work they play no central part.

His primary concern was to discover how one could live a good human life, one that is fitting to the place of humanity in the cosmos and reflects an understanding of how things really are. When he reflected on the world in which humans exist, he discerned the deep ambiguity with which all religion and philosophy begins. Humans are called to goodness, to the pursuit of justice and the hope of happiness. But they are imprisoned by greed, hatred and passion, in a world in which injustice often seems to pay and goodness is swallowed up by death. What sort of world is it that breeds such a tragic ambiguity? And is there any resolution of the tragedy that is human existence?

One possibility, the one that Plato's work chiefly expresses, is to distinguish appearance and reality. What appears in this sense-bound world is desire and attachment, injustice and hopeless love, conflict and death. But there is a reality which this world partly expresses and partly distorts. It is a reality of beauty and goodness, the true home of the soul, but from which the soul falls by the abstractly irrational, yet deeply comprehensible, desire for pride, possession and pleasure. The earthward journey of each soul is its exploration of passion, with all its evident attractions and yet its ultimate self-destructive emptiness. And the proper destiny of each soul is to return, passion exhausted, to the sphere of the stars, beyond corruption and decay, a journey from the world poised between reality and unreality to the world of the real. 'Lead me from the unreal to the real': that prayer from the *Upanishads* is also Plato's prayer. It is addressed, not to the gods, who themselves share in unreality, but to the One beyond all finite being, who orders this cosmos in all its apparent tragedy and ultimate harmony.

Plato was decidedly not a hater of the body, but he was a lover of the soul. He saw the universe as basically good. Indeed, he describes it at the end of the *Timaeus* as 'an image of the intelligible ... a visible god, supreme in greatness and excellence, beauty and perfection, a single, uniquely created heaven'. The perfection of the universe consists in its containing every possible sort of finite goodness – even fish have a sort of watery goodness, despite the fact that they cannot breathe pure clean air. It therefore testifies to a world-shaper who 'was good', and 'wished all things to be as like himself as possible'. The universe exists for the sake of its goodness, of the beautiful and enjoyable things it contains, which reflect in many different ways the one undivided goodness of its origin. Unlike Zeus, this god is perfect in beauty and excellence, and, being without envy, wishes as many different forms of beauty and excellence as possible to exist, and to be like their divine original in different ways. That is the reason for the existence of the universe, that the goodness of the Demiurge might be expressed in a multitude of finite forms.

Yet the universe is a realm of conflict, destruction, suffering and death. For that reason, Plato never says that the Demiurge is the creator. The Demiurge is rather the world-shaper, and what is shaped is already existing matter. 'This world came into being from a mixture and combination of necessity and intelligence. Intelligence controlled necessity by persuading it for the most part to bring about the best result.' Being, space and becoming exist, containing the four elements of air, earth, fire and water, through necessity. They are not brought into being by anything else. When the Demiurge sets out to make the 'visible god' that is the cosmos, it persuades this necessity for the most part to conform to the Forms or ideas of perfection, which are also necessary in their own way.

In Plato's view there are three main factors at work – a sort of chaotic matter, whose properties are necessary; a world of Forms, which is also necessary, and a Demiurge, who tries to impose as much Form on matter as possible, but can never manage a perfect job. The cosmos that results is just right for attracting those weak and starry souls who quite like the idea of a holiday in the world of matter, but are not fully aware of its consequences. In any case, it is not the Demiurge's fault that they choose to become embodied. In fact it was left to the gods (whom the

Demiurge shaped out of thinner matter) to make humans, and the Demiurge washes its hands of the whole of human history to a large extent.

In Plato's view there is no Devil, no evil force setting out to oppose the creator. There is not really a creator. There is intelligence and necessity, and the free choice of souls to live in the material world, which never loses its goodness, and yet necessarily contains the possibility of conflict and destruction, of greed and despair. As Plato says, there is a lot of myth and a lot of imaginative speculation in all this. It may need de-mythologising, and I do not suppose Plato would object to that. But the important core of the stories is the claim that the cosmos has a structure that accounts for the tragic situation of humanity by placing it in a context of the inner journey of souls through a realm of desire, ignorance and necessity to a vision of perfect goodness and intelligibility.

Why did this Platonic worldview not give rise to a Platonic religion? It had most of the requisite elements. It had a charismatic religious teacher, Socrates, who died heroically, obeying the ruling of an unjust state rather than choosing to escape, as he could have done. It had an apostle, Plato, who committed the Socratic teachings, suitably modified for an aristocratic audience, to imperishable prose. It had an appealing picture of the cosmos, and myths telling of the origin and destiny of the soul. It had a high ethical content, and a supreme spiritual reality (or two of them, the Demiurge and the Good). Why is there no Platonic religion?

Well, in a sense there is. It is called Christianity. Or at least Christianity took from Plato many of the most important aspects of his thought, and attached them to its own central teaching that Jesus was the supreme manifestation of God. Especially in its Greek Orthodox form, Christianity preserved the view that the things of time are, or at their best can be, images of eternity (Jesus is, of course, the perfect image of the invisible god, and he is so described in the New Testament, in the letter to the Colossians 1:15). In its liturgy material things become transparent to the underlying spiritual reality. The world of sense is the world of unreality, and a major virtue is *apatheia*, freedom from passion, a main aim of Greek monastic life. The real world is a world of Essences, flowing from the Good, which is the object of monastic contemplation. The Guardians of truth are the bishops, who censor all artistic works which might mislead the populace under their care. And the spiritual quest is the flight from desire and sensuality to the unchanging and eternal source of all goodness, 'beyond being itself'.

Platonism lived on, while the gods, who were never very important to it, faded away, becoming angels (or demons or even saints), messengers of a higher reality. Of course it is a Platonism that has been modified by its contact with the Hebrew religion, and precisely because it is a mutated form of Platonism, it often protests loudly that it is not Platonism at all (forms that are very nearly alike tend to proclaim their differences very loudly, even though the differences are not nearly so apparent to anyone else).

Platonism is naturally at its strongest in the Greek and Byzantine forms of Christianity (so called because Byzantium, later called Constantinople and then Istanbul, was the capital of the Eastern Roman Empire, and seat, as it still is, of the chief Patriarch of Eastern Orthodox Christianity). But it played a decisive role in Latin Christianity too, the form of Christianity that gives its allegiance to the bishop of Rome.

Augustine and creation *ex nihilo*

The greatest architect of Latin Christianity was **Augustine, Bishop of Hippo** (354–430), a city on what is now the Algerian coast. Augustine took Plato's system of the threefold origin of the cosmos, the Demiurge, the Good and matter, together with their rather remote connection to the gods who were worshipped by the people, and wove them into a coherent synthesis which has remained the basis of classical Christian theism to this day. He did so by developing the doctrine of creation *ex nihilo*, out of nothing. This doctrine was not invented by Augustine.

It was widely accepted in the Christian churches by the end of the second century, though it was not formally defined by the Roman Catholic Church until 1215 CE. But Augustine gave it a fully worked out and definitive form.

What he did was really very neat. First of all he conceived all the Forms or Essences, headed by the Form of the Good, as ideas in the mind of God. Then he made God the creator of matter, so that it had no independent existence. And finally he demoted all the ancient gods to angels or demons, servants of the one creator God. Thus he gave the whole cosmos one simple and elegant explanation in the will of a creator God, who was the sole proper object of human worship and devotion.

There was not an independent realm of ideas to which God somehow had to conform. God did not have to look at a separately existing rule-book to find out what was good or possible. Instead, the rule-book, all the possible worlds that could ever exist, and all the moral rules that could ever apply, were ideas within the mind of God, constituent parts of God.

So if you ask the question, 'Does God have to conform to independent standards of goodness?', the answer is, 'No, those standards are ideas in the mind of God.' If you are really objectionable, you might go on to ask, 'But couldn't God have thought of different ideas, and then we might have had very different moral rules. Maybe rules like, "Kill two people on Fridays", for instance?'

Such a question asks whether God could be irrational, making up moral rules for no reason at all. Augustine's answer would be: 'God could be irrational, but why should God be?' To be irrational is to bring things about for no reason, or for a bad reason. To be rational is to bring things about because they are desirable, they give happiness or satisfaction of some sort. God is a being of perfect power and perfect knowledge. So God knows everything God could bring about, and can bring about anything that is possible. For God to be rational is for God to bring about what God wants to bring about, what gives God satisfaction or pleasure. If God could be irrational, God could bring about things that brought no satisfaction or pleasure. But no powerful and wise being would do that. So even if God could theoretically be irrational, God would never choose to be.

So we can say that God brings things about because they give God happiness, and that is rational. But you push things still further, and ask, 'Could God not get pleasure from almost anything?' God might derive happiness from watching people suffer intense pain. Why could a cosmic sado-masochist not exist?

There is an answer to this. God, being omniscient, knows all the possible universes there could ever be. Are some of these possible worlds better than others? Well, in practice none of us has any difficulty in saying that some states are better than others. That is, we prefer some to others. We prefer being happy to being sad, being healthy to being ill, we prefer being free to being chained to a wall, and we prefer knowing how to heal diseases to being ignorant of how to cure them. Some states just are preferable to others, and these states have broadly to do with survival, health, happiness, and a reasonable degree of freedom and knowledge.

God, being omniscient, will know that happiness, freedom and knowledge are more desirable than boredom, constraint and ignorance. There might be lots of niggling arguments about degrees of goodness and badness, their distribution, and what exactly might produce them. But overall we would all agree that a world with lots of happiness, freedom and knowledge in it is better than a world with none of these.

From whose point of view, you might ask? Well, from everybody's point of view. Or perhaps I should say, from the point of view of any impartial observer. We are not telling people how to be happy, what sort of knowledge they should have, or how to use their freedom. We are not laying down all sorts of moralistic laws. We are just saying that better – more desirable – worlds have more happiness, freedom and knowledge in them. They therefore have beings in them that can experience happiness, freedom and knowledge. The more beings there are, and the more of those things they experience, the better the world will be. So it seems as if the best possible world will be one with huge numbers of beings in it which are ecstatically happy, perfectly free, and extremely wise and knowledgeable. It must be admitted this world does not look very like that. But it sounds a very reasonable description of Heaven, or perhaps of some angelic world. And if things were very carefully arranged, so that nobody's freedom ever conflicted seriously with anybody else's, heaven is (possibly) possible.

God, being rational, will desire what is most desirable. So if God decides to create anything at all, God will create one or more universes of beings which are as happy, free and wise as is possible in those universes. In other words, if there is a wise and powerful God, any creation is bound to be good, desirable both to God and to any conscious beings in it. That just follows from the nature of God. God, being omnipotent, can cause matter to exist, precisely in order to allow many happy, free and wise beings to exist. Matter does not just exist without any reason, as it does in Plato. Matter exists because God wills to make it exist, so that many desirable states can exist. It is wholly caused, both in existence and in nature, by God, and is not some sort of eternally existing independent stuff. That is what it means to say that creation is 'out of nothing', *ex nihilo*.

Aristotle and the Perfect Being

For Augustine, God is not compelled to create anything. Although it would be good to create many finite beings who can experience desirable states, it is not obligatory. God does not need to create, because God is already the most desirable thing that could possibly exist. God already has the maximum degree of happiness, wisdom, freedom and knowledge. So even if God never created anything, there would still exist a perfectly desirable – a wholly good – state of affairs. We can explain creation by saying that God chooses it for the sake of its goodness. We can see that God might be supremely good. But does this explain why God exists? Can anything explain that? Augustine and Plato both thought that the existence of God is self-explanatory, that it can be explained simply by reference to itself.

For Plato, this is because the most basic type of explanation is in terms of goodness or value. You explain why something exists by showing that it is good for it to exist, just for its own sake. For instance, if you ask why Mozart's Jupiter symphony exists, you might first of all refer to the life of Mozart, the state of music in his day, and the things that motivated him to write it. (Plato had not heard of Mozart, but that was his misfortune.) In the case of Mozart, after you have found out as much as you can about his culture and training, you ultimately have to say that the symphony exists because the composer thought it was a good thing to produce. The symphony exists mainly because that is what Mozart wanted and was eminently able to produce, a work of art which was creative and beautiful.

The creative process, the exercise of free creative imagination and skill, and the finished product, are just good in themselves, for their own sake. The music may produce happiness, or money or fame, but that is not the reason, or the main reason, for writing it. The music is written, and it is heard, just because it is an intrinsically worthwhile experience to create or appreciate it. So we explain why the symphony exists by saying that its creation and appreciation are of intrinsic value, they are good in themselves. Or at least, any explanation that misses this factor out is radically incomplete.

Thus you explain why something exists by showing that it is of intrinsic value; it is good that it exists. And, while it may be potentially valuable even if no one ever experiences it, the actual value lies in its production or contemplation by some conscious being. For Augustine, we can therefore explain why God exists by showing that the being of God is of intrinsic value, and that this value is consciously experienced by God. It is in that sense that God is good. God contains the highest degree of all intrinsic values, and consciousness of them is itself the supreme good.

Instead of having a conscious being which has to look to the world of Forms to use as a pattern for world-shaping, you now have a God who looks to the divine perfection itself as the pattern of all goodness. This idea of God was already fully developed by **Aristotle** (384–322 BCE), a pupil of Plato who later founded his own philosophical school in Athens, the Lyceum. Aristotle did not share the mystical inclinations of Plato, and says little about an ascent of the soul to the contemplation of the Good. His interest was much more in explaining why things happen as they do in the universe, what we might today call a scientific explanation of things. He rejected the idea of a world of Forms, insisting that forms, or essential natures, generally need to be embodied in matter to be real.

Nevertheless, according to Aristotle, 'it is necessary that there should be an eternal unchanging substance' (*Metaphysics* 12, 6). This will impart change to other things, but will not itself change. Moreover, it will be immaterial, since it is beyond any sort of change or corruption. It will produce change by 'being loved', by a sort of inherent attraction it possesses. It cannot itself change, because all change would be for the worse. And it contemplates the most perfect and best of things, and so exists in pure bliss or beatitude. What is that most perfect of things? Well, it is, so it must be thinking of itself. So God enjoys contemplating the divine being itself, knowing that it is the best thing there is. 'Its thinking,' says Aristotle, 'is a thinking on thinking.' That is, it is the object of its own knowledge, and in such knowledge lies supreme happiness.

Without going into the intricacies of Aristotle's arguments, which have filled volumes of commentary ever since, we can see that he had an idea of God which is of one necessary, changeless, perfect, blissful being, which causes other things to change by their inherent attraction to it. He closed the gap between the Demiurge and the Good by making the best of all beings itself the cause of change in the cosmos. The price of all this is that God, the best of all beings, never actually does anything, but simply changes things by being there.

Aristotle's works were rediscovered – though they were rather mixed up with some works of Plato – by Muslim philosophers, before they passed into Latin in about the twelfth century. In particular, **Ibn Sina** (called in Latin Avicenna, 980–1037) and **Ibn Rushd** (in Latin, Averroes, 1126–98) developed Aristotelian ideas of God which influenced later Christian thinkers considerably. From the first, there was something attractive about Aristotle's idea of the Unchanged Cause of all, perfect in love of the good, drawing the universe to itself (we have seen evidence of this in Dante). Yet there was also something suspicious, for believers, in the apparent rejection of the idea of active divine providence, in Aristotle's idea that matter was without beginning or end, and in the seeming lack of any notion of personal immortality. Partly for these reasons, such speculations rather quickly died out in the Muslim world, where attention passed to more practical issues of how *Shari'a* was to be interpreted. In the Christian tradition, Aristotle was successfully baptised by Thomas Aquinas, and quickly ousted Plato – though Christian ideas of God remained a mixture of Aristotle and Plato, and did not move far beyond the unification of Plato, Aristotle and the Bible that Augustine achieved.

There is for most theists something a little uncomfortable in the thought that God spends the time in self-contemplation, in a sort of unchanging self-love. It is just too much like perpetually admiring oneself in a mirror. But after all, it might be said, God is the only thing really worth loving unreservedly, so God really has no choice. 'I am sorry, but I really am the greatest,' God might say. And this would be right. God is supreme perfection, and the pattern of all goodness.

But for Plato and Aristotle alike, this God is not a creator. Aristotle says that it is absurd to think that time and change ever began. We can see why very easily, if we try to think of a first moment of time, and then ask, 'And what came before that?' It seems that there is always a time before any given time. Therefore time can never have begun. What God does is to change or shape the material world by attracting it into some sort of likeness to the divine. The sort of likeness, and the degree of it,

Plato (pointing upwards) and Aristotle inventing the God of the philosophers in The School of Athens *(1509) by Raphael.*

will depend on the nature of the matter involved. So we can imagine a descent from thinner to thicker matter, and at each level of descent there will be a more imperfect mirror of perfection, until at the lowest level one might have a demonic world, as far removed from the purity and perfection of the divine pattern as it is possible to be.

For Plato and Aristotle, there is no explanation of why matter exists; it is just there, by some necessity we cannot understand, and it largely explains why the world is not as good as it might be. Again, Augustine goes further than both Plato and Aristotle in unifying the constituent elements of reality, and makes matter wholly a product of God. Creation is 'out of nothing', meaning that God does not shape the cosmos out of pre-existing stuff, but God makes the stuff itself. Because God is supremely good, God knows that it is good if other conscious beings, who can create and appreciate values of their own, exist. God does not *have* to create them, but it is good if God does. So God freely chooses to create such beings, and the cosmos in which they exist.

Augustine and Platonism

Augustine remains a Platonist in many ways. He retains the Platonic distinction between appearance and reality, between the world of the senses and the spiritual perfection of God. He retains the story of the soul's journey as one from bondage to the senses to the intellectual or spiritual vision of the Good. But he drops the idea of rebirth, stressing that each soul is created anew by God. And he sees Jesus as the perfect image of God in human form. Although the notion of the *Logos*, the wisdom of God, becoming flesh is quite Platonic, the particularities of the life of Jesus, an obscure provincial carpenter's son who died a criminal's death, give that notion a very non-Platonic form. They give to the material, and especially to manual labour which shapes the material, and to the outcast and disadvantaged, a greater emphasis and importance than the aristocratic Plato had done.

The god who appeared to Abraham in fire had the power at least to provide what he promised for the Patriarch's descendants. The god who spoke to Job out of the whirlwind had the power to control the whole world, for inscrutable purposes of his own. The god who spoke to Augustine in a walled garden (so Augustine wrote in his best-known book, the *Confessions*) was the one and only creator of the cosmos, who freely creates all things for the sake of their goodness, and whose will is that rational creatures should overcome egoistic desire and be led by divine love to the vision of the divine perfection as the fulfilment of their rational desires.

Augustine seemed to have fulfilled the Platonic dream of giving a coherent account of a wholly intelligible universe. The gods are no longer arbitrary figures who come into being for no obvious reason, and who have no particular concern for human lives other than that of interest or amusement, but who might be bribed by sacrifices from time to time. There is one perfect self-existent source of all beings, creator of a universe which itself is both supremely rational and good. God knows all possible worlds, and brings one or more into existence for the sake of their goodness, which dimly and partially reflects the divine goodness. In this creation, there may be necessities which only God knows. They do not constrain God as external limitations, but express what is unavoidable in the divine nature itself, which is necessarily and unchangeably what it is.

The religious life is the ascent to conscious knowledge and love of God, and it is both supremely rational and emotionally and morally satisfying. The intellectual understanding of the universe and the pursuit of the religious life fit seamlessly together.

No longer do philosophers have to be perplexed by the strangeness and ambiguity of religious rituals and myths. A purely rational, and yet spiritually mature, religion can replace them. That is why Augustine was so confident that this new Christian picture (it might equally well have been a Jewish picture, and in Philo of Alexandria it was; or a Muslim picture, but Islam had not yet appeared) of the one perfect creator would drive out belief in the old Roman gods, leaving them as archaic remnants of an outmoded worldview.

But there remain major problems with Augustine's synthesis, elegant and attractive though it is. He saw them himself, and though he did his best to deal with them, they have remained to perplex generations of Christian theologians. Perhaps the biggest problem is how, on Augustine's theory, can there be so much evil and suffering in the created universe?

Indeed, you might wonder why a perfect God would bother to create anything else at all, since nothing could make things any better for God, and anything is likely to make them decidedly worse. However, in a sense creation makes things better by creating lots of other happy, free and wise beings. That might not increase God's perfections, but it would increase the total amount of good that exists, and add to the sorts of goodness that exist.

Why should God care about that? Well, since there is an objective difference between good (which rational sentient beings prefer) and bad (which they would choose to avoid), God knows what it is. God therefore knows that it is good to create happy, free, wise beings, and bad to create sad, constrained and deluded beings. He knows that, not by knowing some external facts, but just by knowing the divine nature, including all the many good and bad possible worlds it contains. It is just irrational to create bad, and it is better to be rational than irrational, so God is rational. Therefore God creates what is good, and not what is bad.

Everything seems to be going along very smoothly – except for the awkward fact that we do not live in heaven, and that there seems to be an awful lot of bad around in the world. We seem to have argued that God has to be good by definition, and so does any cosmos he creates. And for Augustine, that is true. The Forms, including the form of the Good – the knowledge of all possible good, rationally desirable states – necessarily exist in the mind of God, and God necessarily acts in accordance with the divine nature. But while that is all very intellectually neat and tidy, it does not seem to square with the observed facts.

Plato dealt with the problem by saying that finite being results from a mixture of intelligence and necessity. Intelligence produces the good, as far as it can, but necessity limits what intelligence can do. For Augustine, there can be no external necessities, such as the independent existence of matter, space and time, which might limit God. But, just as Augustine turned the Forms into ideas in the mind of God, so he placed necessity, not external to, but inside the being of God. Whereas for Plato necessity constrained the Demiurge from outside, and for Aristotle it prevented the material world from perfectly imitating its divine pattern, for Augustine necessity disappears into the divine being itself. God exists by necessity. God's nature is what it is by necessity. And so in God's creation of the cosmos there may be necessities grounded in the divine nature itself, which we cannot discern.

Anselm and Necessary Being

The idea of necessity is not an added extra for Augustine's God. God is not a being who just happens to be this way, though it could have been very different. There is something necessary about it. Just as mathematical truths such as 2+2=4 have to be the way they are, so God has to be the way God is.

It is hard to get to grips with this idea of necessity, but it is fundamental to Platonic thought. The basic distinction is between things that are contingent, which could be otherwise – my hair could be a different colour, or might not exist – and things that are necessary, which could not be otherwise – such as 2+2=4. Some modern philosophers would say that all truths, except trivial ones (and 2+2=4 is fairly trivial), are contingent. Anything might be different. Anything is possible. But for Plato and Augustine some things are necessary. They just have to be the way they are.

The idea of necessity might seem very strange, but we all feel its attraction. If a stone falls to the ground, we say, 'It had to do that, because of the law of gravity. It had no alternative.' Or if we do something which other people criticise, we might say, 'I had no choice; being the person I am, I just had to do what I did.' The attraction of this sort of determinism is very strong. Things have to work out the way they do. The laws of nature have to be obeyed. People's actions are all determined by their characters, or their genes, or their electrons and quarks. All these are forms of necessity. It is an idea we all use quite a lot.

When we come to try to justify it, that turns out to be very difficult. Why shouldn't anything happen at any moment? Well, if it did, life would be totally impossible. I might turn into a banana, you might start growing younger by the minute, we all might fly out of the window. We would never know what might happen next. Life would be complete chaos. Some sort of order has to exist, for life to be possible at all. And if it *has* to exist, there is a sort of necessity.

Necessity is quite a natural idea, then. And if we could show that something existed by necessity – that it really could not fail to exist, or be any different from the way it is – that would be a really ultimate sort of explanation. The supreme reality, God, exists because it just has to be the way it is. And if, like God, it somehow explains the existence of everything else, like this universe, then we would have the best possible sort of explanation we could ever get. So how could we show, or even suggest, that something exists by necessity?

At this point it is necessary to introduce **Anselm** (1033–1109), Archbishop of Canterbury, who provided a brilliantly short and acute definition of God. God, he said, is 'that than which nothing greater can be conceived'. Remember, he went on, God is greater than anything you can conceive. But God is certainly not less than the most perfect thing you can conceive.

Again, Anselm's arguments for this have provided rich fodder for generations of philosophers to chew over. But he is basically saying that if you can even think of something that would be more perfect than God, then that thing would actually be God. So if you want to get an idea of God, think of every property which it would be better to have than not to have, and think of all those properties existing in the highest possible degree. For instance, it is better to be free, happy and knowledgeable than not, so God will be the freest, happiest and most knowledgeable being there could possibly be. Anselm adds – and this brings us to our present discussion – that it is better to exist necessarily, without fear of destruction or non-existence, than to exist contingently, in such a way that you might cease to exist or perhaps be injured or destroyed by some other being. It is better to be changeless than to be changing – given that you are perfect to begin with. You might want to say that the best thing is to be necessarily all-powerful, all-knowing and without any unhappiness at all. Anselm is in complete agreement with both Aristotle and Augustine – God is necessarily the best thing there could possibly be, and knows this.

It may be as well to add just a word of caution here. What we can conceive, or imagine, might be very different from what can actually exist. In other words, we might think of the best possible thing we can – and it might be a very beautiful and talented ninety-foot-high woman. With this example, it is easy to see that our imaginations are just too limited (it would obviously be better to imagine an immortal goddess than a woman, for a start). But there might be something wrong with our imagination of the best possible being. We ought perhaps to bear that in mind. We could still say that God is that than which nothing greater can possibly exist. But that might be different from the greatest being anybody can conceive.

Our conceptions might not be a very good guide to reality. This point will turn out to have some importance when thinking about why God creates evil. We might feel like saying that we can imagine a better God, one who does not create any evil, and that sounds obvious. But it might be that even the most powerful possible being could not create a universe with morally free agents in it, without creating at least the possibility of evil. Our imaginations are just not reliable enough to allow us to decide on that. So it might be better to say that God is that than which nothing greater (better) can exist, and human thought can at least point us in the right direction, though it is not totally reliable, especially on points of detail. Nevertheless, it seems likely that such a God will be as happy, wise and free as any being can possibly be.

The idea of God's necessary existence has nowhere been better put than by Anselm. As well as defining God as the best conceivable being, and including 'necessary existence' as one of the properties it is better to have than not to have, he invented the ontological argument for God's existence. This argument is absolutely infuriating. Since Anselm's time it has taken many forms, all circling around the one central idea of necessary existence. This is one version of the argument: if it is possible for there to be something that, if it is possible is actual, then it is actual. God is such a thing, by definition. Therefore, if God is possible then God is actual. But God is obviously possible. Therefore God exists.

This argument has infuriated philosophers ever since, because it obviously should not work, and yet nobody can finally refute it. How can God be proved just from a couple of sentences, without even looking at the world? What it does show is that there is something special about the idea of God. God is not something that just happens to exist, even though it might not – that would be a God who existed in some possible worlds, but not in others. And that would mean there could be lots of worlds without any God at all.

Some people say they can easily imagine a world without God, so God cannot be necessary – necessity would mean God would exist in every possible world. However, many theists claim precisely that there could not be any possible worlds if there was not a God. The argument goes like this: everything that happens is obviously possible. If we think of everything that could possibly happen, then we have a complete array of possible worlds. But you cannot have possible worlds just existing, because they are merely possible, and not actual. So, if there really are possible worlds, they must exist in something actual, something that really exists. Now we have an actual real thing in which all possible worlds exist. The nearest we can come to imagining this is to think of an actual mind or awareness in which all possible worlds exist as ideas. That mind is God, and the possible worlds are ideas in the mind of God.

These ideas are necessary, because they are all the possible ideas there could ever be, and there are no further alternatives left. And the mind of God is necessary, because if it did not exist, there would be no possible worlds at all. So now we have the mind of God, which has to exist if anything at all is possible. And we have the ideas of all possible worlds, which have to exist, just as they do, in the mind of God. We can say that God necessarily exists, and knows everything that is possible (God is omniscient).

Furthermore, if there is a possible world in which God (the being who exists in all possible worlds, remember) exists, then that God must exist in every possible world, and there cannot be any possible world in which God does not exist. You may think you can imagine one, but in fact you would be overlooking something. After all, how do you know what worlds are possible and what are not?

But, says the atheist, if you do not know what worlds are possible, you cannot be sure there is a possible world with God in it. That is possibly true. We might have to say, well it looks possible, and if it is possible, then God does exist. But we cannot quite be sure. All the same, we have established that God is either completely impossible or absolutely necessary. Either God exists in all possible worlds, or in none of them. Moreover, it does (possibly) make sense to say that God exists by necessity (in all possible worlds).

This quickly gets very annoying (and perhaps the only remedy is to go and play backgammon with David Hume, see p. 180). Thinking about possibility and necessity quickly makes the head spin. That might make some people give up this sort of rational theology altogether. But it might attract others, and suggest that, while the argument does not altogether prove there is a God, it helps us to understand the idea that God necessarily exists, and that such a God is a sort of firm foundation for the contingent world. God is totally different in kind from anything in the universe, but is always present as its foundation. And there will be necessities in the nature of God which we cannot hope to understand from our finite viewpoint, but which may constrain the sorts of universe God can create.

Evil, necessity and the free-will defence

One of these constraints may be that, in any universe God can create which contains morally free agents, there must be some possible evil. In our universe, and on our planet, this evil has been realised by the evil choices of free agents, and the creator of morally responsible agents cannot prevent it. This is often these days called the 'free-will defence'. Evil exists because of the misuse of free will. As Augustine saw it, Satan was an angel who had fallen from heaven, and his fall had corrupted the whole earth. Then he had corrupted Adam and Eve, so that now all their descendants are doomed to be born into a corrupted, 'fallen', world. This solution is very like Plato's theory of rebirth, in that it locates the origin of suffering and death in past free choices.

Satan and Beelzebub feeling that things are getting distinctly warmer. An engraving by Charles Laplante from the first book of Paradise Lost, by John Milton.

However, there is a big problem with Augustine's version. If Adam fell, that is not my fault. If Satan fell, that was not Adam's fault. And, worst of all, if God created Satan, that was not Satan's fault either. In the end, it does seem to be God's fault, after all. At least in Plato's version, what I suffer is my fault, from some previous existence. But if I never existed before I was born, why should I be held responsible for a miserable state I was born into, which I did not personally choose? That is Augustine's theory of 'original sin' – you are born guilty, and deserving of hellfire, even before you have actually done anything. It does not seem fair, to say the least.

Indeed, for Augustine things are even worse. It may be very elegant to have one perfect creator who causes everything in the cosmos to be the way it is. But if God causes everything, how can I really decide anything for myself? We can say that God causes me to decide for myself, but that sounds a bit fishy. If God causes everything, then God causes my decision. And if God causes it, how can I?

Now we have come up against one of the biggest puzzles in the whole history of human thought. It is this: I should only be punished for what I am responsible for. I am only responsible for a wrong act if I know what I am doing, if I know it is wrong, and if I could have done something else. Nobody forced me, I was free. This is certainly true in English law. To be justly punished, I have to be free to do otherwise.

Now if I am caused to do what I do – whether by my genes, my electrons, my society, my mother, or God – that means there is really no alternative to what I do. If I jump off a cliff, there is no alternative to falling to the bottom.

Most philosophers, whether they believe in God or not, think that everything in the universe is caused. So if we knew the laws of physics or the will of God completely, we would see that things just have to be the way they are. There are no alternatives. But they also think that human beings are properly held responsible for their actions, at least sometimes, and therefore that they are sometimes free to do otherwise. So they have the problem of seeing how somebody can be free to do otherwise, when there is no alternative to what he or she does.

Most philosophers, and not just Augustine, have thought you have to believe both of these things, that there are no alternatives to what happens, and that people are sometimes free to do otherwise. This is called **compatibilism**. Augustine believed it. Aquinas believed it. Calvin believed it. Kant believed it. Spinoza believed it. Almost everyone believes it. It means that causal determination by the laws of physics or by the will of God is compatible with human freedom and responsibility.

The opposite of compatibilism is **libertarianism**. This is not, as some of my American colleagues think, the right to own a sub-machine gun or to live on Venice Beach with a preferred other of your choice. It is the view that a truly free act cannot be wholly determined by any prior state or being or law of nature. A free act might be determined in many ways, but part of it is due to a really new decision of the agent, which is unpredictable in principle from any law. Even God could not predict it, since part of the act is wholly in the power of the agent. Most compatibilists pretend that they do not understand what this means. They say that such an act would simply be random, and therefore irrational. Whatever you think about this, it is a fact that most philosophers throughout history have been compatibilists, and have thought that predictability or determinism does not detract from any freedom that is worth having.

Now, if compatibilism is true, there is nothing in principle wrong with Augustine's theory of original sin, or with God holding people responsible for what God causes them to do. God determines everything that happens, and at the same time people can be held responsible for their actions. Modern secular philosophers may say that people should only be held responsible when their own conscious minds have formed an intention to do something which they then carry out. But that is only a matter of convention. It is obvious that the formation of intentions in somebody's mind is just as determined as everything else is. It is not exempt from universal causal determinism. So it is just as plausible – but not so widespread in a secular society – to say that people should be held responsible when they are the descendants of notorious sinners, or when their minds form intentions to do evil, even though God has ultimately caused those intentions to form.

As Augustine says, humans are justly condemned to perdition by God because of their evil thoughts and actions, even though there is no alternative to them happening. If God chooses to save a few from condemnation, that is unmerited mercy. So if you are a compatibilist, you have no reason to complain about the doctrine of the fall of Satan and original sin. If you do complain, that is a waste of time, since there is nothing you can do about it. But of course you were determined to complain anyway, so you may as well continue – unless you are determined to stop.

Most theologians want to preserve the total omnipotence of God, and God's total knowledge of the future. The price they have to pay, of making God responsible for all the evil in the universe, is high. But it would be widely thought that Augustine was right to explain evil largely as a result (or a condition) of responsible freedom, and to think that such freedom is compatible with total divine determinism (usually called 'predestination', in theological circles). An unfriendly critic might say that this is a free-will defence without any real free will.

Creation as a timeless act

There have been innumerable subtle arguments in theological circles about whether God predestines some souls to Hell as well as predestining the elect to Heaven (that would be 'double predestination'), or about whether people freely choose their own destinies. Yet all these arguments have taken place within a general view of God which means that they are little more than subtle variations on the theme of total divine determination. For with Augustine's view of creation, it has to be true that God in the end determines everything that happens, from beginning to end and in every detail.

This is because creation is not, contrary to popular belief, something that happens just at the start of the universe. God does not sit around wondering what to do, and then suddenly decide to create a universe. Augustine raises the question, what was God doing before creating the universe? His answer is surprising. God wasn't doing anything, because there was no time in which God might have been doing something. Why not? Because when God created the universe, God created both space and time. There was no time before God created it, and so there cannot have been any 'before' (since before presupposes time).

Time, despite Aristotle, did have a beginning (most modern physicists would agree with this). You can always ask, 'What existed before the first moment of time?' – but the question does not really make sense. It is like asking, 'What positive integer exists before the number 1?' The answer is that it is the first positive integer. So, if time is a relation between events, and there is an event that is not preceded by any other event, that is the beginning of time. No problem.

God, however, is the creator of time. So God does not exist before it. God must exist completely outside and beyond it, not in a temporal way at all. God is absolutely timeless. In God there is no before and after, and God does not exist at any time. It follows that God does not now exist. That sounds very paradoxical. Yet that is precisely what Augustine says.

The point is that God does exist. But there is no time at which God exists. The whole of time, from beginning to end, is created by God. Because of that, it is just as true to say that God creates at the end of time as it is to say that God creates at the beginning. If we imagine the whole of time as a line from A to Z, then the whole line is made by God in one and the same act.

When it is 1000 CE, God does not have to wait to see what is going to happen in 1001 CE. God makes 1001 at the same time as making 1000. In fact God makes every time at the same time – or, technically, in the same non-temporal act. That means that God does not 'foreknow' or foretell the future. God actually knows it in every detail, since God makes it at the same time as the past. Nothing is either past or future for God. It is as if God sees the whole of time spread out in one 'timeless present'.

Prophecy is no problem for a God who knows exactly what is going to happen at every time, and can put this information into the minds of any prophets at will. But what about when we pray for something to happen? Does that not suggest that God waits to see what we pray for before deciding what to do next? Not at all. God creates the prayer at the same time as creating the future which is the answer, either yes or no. So God does answer prayers, in that God makes our will, in praying, one of the causes of the event that is future to us, but not to God.

If we return briefly to the question of why God created this precise universe, with all the evil it contains, and remember that Augustine is a compatibilist, we now have a clear and coherent answer. 'God did not alter his eternal resolution in creating the world,' writes Augustine. That is to say, God did not first of all think of all the possible worlds God might create, and then decide to create one of them. Such a process would take time, and would consist of God doing one thing after another – first thinking, then deciding. But God has no time to think. God has to do everything at once – think, and decide, and create. God's decision to create is eternal, fixed, and it exists changelessly in God.

Once you see that, you see that God is not a moral agent, poised between good and evil, wondering which to choose. God is indeed free, because there is nothing other than God to constrain God. God is all-powerful, because there is nothing other than God that can impede the divine will, and all powers come from God alone. God is good, as supremely desirable and changelessly perfect. But the universe God creates – and perhaps, Augustine suggests at one point, God creates many – is not chosen after a process of deliberation. God's decision is without beginning, eternal, changeless. Like God, it has to be what it is. There is simply no point in blaming or questioning God. In that sense, Job was right after all. To see God would be to see that what is must be, even though it is the creation of a wholly perfect and all-powerful creator. In that vision, freedom and necessity coincide. Our truest freedom, as the philosopher Spinoza said, lies in the acceptance of necessity. And, as Augustine would add, in the joyful service of the one whose being can fulfil all our desires, and who puts the desire for the divine perfection into our hearts, making it our deepest will.

Faith and understanding

So Augustine closes the system, having pushed human reason as far as it will go into the mysteries of creation and of the divine will. God remains finally inscrutable, but at least reason can dimly discern the rationality or wisdom that lies at the heart of creation. Our life in this world seems to us a product of chance and fate, so often a chaos of competing wills, of frustrated ambitions, and of tragic misfortunes. What is there for us but to grasp at pleasure wherever we can find it, before we end as we began in the darkness of non-existence? Augustine holds before us the picture of a deeper reality, one of rational necessity and elegant beauty, in which all things take their proper place in an ordered descent from a source of perfect wisdom and beauty. It is possible for us to be liberated from the false picture of appearance, and from the egoistic desires to which it leads. Then we can ascend towards seeing the necessity and beauty of things, and above all towards seeing the one changeless beauty which is the true object of human contemplation. Our wills have been disordered towards lower forms of goodness, or towards that corruption of goodness which we call evil. But they can be turned, by divine help, towards the source and goal of all goodness. We can discover the changeless good in the changing ambiguities of time. We can hope to move beyond time itself to the contemplation of the timeless and eternal, and that is the beatitude which validates creation and seals it as incomparably good.

Is this the god of the philosophers? If it is, it is not a god who is inferred as the remote cause of the universe, as somehow necessary to keep the planets in their orbits. It is not the god of Aristotle, who probably did exist only to explain why the stars and planets moved in their orbits. It is not a god who is a product of mere human speculation, opposed to the revelations to the prophets and somehow having the character of presumption and human arrogance. It is a God who gives coherence and intelligibility to the universe as a divine creation, and integrates the spiritual quest for knowledge and love of supreme goodness with the scientific quest for understanding of the universe and the place of humanity within it.

There will probably always remain a difference of temperament between those who desire such a 'grand narrative' and integrated explanation of all things, and those who think the human mind is too puny ever to succeed in such a task. Some will say, let science do its job as well as it can, and seek to explain the causes of things according to laws in the physical universe. But let religion remain in the realm of faith, of trust in the God revealed to Abraham, Isaac and Jacob, of loyalty to revelation and hope in redemption. For them, the voice out of the whirlwind speaks of a different area of human life from the voice of the Academy. We must speak of one God, the creator of all things, but we can only speak in stories, remembering how far from reality all our thoughts must be, but trusting that God has given stories that will not finally mislead us. The Augustinian approach, which was later followed through in a more Aristotelian way by Aquinas, misleads by threatening to found faith on philosophy, and therefore on the vagaries of human intellect.

To those, however, who feel the need to integrate intellectual understanding more closely with faith, Augustine will remain an outstanding example of someone who tried to do precisely that. He did not first have a philosophy, and then construct a faith which followed from it. All such attempts in human history have failed, and the neo-Platonist philosophers who tried to make Platonism a religion failed along with the rest. Augustine first had a faith, based firmly on a response of the heart to the revelation of the nature of God in the person of Jesus. But he was driven to try to make sense of that faith in the context of the best understanding of the natural world available in his day, however provisional that understanding was.

As Anselm, one of the greatest rationalists in the history of religious thought, put it:

I do not try, Lord, to attain your lofty heights, because my understanding is in no way equal to it. But I do desire to understand your truth a little, that truth that my heart believes and loves. For I do not seek to understand so that I may believe; but I believe so that I may understand. For I believe this also, that unless I believe, I shall not understand.

Proslogion, chapter 1

Many of Augustine's conclusions may have been mistaken. But what he leaves is a picture of the human soul which, on its journey through this world of sense and time, 'being inflamed with God's love loses all temporal concupiscence, and is formed according to God's most perfect pattern, pleasing him by participating in his beauty'. He leaves us with the thought that the quest to understand the universe is itself a quest for beauty and intelligibility, a quest which finds its fulfilment in the final vision of perfect beauty:

> Ah then my hungry soule, which long hast fed
> on idle fancies of thy foolish thought,
> and with false beauties flattring bait misled,
> hast after vaine deceiptfull shadowes sought,
> But late repentance through thy follies prief;
> ah ceasse to gaze on matter of thy grief.
> And looke at last up to that soveraine light,
> from whose pure beams al perfect beauty springs,
> that kindleth love in every godly spright,
> even the love of God, which loathing brings
> of this vile world, and these gay seeming things;
> with whose sweete pleasures being so possest,
> thy straying thoughts henceforth for ever rest.'

EDMUND SPENSER, (1552–99), 'An Hymne of Heavenly Beautie', in *The Penguin Book of English Christian Verse*, p. 57.

Find out more ...

Two dialogues by Plato that have been very influential on subsequent religious thought are *The Republic* (trans. Desmond Lee, Harmondsworth, Penguin, 1995, especially 514A–520C) and the *Timaeus* (trans. Desmond Lee, Harmondsworth, Penguin, 1965).

Augustine writes on creation in his major work, *The City of God* (trans. John Healey, London, J.M. Dent, 1945), book 11, chapters 4–6. His best-known work is *Confessions* (trans. E.M. Blaiklock, London, Hodder & Stoughton, 1983).

Aristotle's treatment of God can be found in his *Metaphysics*, 12, 6–9. There are many translations and editions of this. I used the translation by David W. Ross in *The Works of Aristotle*, vol. 8 (Oxford, Clarendon Press, 1928).

Anselm propounds the ontological argument in his *Proslogion*, 1 and 2. An illuminating discussion of God is found in his *Monologion*, chapters 1–15 (both trans. S.N. Deane in *St Anselm: Basic Writings*, La Salle, Ill, Open Court, 1962).

5

The poet of the world

In which the reader will be introduced to Hegel, who thought he was the Absolute Spirit, and to Karl Marx, who thought he was Hegel standing on his head. The reader will discover that pantheists do not exist, and that process philosophers are all collections of monads, will be comforted to learn that the universe is continually getting better, but disappointed to hear that it is not going anywhere in particular.

The timeless and immutable God

For over a thousand years the classical view of God, shaped by Augustine, Anselm and Aquinas as well as by philosophers of Judaism and Islam, dominated Western European thinking about God. The view is not at all anthropomorphic. It does not picture God as a male human being. Quite the contrary, if it has a problem it is that it is too agnostic, saying that God is so different from anything we can imagine that there is actually little we can say at all.

The classical view says that God is non-material, not limited in any way, not composed of parts, timeless, immutable and impassible (not affected by anything in any way). These very abstract terms all follow in a very elegant way from the basic assertion that God is 'simple', not divisible even in thought in any way whatsoever. We have to deny of

The history of the planet earth as a journey from an alienated world towards the fullness of God.

God everything that is true of the universe. God is totally other than anything in the universe, a completely different sort of being.

Nevertheless, we can say some things about God. For instance, God is, in Anselm's definition, 'that than which nothing more perfect can be conceived'. We can think of God as possessing every good quality we can conceive of, as supremely beautiful and wise and happy – even though we cannot begin to imagine what that is like for God. God does not need to create any universe, for God is already perfect in the divine being, and quite complete without anything else whatsoever. If God does create, it is totally gratuitous. The universe need never have happened.

When we say that God creates the universe, we do not mean that God first thinks of a universe, and then begins to create it bit by bit, amending a piece here and a piece there if things do not go according to plan. The whole universe from beginning to end has to spring from God in one timeless act. We can say that God knows and wills the universe, but these terms are analogies, nothing like human knowing and willing. They really say that the universe is purposive and intelligible, and springs from a being to which such terms as 'purpose' and 'intelligence' apply only in ways we cannot imagine.

When we worship such a God, we clearly cannot be seeking to flatter or influence God by telling God how wonderful God is and what a good job God has done. We must simply be appreciating and attending reverently to the inexhaustible power and the changeless perfection of God, from whom all good things flow, and from whom all evil arises as a privation, or falling away from goodness. God alone is supremely desirable and limitless, and worship is the conscious recognition of that fact, as we try to attend to and feel the divine perfection as much as possible.

All this is a long way from some popular pictures of a God who is always busy listening to prayers, deciding which ones to answer, changing his (people still usually speak of 'his') mind as new events happen, and engaging in long discussions and arguments with the Patriarchs and prophets. It is also a long way from some popular presentations of the Christian God as divided into three parts, Father, Son and Spirit, discussing which one of them should become incarnate as a man, deciding after some hesitation to redeem the world, becoming human, suffering and dying on the cross, and waiting impatiently in heaven before returning to judge the world at the end of time.

It is important to see how different the classical view is from the popular view. Whatever the Trinity is, it cannot consist of three distinct 'parts' in God, who has no parts. Whatever is meant by 'God becoming man', it cannot mean that God changes by taking on human flesh. Whatever is meant by the Holy Spirit working to sanctify the hearts of men and women, it cannot mean that God is actually changing by acting like a finite being in history. All statements about God changing and acting, whether they are in the Bible or not, must be metaphors. All changes are in finite things, and not in God, who is changeless.

So, for example, when God the Son suffers, it is the human nature only that suffers, not the divine. When the Word becomes flesh, what happens is that a particular human life, that of Jesus, is changed to become united with the changeless God in a unique way. When God is said to judge or to save humans, it is not God who changes. It is those human lives that, by the course of actions they have chosen, see the unchanging God as either angry in judgment or loving in grace. The love and the anger of God are the same thing, but seen from very different human perspectives. God does not decide at a particular point in time to redeem the world. The judgment and the redemption are already decided at the moment of creation, which of course, from God's point of view, is the very same moment as the moment of the end of time – and as every other moment in between.

The crucial feature of the classical view is the complete timelessness of God, which entails complete immutability. For anyone influenced strongly by Plato, the changeless is obviously superior to the changing, and nothing that is perfect can change in any way without becoming worse (to say that it might become better does not help, since that entails that it must have been less than perfect to begin with). The classical God does not act as an agent in time, although the whole of time is the unchanging act of God. If you ever speak of God acting in history, you cannot mean – in the classical view – that God decides to do new things that God might not have done. You might mean that God eternally sets up the whole process of history so that some events show the divine nature and purpose more clearly or decisively than others. But God is not actually acting in those events more or less than at any other time.

When you realise the immense difference between the classical and the popular views of God, you realise, perhaps to your surprise, that the classical view is nearer to seemingly very radical views of a God who is not a particular cause or personal agent in the world, who is not a being among other beings at all. So when conservative Christians attack views like those of the twentieth-century theologian Paul Tillich for saying that God is not a person, but is 'Being-itself', the depth and power of being, they are in fact attacking the classical Christian doctrine of God. Sometimes conservatives simply forget what real conservatism is, and those who try to be orthodox Christians simply have not realised how very agnostic and radical the orthodox tradition about God is.

The rejection of Platonism

Nevertheless, some Christians feel slightly uncomfortable about holding that virtually everything the Bible says about God is metaphorical, and that Plato, a pagan philosopher, gives us the key to interpreting the Bible properly. The sixteenth-century Protestant Reformers did not change or criticise the classical picture of God, but some of Martin Luther's writings contain the seeds of what was, in some of his followers, to become known as 'kenotic Christology'. The word *kenosis* is Greek for 'emptying', and the view is that the Word or Son of God emptied itself of some of the divine attributes – omnipotence and omniscience, for example – when becoming human. Without going into the details of this concept, what it does, by implication, is to admit some sort of change in God. God either temporarily loses, or perhaps suppresses, some divine attributes.

This would mean quite a change in the classical view that God does not change at all. For many Protestant Christian theologians the statement that 'the Word became flesh', and suffered and died, does suggest that God changes the divine nature when getting involved in space and time, in the person of Jesus. From a Protestant point of view, there has since the time of Luther been a widespread reaction against the view of God as a changeless self-contemplating perfect being, in favour of seeing God as really changing by entering into human history, sharing human suffering, and responding in new and unpredictable ways to the prayers of human beings.

On a more purely philosophical level, since the seventeenth century the modified Platonism that underlies the classical picture of God has seemed less and less appealing. In fact, one of the major changes in the history of human thinking occurred with the rise of the natural sciences in seventeenth-century Europe, and the collapse of Platonic philosophy. The change can be put briefly in this way: for the old view, the changeless is superior to the changing; temporal things are only half real; and history adds nothing to the perfection of reality, being only a series of shadows of the changeless. For the new view, change, which is the condition of creative action, is superior to changelessness; only temporal things are fully real; and history is the arena of new and worthwhile activities, and the necessary condition of the real existence of values.

This change did not come about instantly. It spread out over three hundred years in the history of European ideas. But it expresses a gradual change of focus from the eternal to the temporal, and to the necessity of time and history to the true reality of everything, even of God. Even in the thirteenth century Thomas Aquinas had used Aristotle, rather than Plato, as the basis for a Christian philosophy. Whereas Plato had seen the world of Forms as more real than the world of the senses, of change and time, Aristotle saw the Forms as embodied in matter, so that this material world is the only real world. Yet as far as God was concerned, the Platonic view that the changeless is superior to the changing, that perfection implies immutability, and that ideas in the mind of God are more real than individuals in space and time, was retained by Aquinas. Aristotle himself may well have been a materialist, and his God was probably a sort of scientific postulate to explain the nature of the cosmos. But Aquinas retained as central the Platonic vision of the journey of the soul from sensuality to the contemplation of the Eternal, and for that vision it was essential that God should be free from even the possibility of change and decay, and therefore from any historical or temporal relationship to the cosmos.

This is a profound spiritual vision, but from the seventeenth century many people began to wonder whether it really gave enough importance to the existence of the cosmos, and to the meaning of human lives which are, after all, lived out in time. Is it really plausible to say that whatever human beings do, whether they are happy or sad, heroically good or demonically evil, it makes no difference whatsoever to God? Is it acceptable to say that God does not change in the slightest, whatever we do, and whatever happens in the world? Doesn't history, and the humdrum events of human life, have more importance than that?

Maybe not, of course, and for the classical view it is part of spiritual training to realise that we are not finally important in the scheme of things. We add absolutely nothing at all to the infinite perfection of God, and our lives are wholly gratuitous. Precisely because God is infinite, nothing can be added to God, and if our little lives have any point and purpose, it is that we are able to have some small experience of faint material images of the infinite perfections of God. We are creatures of the cave, and nothing we do has any effect upon the sun, even though our truest knowledge and highest happiness will come from ascending to see it in the daylight.

As the natural sciences began to grow, however, and the Platonic certainty of a more real world of intelligible Forms began to fade, it was not so clear that there was a perfect sun which contained all the good things of earth, but in a higher manner. If this sublunar world is the only real world there is, must actual perfection not somehow lie in this world, rather than in some realm beyond it? Might 'perfect Beauty itself, beyond all particular beautiful things', not be an abstraction, so that there are really only the beautiful things we know and see here below? Maybe these things have a creator, but does it really make sense to say that the creator is completely beautiful and perfect without them? Perhaps – and here is the radical thought – the creator needs to create actual beautiful things in order to enjoy them. Then they will not be just shadows of greater realities. They will be the realities, however imperfect they are.

Perhaps, even more radically, they are developing realities that need to be perfected in this universe by the actions of created agents within it. Then finite agents would have an important role in the history of being, having the vocation of bringing potential beauty and intelligibility into new and higher kinds of actuality. Humans would not be gratuitous pimples on the surface of a fundamentally unchanging being. They would be parts of a growing, developing universe with the duty to help it grow into its potential fullness in individually and uniquely chosen ways. Perhaps they even play a part in helping God to realise and make fully actual the potentialities in the divine nature.

If this is the case, the purpose of human life will not ultimately be to turn away from the material and contemplate the Eternal. It will be to shape the material itself towards perfection, to create and contemplate values that have to exist in space and time if they exist at all, and to bring into being good things which add to the total perfection of existence, and do not simply partially imitate a perfection that is already complete, and in a sense better without them.

This is a complete transformation of the understanding of the cosmos and of the place of humanity within it. It is not an accident that it developed at a time, from the seventeenth to the nineteenth centuries, when the new natural sciences were giving humans an understanding of the universe which promised the ability to change and improve nature.

It was also a time, towards the end of the eighteenth century, when established authorities, who relied on preserving unchanging and ancient traditions, were being challenged by a new emphasis on 'the rights of man', on the possibility of new social structures, and on a belief that the conditions of human life could be changed. The American and French revolutions, crystallised in the events of 1776 (the Declaration of Independence)and 1789 (the fall of the Bastille) respectively, seemed to show that radical change for the better was possible. The basically aristocratic philosophy of Plato, offering enlightenment to a leisured elite, was undermined by the newly envisaged possibility that common people could change the world by revolutionary effort. Change and becoming, time and history, might be fundamentally important to the nature of being itself.

Hegel and the philosophy of Absolute Spirit

The person who gave definitive expression to the new view was **Georg Wilhelm Friedrich Hegel** (1770–1831), a rather dull student from Stuttgart who became arguably the most unreadable philosopher of all time, and yet changed the face of philosophical thought in Europe. He started his career by training for the Lutheran ministry, but ended it by regarding Lutheran Christianity as a picturesque version of his own more rational philosophical system. He always regarded himself as a Lutheran, and indeed said that he was the first truly Christian philosopher. This may be true, but it must be said that very few, if any, Christians have agreed with him, and very few Christian theologians have been impressed by the thought that their faith is basically a mythical version of Hegel's philosophy.

Hegel proposed that the whole of temporal reality is the self-expression of Absolute Spirit (*Geist*), as it seeks to realise its own nature. So the universe is not just something completely separate from God, as it is in the classical view, it is the way in which God necessarily expresses the divine being. Just as persons might express their thoughts in words, or music, or dance, so God expresses the divine thoughts by creating the universe. You might say that persons would not really be persons if they did not express themselves in some objective way. So Hegel would say that God would not be God if there was not some universe in which the divine being could be expressed, and could thereby come to make actual what it potentially is.

In this process of self-expression, Hegel holds that Spirit has three basic modes of being: 'There are three moments to be distinguished: essential Being, explicit Self-existence, which is the express otherness of essential Being, and for which that Being is object; and Self-existence or Self-knowledge in that other' (*Phenomenology of Spirit,* para. 770).

I will try to spell this out, though any interpreter of Hegel will immediately be contradicted by other people who interpret the same texts in quite different ways. The first moment, 'Essential Being', or 'Being-in-itself', is the complete array of all possible ideas in the mind of God. For Augustine and Aquinas, these ideas, which are basically Plato's Forms, are fully real, and are the objects of a divine contemplation which is perfectly blissful and complete in itself, not needing anything else to be wholly perfect. But Hegel proposed that the ideas in the divine Mind are in fact only potential. They are not fully real, and if God's being consisted only of ideas or Forms, it would be radically incomplete, a sort of pure potentiality for being. To become actual those ideas, or at least some of them, need to be embodied in a physical universe.

So Spirit necessarily creates or actualises some of its possibilities, in a finite temporal universe. There is 'a necessity compelling Spirit to ... make manifest what is inherent'. There is a much more urgent reason for creation in Hegel's philosophy than in the classical view. God has to create in order to realise actually valuable states. The universe is thus part of God's own self-realisation. In a sense, it is part of God, for it realises God's potential nature. So the answer to the question, 'Why does God create a universe?' is that God has to create a universe, in order to exist as a fully actual being.

The second of Hegel's three 'moments' in the life of Spirit is 'explicit Self-existence', or 'Being-for-itself', the stage in which God brings into being an actual universe. This universe objectifies some of the ideas in the mind of God. So God can know them as objects, but at the same time these objects are alienated, or set over and against God as something other or alien. They have to a greater or lesser degree their own life and autonomy, and so in a sense God has given up complete control to allow created beings to follow their own paths. Hegel, no doubt influenced by Lutheran thought, calls this the *kenosis*, the self-emptying of Absolute Spirit.

The universe is not only the self-realisation of God. It is also the self-alienation of God, splitting the divine being, making it into a series of finite temporal objects over and against essential Being. Spirit sees itself as in a mirror which creates an image with its own sort of reality. For Hegel the universe is an image of Spirit, as it is in Plato. But whereas in Plato, the image is a shadow of the fuller spiritual reality, in Hegel, the image is that which makes real and objective the nature of Spirit, even as it becomes an object separate from Spirit at the same time. Yet because the object is separate, it has its own life, and is 'fallen' from Spirit, realising Spirit only in partial and imperfect ways.

The third moment in the life of Spirit is that in which this 'fallen' universe is reconciled and united again to Absolute Spirit, and Being exists 'in-and-for itself'. All the imperfections and ambiguities of the temporal world are reconciled into a higher harmony, and integrated into the finally achieved consciousness of Absolute Spirit, as time is eternalised, and passes for ever into the life of eternity. In this third stage, Spirit is like Aristotle's Prime Mover, blissful in the consciousness that all perfections exist in itself, and that it is itself the supreme object of blissful contemplation. But on the Hegelian view, that state comes only at the end of the history of the universe, as all the universe's struggles and developments are taken into the life of Spirit, with all its conflicts and sufferings transcended and reconciled. Spirit, having realised itself in history, can now exist in completion as a fully actualised reality.

Nevertheless, we should not think of this as a time-bound process, as though God started off as an unconscious and almost purely potential being at the beginning of the universe, and ended up at the end of time as a perfect conscious Mind. Hegel does not really think of Spirit as literally evolving, as getting better from moment to moment. That is how it appears to us, as time-bound creatures. But Hegel says, 'The essential Being is inherently and from the start reconciled with itself.' Time is important to God's self-realisation, but God transcends time, and is from the start the perfectly conscious Absolute Spirit, even at the beginning of the temporal process. In other words, for Hegel just as for Aquinas God is basically time transcending or eternal. The difference is that time is an essential aspect of the being of God, since it realises in time what God is, and without time, God would not be eternally what God is. God does not become a completely time-bound being, but a temporal expression is necessary to God's being eternally what God is.

Hegel saw this as the philosophical truth that the Christian doctrine of the Trinity symbolised in picture-language. 'Spirit-in-itself' is the Father, apart from the universe and generating it. 'Spirit-for-itself' is the Son, generated from the Father as an image of the Father and yet in some way having its own proper historical being. And 'Spirit-in-and-for-itself' is the Spirit, integrating all the good bits of the history of the universe, eliminating the bad bits, and taking them into the completed experience of God. Of course, classical Christian theologians did not thank him for this. Whatever the Trinity was for them, it had to be primarily timeless. For Hegel, his Trinity is a historical process, by which the Father projects itself into the other (the Son), and then brings the other back to itself through the Spirit at the end of time. Even worse for the classical theologian, the Trinity somehow includes the whole history of the universe in itself.

There is a word for this in classical thinking about God: it is 'pantheism'. Hegel has sometimes been called a pantheist, because he makes the universe part of the history of God, because he gives God a history at all, and because as a result the transcendent God tends to disappear without trace into the historical process. Spirit becomes just a Romantic name for the process itself, and the transcendent God ceases to be relevant.

Marx and the dialectic of history

It has to be admitted that just such a thing actually happened. **Karl Marx** (1818–83) used Hegel's theory in his own writings on communism. But to do this he had to stand Hegel on his head, as Marx put it. When standing on his head, Hegel can no longer say the words 'Absolute Spirit'. Every time he tries to do so, out come the words 'dialectical materialism' instead.

Hegel had given the causal priority in all things to Spirit. It was Spirit, he maintained, that generates the universe, which realises its own nature in the events of history, and takes all things into its own completed experience. For Marx, the driving force of history is 'matter'. He did not mean electrons or lumps of inanimate stuff, but the forces of economic production and exchange. History is driven not from the top, but from the bottom, by forces of competition and survival.

According to Darwin's theory of evolution published in 1859, eleven years after the *Communist Manifesto*, animals survive because they compete for survival in a harsh environment, and some lucky mutations win out in the competition, because they are better adapted to their environment. So for Marx history is driven by forces of competition for producing and exchanging goods. It is not a Spirit-driven progress to peace and justice, but a greed-driven process of ruthless competition and elimination.

Nevertheless, there is supposed to be a sort of inevitability in the process. Darwin, no doubt influenced by the evolutionary philosophies current at the time, thought that animals were bound to get better and better adapted through natural selection, so there was no limit to their perfection. So Marx thought that economic history was bound to end up in a sort of Utopian society where everyone had enough of whatever they wanted, and everyone would be free to do just what they wanted. They can hunt in the morning, fish in the afternoon, and rear cattle in the evening, he said, in one of his rare moments of happy optimism (this is from the *German Ideology*).

For Marx history is a dialectical process.

dialectic – a continuing uniting of opposing or conflicting tendencies (*Shorter O.E.D.*)

Because of economic conditions, certain forms of social framework come into existence, and values appropriate to them are prized. Thus feudalism originates through the necessity of organising defence against enemies, and its values include such things as chivalry, honour and loyalty to one's lord. These conditions and values, however, contain the seeds of their own dissolution, internal contradictions which lead to a new form of society with quite different values. Feudalism led to the build-up of associations of peasants, and thus prepared the way for uprisings against the aristocracy, who were after all in a small minority. This led to bourgeois society, whose values were those of the middle class or bourgeoisie – thrift, hard work, the accumulation of private property and respectability.

The dialectic of history is that each social structure that is thrown up by economic circumstances overstresses one set of values (this is the so-called 'thesis'). This leads to a reaction, in which a different and largely opposing set of values takes over (this is the 'antithesis'). And that in turn in time produces a swing of the pendulum back again. So bourgeois capitalism produces large collectives of urbanised workers, who will bring in the rule of the proletariat, and their values of liberty, equality and fraternity. This swing will be at a higher level, because of what has gone before, and so it is called the 'synthesis' of the dialectical process. That synthesis becomes in turn a new thesis, and the dialectic goes on.

History is an alternating play of contradictions, or a continual swinging between opposing tendencies and values in society. So Marx charts human history as a progress from feudalism through capitalism to socialism and, at last, communism. When we get to communism, however, the dialectic stops, because at that point, he thought all contradictions would have been overcome and reconciled. Everyone would be happy and free; the contradictions of history would have been resolved. The truth is perhaps more sombre – all capitalists and bourgeoisie have been eliminated. Only proletarians are left. There are no oppressed people left, as the oppressors are all dead.

Marxism has been a tremendously influential force in recent history. So the philosophy of Hegel is not mere abstract speculation. At least when you stand it on its head, it has a powerful social message and motivating power. It speaks to the oppressed of the world, and tells them to rise up against the oppressors, because the power of destiny is on their side. The revolution they are to accomplish is not some highly risky moral crusade. It is simply taking part in the inevitable dialectic of history. The time is right, and the revolution is bound to happen. After a short period of necessary dictatorship, the classless society of peace and justice will be ushered in, not just by human action, but by internal historical necessity.

Marx opposed the powers of organised religion, which he saw as oppressive and reactionary. But his attitude to religion is more ambiguous than is sometimes realised. Everyone knows the famous quotation, 'Religion is the opium of the people', but not as many know the sentences that immediately precede it: 'Religious suffering is at the same time an expression of real suffering and a protest against real suffering. Religion is the sigh of the oppressed creature, the sentiment of a heartless world, and the soul of soulless conditions' (from the introduction to *A Critique of Hegel's Philosophy of Right*). They could have been written by a devout believer.

It is true that Marx thought religion gave an illusory happiness, pie in the sky when you die, instead of happiness here and now for the oppressed. But might there not be a form of religion without illusions? Might religion not be a force of protest against real suffering, and an affirmation of true human freedom and fulfilment?

A free and equal society? A rally in the 'Square of Heroes' in Budapest, Hungary during communist rule.

As Marx saw the religion of his day, it did not do that. It colluded with oppression, blessing and fraternising with capitalists and neglecting miners and factory-workers. It counselled believers to put up with oppression patiently, and pray for happiness in heaven, and above all not to rock the boat of the established social order. He felt strongly that religion should be about human flourishing in this world, and that if there is such a thing as salvation, it must be possible in the social conditions we actually have, not just in some imaginary never-never land.

In this sense, did Marx himself not actually have a religion? He was Jewish by birth, though baptised as a Christian in infancy, and his stress on liberation and salvation as this-worldly in emphasis seems very Jewish. The Old Testament does not look for deferred happiness in an afterlife. It very rarely mentions any afterlife, and when it does the outlook seems fairly gloomy. *Sheol*, the world of the dead, is a place where ghosts gibber and moan, and darkness reigns. Liberation is about escaping from Egypt or Babylon. The great prophets are social critics of oppression and radical reformers and protesters against the excesses of monarchy. The messianic age will come on earth in future, as the inevitable climax of human history. Does this not sound very familiar, when we read Marx? Religion without illusions is the quest for justice and peace in the social conditions of this world, coupled with the belief that the just and free society is destined to come, because it is written into the dialectical structure of history. Its goal is the classless and free society, its chosen people is the Communist Party, the vanguard of the future, and its prophet is Marx.

We know now that it all went wrong. Upside-down Hegel was not a good prescription for the twentieth century. Revolutionary Marxism tortured and massacred more people in fifty years than the so-called oppressive religions had managed to get through in generations. It was not a small thing, after all, to get rid of Spirit and give the causal priority in history to economic necessity. For Spirit is what validates morality, sets absolute limits to human greed and hatred, and gives transcendent significance to the processes of history.

In Marx's account, morality is only the scum thrown up on the surface of the forces of economic production and exchange. It changes as those forces change. It is no absolute force, and the goal of the just society is therefore not so much a moral goal as simply the necessary outcome of a morally indifferent process. Once revolution is seen to be inevitable, to be the outworking of destiny, it has no moral limits. And the dictatorship of the proletariat, which Marx saw as a temporary phase to introduce the free communist society, becomes a permanent dictatorship of fear and conformity to political acceptability, from which there is no escape.

So there is an unbearable tension in Marx between his outrage at the conditions of the industrialised workers, in early nineteenth-century Britain, particularly his longing for freedom for the poorest and most oppressed, and his recommendation of a revolution which would introduce unprecedented violence and terror into the lives of those he most wanted to help. The combination of belief in an iron necessity of history and the uselessness and hypocritical character of morality opened the way to chaos for half the world.

All this, of course, vindicates the dialectical character of history. The one-sided pursuit of a specific set of ideals leads to a state the opposite of that which one desires, and breeds a reaction which may be equally one-sided. The opposite pole to Marxist communism, which gave Marxism much of its power as an apparent antidote, is fascism.

> **Fascism** – from the Italian word for the bundle of sticks bound around the axe that preceded the ancient Roman consuls in procession; Mussolini adopted this as the symbol of the Italian nationalist and authoritarian political movement, organised in 1919 to oppose communism.

Reacting against the Marxist rejection of the 'bourgeois morality' of the family, of private property and of respect for tradition, fascists stressed the primary importance of family and nation ('blood and soil'), of obedience to authority and the subordination of the individual to the communal will. Fascists, too, can claim a Hegelian ancestry. Hegel had written that Spirit is particularised in the Spirit of a people and culture, and that it may be the historical destiny of some people to bring about a transition from one stage of historical dialectic to another. Oddly enough, he thought it was the Prussians (he was a Prussian) who carried this world-historical destiny in the nineteenth century. And he thought that the world-purpose of a specific age might be best discerned through a great leader (*Führer*), who could see and communicate the purpose of Spirit to his people. Because the dialectic of history is a process of struggle and opposition, achieving a higher stage of development through conflict, it may be that the cultivation of a strong nation, confident of its destiny, bending the world to its will, expresses the inexorable purpose of the world-Spirit to bring to birth the Superman

(*Übermensch*), the human of extraordinary power and will, whose destiny is to teach and lead (or exterminate) the weak (everybody else).

Reading this after the Holocaust and the two world wars of the twentieth century, a shudder of hindsight is inevitable. Is this what Hegel foresaw, or legitimated? We probably have to say that there are ambiguities in the thought of Hegel which were exploited by communism and fascism. But since his work was used in such completely opposing ways, maybe they both missed the point. After all, Hegel claimed always to be a Christian, and as such he was well aware both of the importance of a morality that was binding and absolute and of the divine command to care for the weak and oppressed. In the paradigmatic conflict of the Christian story, the hero who overcomes the powers of evil is one who gives his life on the cross, not somebody with the extraordinary powers of a Superman. In all probability, Hegel's works are, truth to tell, so long and boring that few have ever fully read them. People just took snippets of thought that suited them. Nevertheless, it should be quite clear that Hegelian thought has had an immense practical influence, even though this influence has not always been for the best.

One important fact is that both fascism and communism have rejected religious (theistic) interpretations of Hegel, in favour of speaking of the iron necessities of the historical process itself. They have wanted Hegel without God, a Hegel whose 'god' is only the historical process. And that is surely unfair to Hegel, whose whole work might better be taken as a (very) extended reflection on the nature and purpose of God.

Pantheism and panentheism

Hegel did want history to be much more important to God than it was in the classical view. But he did not want to dissolve God into history, leaving nothing over. The word 'pantheism', so often applied to Hegel, suggests such a dissolution.

pantheism – the identification of God with the forces of nature (*Shorter OED*).

It is very doubtful whether anyone has ever been a pantheist. It is one of those words that you apply to other people when you want to criticise their opinions without actually reading them. Who has ever said that God is just the wind, the rain and the storm? Even the gods of the *Iliad* were not just natural forces. They were associated with and expressed in natural forces, but they also had lives of their own. The sea-mist never flies up to Mount Olympus to have a conversation with Zeus, but Thetis does, so she is obviously more than just a force of nature.

The people who are most often said to be pantheists or at least 'monists' are the best-known philosophers of the Indian traditions.

monism – a philosophy or system of thought that recognises one ultimate principle or being.

But the use of these terms is almost always misleading. Many Indian philosophers (e.g. **Madhva**) were straightforward theists, accepting a personal Lord who is distinct both from matter and from individual souls. In the eleventh century **Ramanuja** developed the metaphor that the world is the body of God, which came into fashion again in the twentieth century in the West, and which could sound like pantheism. But in fact by 'body' he meant something completely under the control of the self and completely and directly known by the self, so Ramanuja's view turns out to be very similar to the common theistic view that God knows and can control any part of the universe. The personal Lord is certainly more than, and is in complete control of, the 'body'. Ramanuja did think that God necessarily has a body, but again the difference from Aquinas and the European classical tradition is very largely verbal, since the Lord forms his 'body' in free and joyful play. When compatibilism is accepted, the difference between freedom and necessity is a very subtle one.

The eighth-century philosopher and saint Sankara might be called a monist (or non-dualist), but he has already cropped up as a philosopher who agrees with the common classical view that God (*nirguna*

The eighth-century Hindu philosopher Sankara trying, with some success, to be one with the universe.

Brahman) is completely incomprehensible. God, for Sankara, also manifests as *saguna Brahman*, a Lord who is omnipotent, omniscient and wise, so again is a personal Lord. In Sankara's case, it is true that he argues that all things are really identical with *Brahman*, but he does so, he says, only because the revealed scriptures, the Upanishads, say so (he clearly states that in his commentary on the *Vedanta Sutras,* in Max Muller's (ed.), *Sacred Books of the East,* vol. 34, p. 350). And what he means by 'being identical with' is that the universe has no independent source of existence other than God. Any classical theist would agree with that. Sankara is at pains to say that almost all human beings are ignorant and bound by sensuality, whereas *Brahman* itself is all-knowing, perfect intelligence. There is much more to be said about Indian thought about God, but it should be obvious that to call it 'pantheistic' is incorrect, if that suggests that there is nothing to God beyond the physical universe.

Even to call Sankara 'monist' is misleading if it leads you to think that in his system there is no personal creator of the universe. When you see what somebody like Thomas Aquinas says about the personal creator, you might well think that he is the one to deny a personal God – but you would, of course, be wrong. Believing in a personal God is just a bit more complicated than you might think.

The Indian traditions about God in general are perhaps more like Hegel than like Aquinas, because they tend to see the universe as in some sense a necessary self-realisation of *Brahman*, a word which it would not be absurd to translate as *Geist*, or Spirit. But since I am in the process of denying that Hegel was a pantheist, that does not make them pantheists either. Evidently genuine pantheists are very hard to find (though in the final chapter of this book I will uncover some Germans who tried their hardest to be pantheists).

The philosopher in the West who is most often accused of being a pantheist is **Baruch Spinoza** (1632–77), who did speak of 'God or Nature' as the highest reality. Spinoza influenced Hegel considerably, and his radically new view that God's infinity includes the whole finite world, instead of excluding it, was adopted by Hegel. When you come to think of it, it is odd to say that God's absolutely unlimited reality excludes, and is therefore limited by, the whole physical universe. If God is really infinite, God will probably have to include the universe in one way or another.

Spinoza certainly believed that. But he clearly added that mind and matter were just two of the infinite attributes of the one primal Substance which he called God. So God is obviously infinitely more than nature, and cannot just be identified with it. The arch-pantheist, therefore, is definitely not a pantheist. And neither are most people accused of being pantheists.

There is a better word for people who think that nature is part of God, even though God infinitely transcends nature. This word was invented by Karl Christian Friedrich Krause (1781–1832), even though it is not included in the Shorter *Oxford English Dictionary*. It is the word **panentheism**, and it means that the whole universe in which humans live is a tiny part of the infinite reality of God.

What is so objectionable about that? Well, it does mean that God will have lots of ugly bits. God will be constantly developing and changing, as the universe develops and changes. So God will be a partly imperfect and limited sort of God. And perhaps it means that, if everything is part of God, we ought to worship everything – including murderers, thieves, frogs and tadpoles, as well as stars and beautiful sunsets. Just to drive the point home, I certainly do not feel that I am God, and I hope you do not either. So I might want to make quite a distinction between you and me and God, and hope that God is much wiser and better than either of us.

Time and creativity

That may seem pretty conclusive. But if we examine it more sympathetically, things may look a little different. First of all, what about change, development and imperfection in God? The sorts of changes that human beings experience will be very different from the sorts of changes that God experiences. Human beings are never quite sure what is going to happen next. Changes happen to us, good and bad, and we are always at the mercy of an unknown future. Change is something we fear, because it is so often for the worse, and it is not under our control.

On the other hand, change can be very good. Anybody who has sat doing nothing on a wet Sunday afternoon knows that change can be an extremely good thing. We like having new experiences. We look forward to holidays, or to new places to see. If there was no change, we could never do anything new, get to know new people, or do creative things. Change would be very good indeed if there was always something new and exciting to look forward to, and if we did not suspect that something bad might be lurking just around the corner.

Change therefore, is not all bad. It might be quite good, if we could ensure that unexpected bad things did not happen. It would mean we could always do new, creative and interesting things, and would not get bored by always doing the same thing. So might change not be good for God, in a similar way? God could control the future completely, so nothing unexpected could ever happen. Nothing really bad would ever happen to God, because God would simply stop it happening. And God could be continually creative, doing new things just for the fun of it.

We get the idea of the classical God by asking what is the best sort of life we can possibly think of. Well, perhaps the best sort of life is one of continual creativity, energy and activity, which is beyond the reach of decay and destruction. By comparison, the life of the classical God, who cannot ever do anything new, being completely changeless, might look rather boringly monotonous. Of course God would never realise how boring it was, because God wouldn't have time to be bored, so it wouldn't be as bad as doing exactly the same thing for ever and ever. Nevertheless, it might be even better to have the chance of creating completely new things.

God is, after all, the creator, so we might expect God to be continually creating all sorts of new things, and to enjoy the activity of creating. God could be like an imaginative artist, rather than like the changelessly self-contemplating (and possibly self-absorbed) intellect of Aristotle. Of course, this picture of a changing, continually creative God is a product of nineteenth-century European Romanticism. 'Art for art's sake' became the motto of a thousand starving painters, who just liked being creative, and didn't seem to make much money. So maybe God, they thought, was like a supreme artist. Since God didn't need any money, such a God had the best sort of life. The Platonic ideal of mathematical contemplation was replaced by the Romantic ideal of 'the poet of the world', imagining it into life for the sheer joy of creating (the expression comes from A.N. Whitehead's *Process and Reality*, p. 346 – 'God is the poet of the world, with tender patience leading it by his vision of truth, beauty, and goodness').

So God the supreme artist can't get any worse; that is no doubt a relief. But isn't it a bit odd to think that God might be getting a little better every day? If God is supposed to be perfect, how can God ever get any better? Well, of course God doesn't improve as an artist. God's technique doesn't get better the more things God creates. God is always a perfect artist, accomplishing exactly what is desired every time. New things are always coming into existence, so you might say God is always knowing more beautiful things, and will know many more in the future.

Should we call that becoming more perfect? At every moment God knows everything there is to be known. There couldn't be any being who knew more than God knows. Nothing can exist, or even be possible, that God doesn't know about. It's just that, since there are more actual things every minute, God knows more things every minute. If God didn't there would be something wrong. The sensible thing is surely to say that God knows everything there is to be known, and that is the most perfect knowledge there could be. But God also knows more things every minute, simply because there really are more actual things every minute, and God has put them there. God's knowledge is always increasing, but that is not an increase in God's perfection, which lies in the fact that God always knows every actual thing there is.

So God changes and develops in knowledge, without getting any more perfect. Indeed, if God didn't change and develop God wouldn't be perfect, because God couldn't be creative and do new things, and wouldn't realise that more new things exist every minute, that they don't all exist at once. The classical God has trouble with this one, because on that view time has to be all spread out at once. Since time is not really all spread out at once, but things really do happen one after the other, the classical God cannot really see things as they are – or so it seems to people who take time more seriously than Plato did.

The redemption of suffering

Surely, however, a perfect God cannot share in the imperfection of the world, in its suffering, conflict, frustration and frequent defeats? That does seem blindingly obvious to classical theists. But then they have the huge problem of explaining how God can truly know suffering and evil if it makes no difference to the divine being, if God has no real experience of it. Given that there is suffering in the world, would it not be a God who would empathise with it, feel it, and know what it was like, who would be more perfect than a God who has an intellectual knowledge that it exists, but is not moved by it?

God ultimately causes all the pain in the world, so it might seem only fair that God should feel it, too. It hardly seems right for God to say, 'You have great suffering, but it will be overcome by joy in the end', unless God can also say, 'I have that suffering too, and we will overcome it together'. Hegel's idea of dialectic suggests that a perfection and joy that is won through struggle and pain might be fuller and deeper than a bliss that never gets less, however much suffering there is in the universe.

What lies behind all these strands of thought is that a God who is really related to the world, and especially to sentient beings in the world, might express a sort of perfection which is the perfection of love, sharing experience with other consciousnesses and working with them to achieve fuller life. At the very least, such a loving God would not be less perfect, though in a different sense of perfection, than a supremely blissful God.

Such a God would not prevent all harm, but would also not be untouched by harm. That harm, for Hegel, would proceed by necessity from the being of God. God would share in the experience of it. But God would overcome it, bringing good out of evil and promising final fulfilment at the end of the necessary dialectic of history. Hegel's word for the overcoming of evil is *aufhebung*, which means to negate and yet fulfil at the same time. The usual English translation is the little-used term 'sublate', but another possibility would be 'redeem', if you think of that as a sort of transformation, which retains all the elements of experience while cancelling out their negative aspects and fulfilling the possibilities for good they contain.

Consider the death of a young child which leaves the parents distraught. According to the panentheistic view, God would share in, would actually experience, that sorrow, and over time would seek to heal it and cover it with forgetfulness of the intensity of the pain. The sorrow would never be forgotten, but it would fade in intensity, and could help to make possible something like a feeling for the pains of others, a true empathy with the alienation of human life. God could bring out of that sorrow a deep solicitude on the part of the parents for the sufferings of others which could bring strength to many lives. Then, if you allow the possibility of a life beyond death, God could give both child and parents a knowledge of how that death had been woven into the necessary structure of history, how it had been used to bring about new forms of goodness, and how it could now be included in a wider experience of being reunited in love for each of them. The child's life, however short, is a life that would not have existed, except as part of the tragic process of history, with all its pain and struggle. Having been brought into existence, child and parents alike can now share in the vision of completed goodness and muted pain that is God's consciousness of the sublated or redeemed world, and continue to work out their own tragically interrupted relationship in a world beyond tears.

We should not think of God as planning suffering because of the good it will bring. The suffering is not planned or intended by God. It arises from the dialectical expression of the divine nature in time. It is part of God, and God consciously experiences it. But the perfection of this God is that the dialectic ends in fulfilment, and even the terrible parts of experience are woven into a total experience in which pain is not forgotten. It is dulled and changed into sympathy and fortitude, used to complete the expression of a divine nature which passes through and includes sorrow within its final experience of an overwhelming joy.

This is a joy that includes and transforms sorrow, works through abandonment to reconciliation, and blends oppositions into a finally experienced harmony of being. Some might prefer untouched, immovable bliss. But others might find in this movement through sorrow to sympathy, through estrangement to union, a sort of perfection which is supremely worth having. Anyway, for Hegel the divine nature is necessary both in its existence and in its self-expression. There is little point in asking why things are so when we understand nothing of that nature in itself. But we may believe that it is God who is self-emptying and who suffers in creation. And that *kenosis*, that emptying, is a necessary part of a binding into the divine experience in which all oppositions are reconciled and the 'third moment' of the divine experience (which is for Hegel timelessly complete) is declared supremely desirable and good.

History and the purposive cosmos

From a Hegelian point of view, God is not omnipotent in the sense that God can choose to create absolutely any state we can imagine – a good world without any evil in it, or a world in which everybody is always ecstatically happy. God is omnipotent as the one and only source of all being. God is the only self-existent, from which all beings flow, by necessities we cannot begin to imagine. God is the power that can overcome evil with good in the historical process. And God is the power that will guarantee the victory of goodness in the final consummation of history. Nothing can frustrate divine power, and God's will is free because it expresses exactly what God is and must be.

This God is obviously not good in the sense that absolutely everything God does is good. This would in any case ignore the conflict and suffering in the world completely. From God flows, by an inner and uncompelled necessity, the dialectic of darkness and light, negation and affirmation, conflict and reconciliation. God is good in that what God *intends* is the final reconciliation, the creative realisation of many unique forms of goodness, and the redemption of evil by its cancellation and enfolding into a wider completion. God is good in that God includes in the completed divine being the greatest array of the most intense values that can be, and have been, envisaged in the world-process, and so God will bring all the good things of our lives to fulfilment. God is good in being supremely desirable, a perfect goodness which can only exist because of the long creative process that constitutes and realises it.

Divine goodness is not unchanging bliss untouched by pain. It is a completed process of abandonment and rediscovery, estrangement and union, a journey undertaken in love, continued in anguish and completed in exultation.

Human existence is seen, in this context, as part of the divine process of self-realisation, which is also a process of estrangement and reconciliation. The process is one wherein all things can be taken up into a final good which can only be precisely what it is because of the whole process that preceded it, and of which we are therefore essential parts. We are parts of God, not because we are already perfect but have not realised it, but because we are important parts of the process by which God expresses, objectifies and sublates the divine nature itself, which is infinite Spirit.

Human life has a purpose, as all life in this universe does. That purpose is to fulfil a unique role in the self-realisation of Spirit. The fact that the universe expresses Spirit as its deepest reality means that all things in our lives can be used for good. We have an important role in the struggle for the realisation of being, of the unique values that God is to create and appreciate in and through us. God sets the purposes. We can mediate, and know and feel, God's creative power as it realises itself through us. In this world, evil is our estrangement in ultimately self-destructive egoism, which frustrates the divine purpose and loses the sense of the presence of Spirit. Worship is not turning from finite beauty to some abstract form of Beauty. It is revering goodness in all its finite forms, committing oneself to create new imaginative forms of goodness, and hoping for their fulfilment in the fully realised nature of God.

We are indeed parts of the process by which God becomes God, with the precise nature God has. We are parts of the divine, but we exist in estrangement from the source of our true being. The religious path is one of turning from self-centred concerns which block the process of divine self-realisation, and realising our own true natures as channels and instruments of divine realisation. As in the classical view, we are to turn from self to contemplate supreme goodness. But now there is a stronger emphasis on contemplating that goodness in the beauty and intelligibility of the material world itself, and on enacting supreme goodness in the world, on changing the world, and so helping the divine self-realisation, on practical commitment to realising goodness.

In many ways Hegel is the very opposite of a pantheist. He does not reduce God to natural forces. He comes near to reducing natural forces to God. He does not have a view of history as a process without morality, driven by blind necessity. He sees history as directed by what he calls 'the cunning of Reason', so that it has a deeply moral order, and events in it reflect a dialectic of Spirit in which oppositions are to be reconciled into a higher moral unity. It is directed by necessity, but not a necessity that is blind. Though it moves dialectically and largely through conflict, it realises a fully self-conscious Spiritual reality, of which its process is a proper outward and visible sign. History and nature become the sacraments of Spirit, and the prophet discerns the secret movements of Spirit in events of history which are only apparently chaotic.

The Hegelian view of God offers an interpretation of the biblical prophetic tradition which raises it to truly cosmic dimensions. The gods of the *Iliad* had purposes, but they were many and conflicting, and fitted into no overall plan. The gods plotted and feasted and lived for ever, but the question of whether the gods themselves had any point was never raised.

Jahweh, the God of Israel, has one purpose which is to be worked out in human history. God's sovereignty over history is absolute. 'Does the clay say to him who fashions it, "what are you making?"' (Isaiah 45:9). God raises up tyrants to punish sin, and promises to Israel that they will be freed from slavery and exile: 'I have given you as a covenant to the people, a light to the nations' (Isaiah 42:6). Human history is an arena of judgment on sin and salvation from evil, which is to be brought about through Israel. Yet this conception is still limited. It is centred on the destiny of Israel, and it leaves God's choice of Israel and any greater purposes for the world largely unexplored. There is, not surprisingly, no idea of development, evolution or emergence of the new. Those ideas had to wait until the eighteenth and nineteenth centuries for their formulation.

Hegel took time, change and evolution seriously for the first time, and made them the foundation of his conception of God as Absolute Spirit. The evolution of the cosmos itself is now seen to have a purpose, and its purpose is the self-realisation of Spirit in finite forms of goodness and in free creative activity. All sentient beings are participants in this process. They are instruments of the divine creation and contemplation of finite goods. Because of their estrangement by being set over against Spirit, they may 'fall' into egoistic desire, and cut themselves off from the kenotic, self-emptying and reconciling activity of Spirit. Even so, they cannot escape the dialectic of history. They remain parts of the world-process wherein estrangement is overcome by the cosmic patience of reconciling love. So the history of the cosmos is a journey into the fullness of God, from the alienated world which is itself an expression of the divine nature in its negativity, and which, from the first reconciled to itself, has to discover in time and through finite consciousnesses that final positivity, the negation of negation which is the deepest meaning of the cosmic process.

Like the Augustinian/Thomist view, the Hegelian view of God possesses intellectual depth, coherence and elegance. When it retains its connection with a Christian background, it has spiritual depth too. For it enables human beings to locate the meaning of their lives in an intelligible and practical context. A life has meaning if it is able to realise unique and distinctive values, if the realisation of such values can be seen as an intelligible purpose to adopt, and if the events of that life can be seen as patterned to make such a purpose and its realisation possible. The elements of value, purpose and pattern are important to the perception of human life as spiritually meaningful. The Hegelian system makes the cosmos itself expressive of value, purpose and pattern, and so it gives human lives significance as contributory parts to a meaningful cosmic process.

But for some a reservation may remain. If cosmic history is the story of God working out the divine nature in time, where do we come into it? The decay of Platonism happened partly because actual space-and-time individuals were seen to have more importance and reality than changeless Forms or Universals. But if we are just parts of a cosmic process, have we not in fact been reduced to cogs in a machine, means to ends greater than ourselves? When time is fundamentally real, creativity can be a fundamental value. But are human beings really creative, if they are only working out a predetermined historical plan? Where has their responsibility and personal creativity gone? It might be nice to think that I am a part of God – part, as Ramanuja would put it, of the body, the spatio-temporal manifestation, of God. But if I am, perhaps, only a fingernail I might want more individuality than that.

This is hardly a new problem. Augustine was quite familiar with it, and it has been a central debate among believers in God since human thoughts were recorded. Do we have any real say in how the future goes, or are we the playthings of the gods? Do we play out our predestined role in history, or are we so radically free that the future actually depends on what we decide today? If we choose the path of evil and egoism, is that really our responsibility, or is it what is decreed for us by a fate which is working out its own inevitable course?

The majority of philosophers and theologians have been compatibilists, and have thought that, whatever human freedom is, in the end it is God (or Nature) who determines how things go. The secular version of this is that actions are determined by our genes, or our electrons. Both versions find talk of human responsibility, reward and punishment, difficult though not impossible.

Process philosophy

There is one twentieth-century philosopher who has made individual freedom absolutely central to his view of the world. That is **Alfred North Whitehead** (1861–1947). If Marx stood Hegel on his head, Whitehead cut his head off, or at least greatly diminished its ability to control its body. Whitehead retains the basic Hegelian framework. God has a threefold character, which Whitehead calls primordial, consequential and superjective. The primordial nature sets out all possibilities, but is 'deficiently actual'. The consequential nature is the perfected actuality of the divine experience, as all events of history pass into the divine consciousness. The superjective nature is that in which the perfected actuality flows back into the temporal world as an influence on the future.

Hegel's first and third 'moments' of Absolute Spirit are preserved (now called the primordial and the consequential), but the second moment is radically revised. Instead of Spirit necessarily realising itself in history, history is now created by an infinite number of free creative events. In this process, God is confined to influencing or 'luring' their decisions in a specific direction. But God does not determine the future, or even have very great control over it. God is the 'great companion – the fellow-sufferer who understands', rather than the sovereign Lord of history. God used to control everything. Now God just has to try hard to persuade events to follow God's good advice. The Great Dictator has become the Great Persuader, watching as countless numbers of tiny agents decide what the future will be, and God just has to accept it.

These events are tiny, and each one exists only for an instant of time. This part of Whitehead's thought derives from **Gottfried Leibniz** (1646–1716), a Prussian scientist and philosopher who held that the universe, and everything and everyone in it, consists of an infinite number of monads. Every monad is a little substance which reflects the whole universe from its own point of view. The monads do not have any windows, so there has to be a sort of pre-established harmony among them so that all their little experiences correlate in the right way. Monads are arranged in an ascending scale from very simple monads in rocks to very complex monads, with God at the top. Human beings are somewhere in the middle, one dominant monad, which we call ourselves, dominating millions of smaller monads which form our bodies.

Whitehead called these monads 'actual occasions' or 'events'. He put in windows to let them have real causal relations with each other, and decreed that each one could only exist for an instant before perishing. So what we call the world of relatively stable physical objects is actually a dizzy series of perishing monads, nothing ever remaining the same for two successive moments. The appearance of stability comes from the fact that each event passes on most of its properties to its successor. Each event 'prehends', or receives information from, all its preceding events. It integrates this information in a unique way, from its own point of view. Then – and this is Whitehead's new proposal – each event by a tiny creative act reorganises its data into a new form, and projects it into the future. As each event perishes, it makes a creative advance into the future by passing on new information to its immediate successors. The whole series is a receptive and creative process in which millions of events are involved, at many different levels of complexity and organisation. That is why it is often called 'process philosophy'.

What is original about Whitehead's scheme is that all the causal work is done by millions of tiny events, co-ordinated and held together by the primordial nature of God. And the basic feature of the whole process is creativity, the fact that really new and original features come into existence at each moment. The degree of novelty depends on the structure and complexity of the events. So events in outer space do not do dramatically creative things – fortunately for the laws of nature, which remain pretty regular. But very complex events in the human brain, for example, may do radically new and creative things, so that they are unpredictable, even by God.

In the Whiteheadian world, it can no longer be Spirit that realises its own nature in the processes of history. Spirit, or God, sets the possibilities, and then has to wait to see which ones the millions of creative events will actualise. It receives the results of their free choices, integrating them into a generally harmonious experience. Then it uses this to influence their choices in future. The process goes on for ever, without beginning or end. So the universe becomes radically open and unpredictable. Even God does not know just what is going to happen next. Nevertheless, since God sets the possibilities and is a major influence on how things go, it could be that on the whole things are getting better. There is no final goal, however; just the process, infinitely realising new forms of beauty and goodness – but also, it seems, new forms of conflict and suffering produced by unwise or egoistic choices.

Whitehead's view lacks the explanatory completeness of Hegel's. There is no explanation for why the beginningless and infinite series of events exists. There is no hope for a final consummation of all things, since conflict seems inevitable where infinite agents are always making their own creative decisions, and people do not exist long enough to have a life after death anyway. They do not even exist long enough to have a life at all. What they have is a succession of momentary lives, which they might mistakenly call the life of one continuing person. Even God seems condemned to being an everlasting sufferer, a sort of cosmic rubbish dump for whatever experiences are thrown up by countless perishing events. The process God is not an entirely happy God – while being very sympathetic to our plight, there is nothing much God can do about it.

Why, then, has a process view of God become so popular among many Christians? First, it may be because few people read and understand Hegel. Of course, no one understands Whitehead either, but at least he writes in English.

Furthermore, the idea of a God who suffers, who really empathises with pain, is very attractive to many people. If God has created a universe with so much pain in it, many people feel that it is hardly a perfection to ignore it altogether.

Again, the existence of suffering itself is easier to explain on the assumption that God did not create it at all. It is just an essential part of the process, flowing from the conflicting free choices of millions of actual events. In God's perfected experience, that pain may be mitigated in some way, but God certainly had no part in bringing it into existence in the first place.

Another strength is that individual decisions are given full weight. Persons are responsible for their acts, and no one, not even God, causes them to act as they do. A great deal of evil is caused by human choices, and even God cannot simply overrule those choices to produce a perfect world. Creativity becomes of primary importance, but destruction is always a possibility for radically free agents, so the future is and remains our responsibility.

The idea of a God who persuades by love rather than dominating like a tyrant has proved attractive to many. Here is a God of patience, of encouragement and of companionship, who may help us on our journey, but will never compel us either to be saved or to be damned. The Lutheran idea of *kenosis* finds one philosophical expression in the process view that God does not possess unlimited power or unlimited knowledge. God is one who shares creaturely experience, in all its tragic dimensions, and seeks to persuade it towards goodness, so far as it will respond to the call of love.

Finally, since God is the all-inclusive mind which forgets nothing, all good is conserved in the divine memory for ever. Whitehead calls this 'objective immortality', meaning that you will not live for ever, but God will remember for ever that you once existed. In that sense, nothing you do is in vain. It will play its part in forming the future throughout infinite time, and will not simply pass into non-existence. For many people, that is immortality enough. It is even preferable to having to think of something to do for billions and billions and billions of years.

The collapse of the metaphysical vision

Hegelian idealism (so called because it makes the whole material world an appearance of pure Spirit or Mind) and process philosophy are very different in detail. For the former, Spirit is the one ultimate causal principle, which expresses itself in the events of time in order to achieve the full perfection which is knowledge of its own realised nature. For the latter, there are billions of ultimate tiny causes, all the events that make up the universe, and there will be no finally perfect state, but only the ever-new creative realisation of values throughout endless time. God is the totality of the process, a persuasive all-including unity with an eternal abstract nature, but God is not the one ultimate cause.

Nevertheless, these two schools of thought share the common basic thought that time, change, creativity, and history have an importance that they did not have for Plato. They give human beings a more active and dynamic role in playing out or frustrating the purposes of the divine being. And they see God as more involved in the sufferings and struggles of history than the one immutable and impassible Supreme Being of Plato and Aristotle could ever be.

The gods of the *Iliad* have been sublated, cancelled in their arbitrary indifference, and fulfilled in their intimations of a life beyond injury and pain. The god of classical thought has been lured out of the blissful life of self-contemplation into a real relationship with the joys and sorrows of the world. Towards the end of the second millennium in Europe the many spirit powers and presences of ancient Greece were transmuted into the one all-including Absolute Spirit who enters into the sufferings and struggles of temporal beings as they strive to realise values in a world of conflict and decay. The whole historical process takes on transcendent significance as it is taken up into the completed consciousness or consequential nature of Absolute Spirit, which enfolds the whole of time and history.

For this picture, the truly human life is a life of discerning and honouring goodness in all its forms, of gratitude to the origin of goodness which is itself supremely desirable, of committing the self to create and revere new and uniquely created forms of goodness in the face of suffering and conflict, of mediating the divine power of reconciliation which, though largely in hidden and ambiguous ways, either drives or persuades the historical process, and of looking for the final completion of our life's struggle in God, when history is transmuted into eternity.

By the law of the dialectic of history, however, every position is destined to pass over into its opposite. And almost as soon as this understanding of God was becoming known, it began to collapse. Now, as this is being written about a century later, it is a belief held only by a tiny minority. It is likely that most people are completely unaware that this was the dominant philosophical view in Germany and in Britain at the beginning of the twentieth century. Its collapse was sudden and complete. The very mention of the names of Hegel or Whitehead is likely only to cause a knowing and dismissive smile among those acquainted with philosophical fashion.

Absolute Spirit was not argued out of existence. It just disappeared, undermined by forces far deeper than intellectual argument. Those forces are nowhere better expressed than in Matthew Arnold's poem 'Dover Beach':

> The sea of faith
> Was once, too, at the full, and round earth's shore
> Lay like the folds of a bright girdle furl'd,
> But now I only hear Its melancholy, long, withdrawing roar,
> Retreating to the breath
> Of the night-wind down the vast edges drear
> And naked shingles of the world.
>
> Ah, love, let us be true
> To one another! for the world, which seems
> To lie before us like a land of dreams,
> So various, so beautiful, so new,
> Hath really neither joy, nor love, nor light,
> Nor certitude, nor peace, nor help for pain,
> And we are here as on a darkling plain
> Swept with confused alarms of struggle and flight,
> Where ignorant armies clash by night.

Find out more ...

There are no easily readable books by Hegel. The account here is largely based on *The Phenomenology of Spirit* (trans. A.V. Miller, Oxford, Oxford University Press, 1997 [1807]). This is a helpful edition with an analysis of the text by J.N. Findlay. One of the most relevant passages is entitled 'The revealed religion', and runs from paras. 748 to 787.

Perhaps the most readable general introduction to the thought of Hegel in English is Charles Taylor, *Hegel* (Cambridge, Cambridge University Press, 1975).

A good selection of Marx's writings can be found in T.B. Bottomore and Maximilien Rubel, *Karl Marx and Social Philosophy* (Harmondsworth, Penguin, 1963).

A.N. Whitehead's major work is *Process and Reality*, which exists in a good corrected edition by David Griffin and Donald Sherburne (New York, Free Press, Macmillan, 1978). Part 5, chapter 2 is most relevant.

A good introduction to process thought is John Cobb and David Griffin, *Process Theology: An Introductory Exposition* (Philadelphia, Westminster, 1976).

6

The darkness between stars

In which the reader will discover a radical difference between the facts of science and the beliefs of religion, will discover just how far Kierkegaard leaped, and just what language games Wittgenstein did not play. The reader will find out the usefulness of praying without believing in God, and why clergy at funerals do not spend time calculating the chances of their clients going to heaven, and may find that so-called radical theology and so-called traditional theology are closer together than either is to popular thinking about God.

Pascal: faith and scepticism

'If we take in our hand any volume of divinity or school metaphysics, for instance, let us ask, Does it contain any abstract reasoning concerning quantity or number? No. Does it contain any experimental reasoning concerning matter of fact and existence? No. Commit it then to the flames, for it can contain nothing but sophistry and illusion' **(David Hume** (1711–76), *An Inquiry Concerning Human Understanding,* section 12).

Thus the great Scottish philosopher threw down the gauntlet to all speculative theologies and grand metaphysical schemes. Hegel and Whitehead are consigned to the flames, or at least their books are. All that remains is mathematics and experimental reasoning, the two planks upon which scientific method is firmly based.

Darkness illuminated by a million suns; the Horsehead nebula.

Hume was well aware of the paradox that if anyone agreed with his statement, they would never read the book in which it was written. For they would already have burnt the book, it being neither mathematics nor experimental science. But Hume accepted paradoxes wholesale – he could demonstrate no natural necessities in things, but believed there were some. He could not find that he had any such thing as a continuing self, but he believed he was one. He could by no means make sense of the idea of a continuing substance, but he believed that trees and chairs and houses continued to exist nonetheless. He could not even justify thinking that the future would be reasonably like the past, but he did not hesitate to get out of bed in the morning without wondering if the floor was still there. So much faith from such a sceptic was only resolvable, as he put it, by playing backgammon, and making merry with his friends.

Some people think that the Enlightenment was a time in European history when philosophers rejected religious authority and placed Reason – of course with a capital 'R' – in place of God, as the supreme authority which would lead to universal peace and tolerance. This is not a wholly accurate picture. There were Rationalists around in the seventeenth and eighteenth century – Descartes, Leibniz and Spinoza might well be called Rationalists. But the greatest Rationalist of all time was the eleventh century Anselm, who could even prove by Reason how many people would be saved (the same number as the number of angels who fell), and could explain to God why God had to become man, and why God simply had to exist. Rationalism, the belief that there is a reason for everything and that we can work out what it is, is not at all anti-religious. Indeed, all these people thought they could prove God had to exist. It is very natural for a Rationalist to think that the whole universe is a product of Reason, and what is that but God?

So it is not Rationalism that corrodes belief in God. It is precisely the suspicion of Reason that does so. David Hume was not a Rationalist, though he is one of the greatest figures of the Enlightenment. He is a man who thought that Reason was 'the slave of the passions'. It could not prove anything. So human life had to be guided by natural common sense, and by reasonable and humane passions.

Even Hegel is not the sort of Rationalist some people take him to be. True, he did say, 'The real is the rational and the rational is the real' – one of those statements that haunt politicians for their whole lives. But it is important to realise that for Hegel the Understanding is what grasps things by means of concepts, whereas Reason is a much more imaginative and intuitive faculty, which can hold together the contradictions that Understanding generates as it tries to think of ultimate reality. Here Hegel agrees with Hume, but adds that Reason can transcend the contradictions of conceptual thinking in an intuitive grasp of higher unities which can only be expressed poetically (or in the language of Hegel, which is unintelligible to ordinary mortals).

The battle was not between Reason and religion. It was between a scepticism about Reason which ended by confining rational activity severely to the world of experimental observation, and an insistence that one could still talk meaningfully about matters which Reason is not in a position to establish. It was also, ironically, between two sorts of scepticism – one which is so sceptical of the achievements of Reason that it sticks severely to empirical observation, and another which is so sceptical of the limitations of Reason that it can happily assert that 'the heart has its reasons, of which Reason knows nothing' (**Blaise Pascal** (1623–62), *Pensées.*)

Which sceptic wins? If you are truly sceptical about Reason there is no reason to be confident that it is more reasonable to stick to experimental observations than to metaphysical theories. So theoretically Pascal wins. Reason cannot tell us to stick to experimental observation, and nothing else can either – especially since, even in coming to this decision, we cannot be relying on any experiments. What experiment could tell us that it is more reasonable to stick to the plain facts than to follow the passions of the heart? Why should we appeal to reason at all to decide such questions? We begin to feel the force of Kant's comment that the renunciation of knowledge does indeed leave room for faith. If we have the passion of faith, why should we not follow it?

In practice, however, David Hume and Immanuel Kant won, with their passionate insistence on confining knowledge to experience and experiment. The trouble is that once we go beyond experience there are so many differing views, with so little to choose between them. And maybe we can live without any of them, since science can enable us to improve nature sufficiently to meet all our needs without recourse to faith. To put it bluntly, prayers for the fertility of the crops might help, but fertiliser is more efficient.

A.J. Ayer: the death of metaphysics

Francis Bacon (1561–1626), one of the great pioneers in formulating the new scientific approach to nature, wrote in the *Proficience and*

Advancement of Learning (1605) that science, unlike philosophy, offered cumulative knowledge which was useful for 'the relief of man's estate'. Philosophy only seems to offer endless dispute, with no cakes and ale. Science was bound to win. It brought agreement, ever-increasing knowledge, and eventually steam-engines and television, flush lavatories and sliced bread.

However, if you confine human knowledge to counting and sense-observation, as Hume advised, the possibilities for thinking about God are abruptly abbreviated. God cannot be either counted or experimented on, so you can no longer speak of God. And what is Nature without God? It can no longer be seen as the appearance that conceals a deeper spiritual reality. It must be what it seems to the experimentalist to be, precisely an object to be experimented upon, weighed, measured and, if necessary, dissected. Nature is, in a word, depersonalised, cleared of all hints of underlying personality, whether Greek gods, Hebrew God, Thomist Unmoved Mover or Hegelian Spirit. And what happens then, when this process is complete?

When I was young I had a philosophy teacher who was well known for declaring that metaphysics was dead. Metaphysics, consisting of a speculative theory about the nature of ultimate reality, was not just dead, it had never really existed. Its theories were just not testable by experiment. Therefore they were not really theories at all. They were strictly speaking nonsense, without meaning. This teacher held that, to have meaning, a statement had to be verifiable, or at least falsifiable. That is, there had to be some possible observations which would show it to be true or false. If you could not think of any such observations, any statements you made were meaningless. They said nothing at all, and therefore they did not really exist. That is why metaphysics had never really existed – all that had existed was the delusion that nonsense was in some obscure way very profound.

Heidegger was usually held to be the greatest propounder of nonsense in the history of human thought, worse even than Hegel. Heidegger's statement, when dealing with the question of what the

Nothing does, that 'the Nothing noths (*Das Nichts nichtet*)', was held up as the paradigm of gobbledegook. No observations could possibly show that it was either true or false. You might as well say, 'The universe is a large piece of round square cheese, without any cheese in it'. Perhaps somewhere that could be taken as a profound statement, to be meditated on devoutly. But in our enlightened times we see that these two statements are equivalent, since both are completely devoid of sense.

A student once asked this teacher if you could make any true general statement about meaningful statements. 'Yes,' he replied. 'You can say that all meaningful statements must be verifiable in principle.' 'I see what you mean,' said the student. 'But how can I verify that?' 'I am glad you asked that,' said the philosopher. 'You cannot verify it. But it is not really a meaningful statement; it is just a rule for using language.' 'Whose rule?' 'Well, it's my rule, really. But it is a very useful one. If you use it, you will find you agree with me completely. I think that would be very useful.'

However, not everybody thought it would be quite so useful. In fact that philosopher, whose name was **Alfred Jules Ayer** (1910–89), did not even agree with himself. (His short book *Language, Truth and Logic* is a clear and readable exposition of what he called 'logical postivism', and gives a good exposition of the verification principle and of the view that talk about God is meaningless.) Ayer said, late in his life, that the only thing wrong with his earlier philosophy was that it was completely mistaken. Putting this in a slightly more technical way, the verification principle, to be useful, had to be interpreted in a very wide sense. Meaningful statements had to be such that some observations remained relevant to their truth or falsity, in principle. And this definition is so wide that it includes almost anything, including God, and also Hegel.

Ayer continued to think that statements about God were vacuous. Though he was prepared to allow them as explanatory theories, and so as meaningful, he did not think they succeeded in actually explaining anything. If you explain some event, perhaps a thunderstorm, by saying, 'God did it', nothing has really been explained.

Ayer is right about that. Scientific explanations help us to predict and control and repeat events under controlled conditions. Talking about God does none of these things, since the purposes of God remain almost wholly unknown to us. It might actually make a difference if there is a God who has some purpose, but we cannot use that theory to help us to predict what is going to happen next. As a scientific hypothesis, God is pretty useless.

Scientific hypotheses and existential questions

But maybe God is not meant to be a scientific hypothesis, anyway. We adopt scientific language largely because it is useful 'for the relief of man's estate'. Language about God may be useful in some other way. Naturally we want our estate relieved. We want more health, leisure and freedom. But what do we do when we have them? Are there not questions that remain, even when we have all the material and social things we want, questions about the point of our lives, their significance and value? Do we not need ways of talking that address these questions?

Such questions may have no answers, in the sense of agreed and established solutions, that put an end to any further questioning. Maybe their meaning is in the questioning itself, in reflection on our life and its significance, in the process of putting ourselves in question.

Such questions are real and of vital significance. But they must occur in the context of the world disclosed by the experimental sciences. And that world turns out to be very different from the traditional view of the universe as the deeply purposive and morally ordered transcript in matter of ideas eternally existing in the mind of the Most High. The traditional view was shattered by two hammer-blows. First, Isaac Newton, though a devout believer in God, eliminated purpose from nature and subjected it to impersonal and absolute laws. This brought many writers enthusiastically to canvass the idea of God as the great designer, the cosmic clockmaker, who had wound up the universe and whose role was mainly confined to guaranteeing that it would keep perfect time (since God created time, this was easy). If God wanted to act in particular ways God had to break the very laws that God had made, which seemed very unfair and not very tidy. Inevitably it was not long before the clockmaker was pensioned off, as an unnecessary appendage to scientific laws which were totally self-explanatory.

Second, Charles Darwin, though again not quite an atheist, gave an account of evolution by natural selection which made the whole existence of human beings come to seem an accident on a cosmic scale, the result of millions of random mutations, selected by ruthless competition, at the price of millions of extinctions, and of almost universal suffering and death. The all-wise loving God who created all things good was replaced by a universe whose processes are impersonal, accidental and indifferent to happiness and pain alike. Far from being the crown and glory of creation, human beings become a freak accident with a peripheral and flickering existence on the edge of galactic space.

Matthew Arnold's poem 'Dover Beach' was written eight years after the publication of Darwin's *Origin of Species*. While there is no evidence of direct influence, it is scarcely coincidental that Arnold writes that this life 'has neither joy, nor love, nor light, nor certitude, nor peace, nor help for pain'. Or is this an unduly pessimistic outlook, even if there is no God, and if the universe is as Newton and Darwin say it is? People can get depressed at the thought of a vast impersonal universe, with no apparent purpose revealed by science, and no concern for human lives at all. But then people can get depressed at the thought of a God who is always watching what they are doing, and whose concern stifles all originality and adventure.

Might it not be possible to look the universe in the face, just as experimental science sees it – a vast system of impersonal laws in which human existence has come about by an almost freak series of accidents, and which will inevitably run down and die as it loses energy, exterminating every species of being which has ever managed to exist in it – to look this universe squarely in the face and remain optimistic and joyful?

Isn't there, after all, something slightly odd about someone who says, 'I am terribly depressed. Do you realise that all life will come to an end and pass into nothingness? The earth will be swallowed by the sun in five thousand million years, and all human strivings and ideals will cease.' Five thousand million years? What difference will that really make to you? What existed five thousand million years ago? Certainly nothing resembling a human being. Is that depressing? The fact is, we are here now. We will die. We have to make the best of what we have. Five thousand million years is far beyond our horizon, and we would do better to ask how we can cope with the present and the immediate future. That may be very good, even if it all ends with death – as of course it does.

It is rather odd that someone should be depressed about what happens to an unknown race of beings five thousand million years in the future, when all they really have to worry about is a few years of life on earth. That will, of course, come to an end. But why not seize the moment, and enjoy what offers itself now, instead of saying, 'Ah, but it will all end in tears.' Will it? Will it end in tears, or just in the sense that one has lived well, and has had enough? Yes, the thought of death is slightly depressing. But, as the philosopher Boethius said long ago – and this he thought of as one of the greatest consolations of philosophy – is it really anything different from sleep, a cessation of consciousness, a rest from pain, and a relief from struggle? When we are having a really good time or attending a party perhaps, do we say, 'Ah, but it will all end. Tonight I have to go to sleep. Unconsciousness will wipe out the sun. How tragic that each day ends in sleep'? We might feel, on the contrary, that a little sleep every now and then is a very good thing. And so is death. Life can be good, exciting and vibrant. But as one grows old, if one is lucky enough to grow old, its possibilities narrow, and finally one is relieved to give up its burdens. Each life has its proper task, its due moment, and then its time is past. Is that depressing? Or is it the occasion for a certain satisfaction, that something has been done, and now its time is over?

Even Nietzsche, no lover of religion, said, 'The kingdom of heaven is a condition of the heart' (from *The Anti-Christ*, section 32). It is not some future or post-death state. Is peace and help for pain not to be found here, in the heart's acceptance of the present moment as the true sacrament of eternity? And if so, what does it matter what happens tonight or in five thousand million years? Some people complain that they will not live for ever, but cannot think of things to do on a wet Sunday afternoon. If you are bored and depressed now, an endless life will only make things endlessly worse. If you are happy and creative now, you need no future compensation for present pain, and you are free to let the future be what it may. 'Sufficient unto the day is the evil thereof.' As the great Indian scripture, the *Bhagavad Gita* puts it, 'He attains peace who, giving up desire, moves through the world without aspiration, possessing nothing which he can call his own, and free from pride' (chapter 2).

Perhaps peace and help for pain can be achieved by learning to renounce desire, ambition, possessiveness and pride. Or perhaps, as Nietzsche said, what he called such a 'Buddhistic' solution is in fact a negation of life, and one should strive for freedom, beauty and the will to power. There will be different solutions to life's questions, each of them reflecting the existential choice we make for ourselves and the way we live. But the questions are not scientific questions, and the reflection is not by means of measuring and experiment. We are in a different area from observation and experiment, more personal, more involved, more passionate and subjective. Yet this is the most important area of all for each human life. This is the area of heart and will. This is the area – not an area either of scientific observation or of intellectual hypothesis – where words about 'God' move, whether they are passionately accepted or rejected.

Kierkegaard: truth as subjectivity

Thus it was that **Søren Kierkegaard** (1813–55) rejected the Hegelian speculative metaphysics that he called 'the System'. 'The present writer,' he says, 'has not understood the System, does not know whether it actually exists, whether it is completed; already he has enough for his weak head in the thought of what a prodigious head everybody in our day must have, since everybody has such a prodigious thought' (from the Preface to *Fear and Trembling*).

The trouble with systems is that they are so very grand. How can such stupendous schemes come out of such petty little animals, scuffing about on the surface of a small planet? What hope have we of getting the System in place? Furthermore, precisely because they are intellectual hypotheses, they must have a provisional character, a certain sort of tentativeness. But religious faith, at least according to Kierkegaard, is a matter of absolute commitment. If you go to church, and the preacher says, 'I am fifty-six per cent sure there is a God, though the arguments are very finely balanced', will he then go on to say, 'Let us pray, with a fifty-six per cent probability of being heard'? Or he might say, 'Let fifty-six per cent of us pray.' Or 'Let us pray with fifty-six per cent of our attention.'

There is something very odd about making faith in God a matter of probability, or of speculation. Such a God would always be a matter of debate, and we would always have to be on the lookout for new arguments which might increase or decrease the probability of God's existence.

The fact is that we do not regard the existence of God as a factual matter, in any ordinary sense. We do not send out search parties – though the first man in space, Yuri Gagarin, did report that there was no God circling the earth. We do not carry out experiments to find out if God is making a difference (well, some people do, but again there is something odd and even distasteful about that).

Francis Galton once tried to correlate the number of prayers said for the British royal family with their general health and longevity. He decided that there was a negative correlation. That is, the more they were prayed for, the more quickly they seemed to die off. Of course, maybe the prayers were not intense enough. Or they might have died even younger had they not been prayed for. Or maybe they felt better, even as they were dying. The evidence is very hard to assess.

For Kierkegaard, any such procedures would be ludicrous. Faith in God is not based on the amount of evidence we have collected that he is answering our prayers. It is not based on evidence at all. It is 'an objective uncertainty held fast in an appropriation process of the most passionate inwardness'.

You can ask somebody if they think there is a God, and they may give a calm, dispassionate, measured answer. But if you ask, 'Do you really believe in God?', you are asking a different sort of question. It is not like, 'Do you believe in fairies?' It is not like saying, 'I agree with everybody that there are trees, and houses, and chairs and people. But I also have an extra belief, that there is a God in addition to all these things.' Believing in God is not believing that there is one extra thing in, or just outside, the universe.

What is it then? Kierkegaard, in a startling phrase, said that 'subjectivity is truth'. He distinguishes objective truth, which is the correspondence of beliefs to facts, and which can be stated without passion, from subjective truth. The latter is the truth of what it is to exist as an individual, finite, passionate, growing or decaying person. Any psychotherapist will tell you that to know the truth about yourself is extremely difficult. It is not just a matter of peering inside one's head and reporting what is there. It is uncovering motives, desires, ideals and attitudes that are often deeply hidden. And the process of uncovering them actually changes the person I am, so that the observing, and the way I observe, shapes what I observe and what I am.

A person with self-knowledge is not the same as that person would be without self-knowledge. So coming to know what I am changes what I am: this sort of knowledge, knowledge of subjectivity, is creative, not just descriptive. And it is passionate, since what I discover, as I enter into myself, are reactions and responses which express and conceal and disturb my innermost self, my inwardness. I cannot report neutrally that, if I am a man, I desire to possess my mother and kill my father, as

Freud would hold that I do. I will be shocked, horrified, startled. I will need to come to terms with that. And that coming to terms will define my way of being for the future.

So Kierkegaard outlines the human condition as one of *angst*, of dread or anxiety before the knowledge of my own desires, my own hatreds, my own trembling on the edge of existence, confronted by inevitable death. To come to realise that is to come to know my own personal individuality, my subjectivity.

Sartre: freedom from a repressive God

But where does God come into this? Well of course God may not come into it. Some of those philosophers who are indebted to Kierkegaard – philosophers such as Martin Heidegger and Jean-Paul Sartre – were glad to be rid of God. For **Jean-Paul Sartre** (1905–80), God was the hidden watcher, always observing what you were doing, so that you could never escape the censorious eye of the almighty. Even in the lavatory there might be a little embroidered sign saying, 'Thou, Lord, seest me' – which would be more than a little off-putting. God would also be the Great Dictator, the one who laid down in advance what you had to be, so your whole life would be nothing but a journey down tram-lines from which you can never escape.

Sartre felt a great sense of relief in getting rid of God. Then, and only then, he thought, we can be truly free, able to be whatever we choose, free of convention, of religion, of faith, and above all of God, who is the ultimate bourgeois moralist. 'Existence precedes essence,' he said – by which he meant that there is no ideal laid down in the divine mind for us to follow. We can be what we choose. Life is absurd, it has no meaning, objectively speaking. It is for us to give it meaning ourselves, in whatever way we choose.

Self-knowledge, for Sartre, is the knowledge that one is not in fact bound by social conventions or religious or metaphysical beliefs. Such knowledge changes life, as we take on full responsibility for what we are.

At the end of life we can say, with that great sage Frank Sinatra, 'I did it my way.' (It is a curious fact that this is the most frequently requested song at crematoria in Britain at the end of the twentieth century. It certainly differs from the traditional religious view that one ought to celebrate the end of a life by singing, 'I did it His way'.)

There is a great deal of insight in Sartre; he was not a major novelist and playwright for nothing. Talk of God can seriously damage your health. It can be repressive, and it can be used to gain social power over others, or to disguise your own neuroses. If somebody says, 'This is God's will', they might well mean, 'I want you to do this, and I will apply this psychological technique to get you to do it.' Of course, this would only succeed with those who already acknowledge God's power. The psychological technique would not work if people did not feel that there is some sort of objective obligation bearing down on them, constraining their life choices.

For Sartre, this widespread belief is 'bad faith', it is an evasion of responsibility. And the belief is always harmful, it represses desires, restricts choices, reduces persons to automata. It gives a picture of life which sees the individual as dominated by a supernatural Big Brother, who makes you feel guilty so that he can then offer you forgiveness – but always on his terms, which are those of total surrender. To become truly human you have to eliminate this picture.

Is that, however, the picture of God that believers have? It would be a poor evangelist who said, 'There is this prying, tyrannical being who requires us to give up all our freedom and submit to his every whim, who fills us with guilt and punishes us unremittingly. I would like to share this vision with you, so that you too can become as miserable and repressed as I am.'

What is striking about most evangelists – at least on American television – is not that they are so miserable, but that they are so unbearably happy. They seem to smile all the time, and their God apparently gives them cadillacs and perfect sets of teeth to smile with. What they seem to say is, 'There is this loving, caring being who requires us to give up our selfish ways and accept his love in return. If we repeat his name, and wave our arms in the air, he will give us Cadillacs and perfect sets of teeth.'

Somewhere between the pessimism of Sartre and the optimism of American television evangelists there must be a happy medium. Perhaps the human situation is not always one in which we are either repressed by forces of social and moral obligation or wrapped in a cosy blanket by a loving and overprotective parent. In coming to terms with our own existence, we might find (but of course we might not) some sense of a reality greater than our conscious egos in which we can participate, but of which we are normally unaware.

What Sartre thought he had found was only an abyss of nullity, leaving us entirely, heroically, on our own. That we might call the wholly atheistic perception. There is no need to speak of God. There is even an obligation not to speak of God, for such speech will imperil our freedom.

Heidegger and Kierkegaard: the absolute paradox

Martin Heidegger (1889–1976) was less dogmatic about what was not there. He thought he found not just nullity, but what he called *das Nichts* – the Nothing, which sounds rather silly in English, but for some reason so much more profound in German. The Nothing is a sort of infinite horizon which relativises all our finite anxieties and concerns, and bundles them up into one gigantic *Angst*, anxiety in the face of Nothing. That is why the English and the Germans sometimes find it so difficult to communicate. An Englishman will say, 'I am afraid of nothing', and a German will reply, 'Ah yes, I understand, it must be terrible'.

Such anxiety is overcome by having the courage to commit oneself to a possibility which, though bounded by death, is uniquely and authentically ours. We find our individual vocation not in relation to a tyrannical or a paternalistic god, but in relation to that unbounded horizon, that which is not a thing but which sets bounds to all things, and which summons each individual being to its own unique temporal realisation. For Heidegger, the journey into the self takes us to a place where the self stands before a sort of infinity, but one of which nothing can be said. That is a perception bordering on the mystical, but perilously (even dangerously) ambiguous (it is hard to overlook the fact that Heidegger was the rector of Freiburg University under the Nazis).

What Kierkegaard thought he found was not nullity, and not infinity. He found what he called 'the Absurd', the absolute paradox. 'The absurd is that the eternal truth has come into existence in time' (*Concluding Unscientific Postscript*, part 2, section 2, chapter 2). For him, religion does not move in the arena of historical or metaphysical probabilities. It moves in the arena of inwardness, of self-knowledge. In that arena, he thought, the individual finds it impossible to escape from the egoism, despair and guilt that dominates human existence. Searching for release, it may come across that which is an affront to reason, that the eternal has entered time in order to release those who cannot release themselves. Then, in the risk of faith, prompted by the passion for the infinite, an individual may embrace the paradox, and thereby find that truth which is subjectivity – becoming an individual placed in an absolute relationship to the absolute.

In Kierkegaard's view, faith is not the acceptance of propositions on authority – theoretical acceptance that there is a God because someone, perhaps someone you have never heard of, has proved it, or even because someone will prove it one day. Faith is total commitment to a discernment that the eternal has entered into time, a commitment which arises out of the need of passion. This is the well-known 'leap of faith', which takes place when reason has run out of steam, or has even halted in self-contradictions (which Hegel renamed 'dialectic'). There, where reason runs up against its limits, we can take the risk that embraces the eternal – but which is only enabled to do so because the eternal has first embraced it.

For Kierkegaard reason runs into contradictions when pressed too far. These will not, in his opinion, be resolved by simply saying that they are sublated in a higher synthesis, as Hegel did. Reason offers no path to God. Each individual is passionately concerned about his own subjective existence, his struggle with passion and desire, his need for peace and fulfilment, his battle for self-acceptance and affirmation. Many of the key decisions of life are taken as a risk which goes well beyond any evidence, but which commits one's life in a specific direction thereafter. Faith is a commitment made in objective uncertainty, with the risk of irrevocable commitment, in response to an encounter with a reality which reason cannot comprehend.

Kierkegaard, who was a Christian, thought of Jesus as the one carrying the message of the absolute paradox, that the eternal has entered into time, being born, living and dying as a man. This paradox he called the 'absurd'. But he does not mean that it is just ridiculous nonsense. The paradox is absurd only from the point of view of Reason, which seeks to get everything into a coherent system. Its affront to reason is – paradoxically – a tribute to rationality, for, as Aristotle said, to be truly rational is to see where the limits of reason lie. When you see the impossibility of objectively answering ultimate questions about the nature of human life, and yet feel a passionate need to commit yourself to some viewpoint in practice, then you may feel the necessity to make a 'leap of faith', a leap beyond reason to an absolute commitment to what is absolute.

Kierkegaard was highly critical of all organised religion and churches, and did not really think we need to know much, if anything, about the historical Jesus. He insisted that each individual faces the encounter with the eternal in time within his or her own experience. It would be easy to adapt Kierkegaard's thoughts to any faith, since the eternal can exist in time as the Qur'an, the Prophet, an avatar, a guru, or as an enlightened one who embodies the eternal in time through the experience of final liberation. All he requires is that at some point the individual in passionate need encounters that which is incomprehensible by reason (the paradox), but which enables life's questions to be, not answered, but dissolved by a response of total commitment.

Does 'the eternal in time' repress or release? As with all knowledge of subjectivity, it depends on how we approach it. If we approach it with the belief that all knowledge is limited to experimental observation, we are liable to dismiss it as a subjective aberration. If we approach it with fear and anger unresolved, then we may find in it the monstrous projection of our own prejudices. If we approach it with a humility and resignation born of recognition of the ultimate emptiness of all our projects, then we may find it brings depths of new discernment, opportunities for new commitment and empowerment for realising our unique potentialities.

In the light of all this, we might say that God is not a supernatural being who keeps interfering in the universe, to adjust the laws of nature or perform a few (but not enough) miracles. We should not think of the word 'God' as referring to any sort of being. We might rather think of it as making possible and expressing a certain mode of apprehending our own subjective existence – not any mode, but a particular set of modes. In these modes we discern, or seem to discern, what is more than any finite describable entity, which speaks of value and possibility, but speaks in silence and mystery. And that discernment calls from us a new level of commitment to realise the goodness we have sensed as possibility.

Tillich: religious symbols

The difference between describing a being and expressing a mode of being is fundamental. What can be described can be debated, analysed, more closely defined, and fitted neatly into the System. But there may be things that can only be expressed. Dance expresses; poetry expresses; songs express; and perhaps words like 'God', when they are actually used as opposed to being discussed, express. They say what they say, and there is no way of saying it better.

In this view, to make such an assertion as 'God is love' is perhaps to have discerned in our lived experience of loving and being loved by others something worth ultimate commitment. That commitment does not depend on any prudential consideration – that it will pay, even in the very long run, or that it will bring happiness in future. It is more like an insight that this is the deepest truth of our being, that it is something which calls us to realise it in our own lives. Love is seen as an objective, changeless, eternal truth, by which our lives are judged and by relation to which our lives can be transformed. It is not an empirical fact, not even a supernatural fact with particular causal consequences. It has its own form of reality, and that reality may be confirmed for us in a particular social practice, the practice of prayer, within which alone we find out what it means to say that 'God is Love'.

As the twentieth-century theologian **Paul Tillich** (1886–1965) put it, such love becomes our 'ultimate concern', a concern which excludes all others, which is unconditional, total and infinite. To be religious, to believe in God, is to have such a concern, and God is the power of being that answers the problems raised by our many failed and changing forms of love by enabling us to participate in a love stronger than death – but not by working miracles which change the causal laws of nature. So Tillich rejects 'theism', the view that God is a personal being who is omnipotent and omniscient, and who has particular causal effects in the universe.

Tillich prefers to say that God is the power and ground of being: 'Within itself, the finite world points beyond itself.' God is the transcendent depth of things, not an additional thing. So all statements about God are symbolic. They cancel their literal meaning while pointing to the power and meaning that is discerned and mediated through the symbol.

We might think of the image of Christ on the cross as such a symbol. It is most unlikely that he looked like the bearded figure depicted on crucifixes – we have no idea what he looked like. It is very odd that a picture of a tortured man could be an object of reverence at all. Taken literally, the crucifix could well seem to be the product of a sadistic imagination, and we might well want to ban it on television as unsuitable for children.

Yet what St Francis saw in the crucifix was the suffering of God for humanity, the power of self-sacrificing love. The crucifix, in order to speak religiously, must cancel itself as a literal representation. It must lead to a discernment of the unconditional power and challenge of unconditional love, and it must mediate that power to the one who seeks to participate in its meaning. When the crucifix spoke to Francis, there was no hidden person behind a screen saying words in Latin or Italian. There was the power of sacrificial love, claiming his total allegiance, whatever might happen.

In a similar way, few Christians reading of the temptation of Jesus in the wilderness by the Devil believe that there was a physical Devil – some do, of course, but even for those who have such unusual factual beliefs, the facts are not what is important. What is important for believers is that Jesus was tempted by the corrupting possibility of an evil will, a desire for popular success or for material power. 'The Devil' has become a symbol for the powers of evil, which continually beset us.

'God' is a symbol for the powers of good, for the possibilities of goodness in our lives, which can challenge and inspire and empower us. Some still take talk of God literally, and think of God as a person who watches over us and hears us pray. But the reality beneath such symbols and metaphors is the reality of eternal goodness, which puts our lives, so often devoted to temporal desires, in question.

Religion does not provide answers to life's questions; it puts our lives in question. It places before us possibilities of action in relation to that which is of infinite value. That is why the questioning, the facing up to such questions, is more important than any specific answer we might, probabilistically and speculatively, come up with. When we discern that which puts our lives in question, we are held fast by religion. We may then say that God chooses us, we do not choose God. The power of eternal goodness holds us fast, and in that moment – then, and not years later, or even for endless time – we know eternal life.

Wittgenstein: pictures of human life

Religious language, then, does not speak about facts in a dispassionate, objective way. It has a very different role in human life. This point has been made most strongly in twentieth-century philosophy by **Ludwig Wittgenstein** (1889–1951), who once said that Kierkegaard was his favourite author. Wittgenstein wrote very little directly about religion, but he is reported to have said, 'I am not a religious man but I cannot help seeing every problem from a religious point of view.' While it is very unclear what this typically gnomic remark means, it could mean that, although he did not go to church, he was captivated by a deep concern with ultimate questions of life's significance. His early work the *Tractatus Logico-Philosophicus* never mentioned religion, but it might be said to be all about religion. The book is divided into seven sections. The seventh simply contains one sentence: 'Whereof we cannot speak, thereof we must be silent.' The *Tractatus* is about what can be said, with what can be said clearly, and with what cannot be said. The mystical lies outside the realm of speech, but it is of fundamental importance. 'It is not how things are in the world that is mystical, but that it exists.'

The *Tractatus* induced a group of philosophers in Vienna to invent logical positivism, which held that all knowledge is experimentally verifiable ('positive'), and all meaningful sentences must refer to experimental facts ('logical'). Unfortunately, this had the consequence that almost all the sentences in their books were meaningless, so that nobody could understand them. Nevertheless, A.J. Ayer popularised these views in Britain, and few people noticed that they were literally senseless. Logical positivism was in fact a travesty of Wittgenstein's early views. In Ayer's version, the ideal of 'the mystical' disappeared. *Das Mystische* had an importance for Wittgenstein that the logical positivists missed. Indeed, while they acknowledged his influence on their work, he merely said that they had completely misunderstood him. It might have been true for him at that time that everything that could be said belonged to logic and science. But the whole realm of the

A 1930 picture of Wittgenstein, who remarked that persons should be judged by their thoughts and not by their appearance.

ethical – and of the religious – did not belong there, in the realm of the sayable.

In his later work, Wittgenstein became rather more relaxed about the ways in which things might be said, and about the sorts of things that could be meaningfully talked about. He had begun by supposing, with Bertrand Russell, that the meaning of a word was the thing that it stands for. Russell had trouble with words such as 'if'. But Russell was never at a loss for an absurd theory, and he proposed that the word 'if' stands for the feeling of hesitation in the mind when one is surveying alternatives. But what if someone does not have such a feeling, when he utters the word 'if'? Is the word then meaningless? And if it still has meaning, is the mental feeling really important?

The theory that words stand for things, and sometimes for very odd and immaterial things, came to seem less and less realistic. Wittgenstein had no general theory about how words have meaning. But he did note that we often learn to use words in the context of little pieces of behaviour, and the words are themselves part of the behaviour – part of the ritual, we might say. So you might learn the words of a song which is used in a certain dance. Those words might become very important to you, but you might never ask what they stand for or refer to. They are parts of a ritual you have learned, which might be associated with all sorts of profound feelings and memories.

Or they might provide a picture, which has the role of 'regulating for all of one's life'. Those who do not have that picture do not contradict it; they simply have no use for it. Thus someone who says of the painting of God in the Sistine Chapel, 'God is not like that', is not contradicting the picture. Non-believers do not use religious pictures or images, such as that of the Last Judgement. But there are people who see their whole lives in the light of such pictures, viewing each event as seen by God, seeing pain as punishment, perhaps, or as a trial. This picture cannot be contradicted, if we do not use the picture in that way. Wittgenstein says, 'I think differently, in a different way. I say different things to myself. I have different pictures' (*Lectures and Conversations*,

p. 55). It is not that he has no pictures, no regulatory picture of how his life is being lived out in the world. He just does not have this picture of the Last Judgement.

Among the many other pictures one might have there is the picture of oneself as a lonely hero, committing oneself to inventing meaning in the face of the meaninglessness of the universe. Or there is the picture of oneself as a child of God, held fast by love and drawn to see life as a growth towards maturity. There are a great many pictures, and 'God' functions in many of them as the focal concept of a certain sort of self-understanding which gives rise to a particular way of being in the world.

Is it reasonable to have such a picture? 'Not only is it not reasonable, but it doesn't pretend to be,' said Wittgenstein. Reason does not decide that Michelangelo's painting is great art, and reason does not justify having the picture of the Last Judgement in one's mind. Those who appeal to evidence for religion precisely misunderstand how religious talk is used, the living contexts in which it functions. They try to turn religious belief in God into scientific belief in God, and God is just not a scientifically usable term.

Religious language and forms of life

The difference between words used in ritual and words used in science is brought out quite well by a story about the Cambridge philosopher Richard Braithwaite, who wrote influentially on the philosophy of science. He decided quite late in life that he wished to be baptised as an Anglican. Accordingly he attended a short course of instruction. All went along very well, until it was pointed out to him that in the baptism service he would have to say the Apostles' Creed. This creed contains all sorts of apparently factual statements about the virgin birth, the resurrection and so on.

Braithwaite, who was one of the few philosophers who admitted to being a logical positivist, felt very uneasy about this. He certainly did not believe such things had literally happened. But his feelings were reassured when he was told that he could sing the creed if he wanted. So he sang it. Singing was preferable to him, because you don't have to mean what you sing. Or at least you don't have to mean it literally. It is more like a story, a narrative. And indeed it could be said that the main point of reciting the creed is not to give a list of strange beliefs, but to praise God, to affirm a certain sort of personal commitment. It gives a sort of shorthand account of the sort of God you are praising – a God who gives life freely and unconditionally, and whose love overcomes the power of death. This is much clearer when you sing something, so Braithwaite's attitude is perfectly understandable.

It should come as no surprise to recall that the word 'God' is used primarily in rituals. It is used in the context of celebrating births, marriages and deaths (if celebrate is the right word for that). Priests say, 'God bless you,' and presumably they are not summoning up a supernatural Spirit, however grand, to give you good luck or protect you from evil. It is a priest's way of saying 'Ciao', or even 'Cheers'. But it has a special holy meaning attached, which is signified by the word 'God'.

What is that holy meaning? Well, it is a matter of connecting up what you are now doing with whatever is of ultimate significance and value for you. We might say, 'May all your deepest values be realised, your deepest desires be fulfilled, and may what you fear be far from you.' It is a wish for your well-being, a kind thought, and a thought with power. For might not the good wishes of others, seriously meant, encourage and sustain us in hardship and inspire and enthuse us in our undertakings?

So a religious person might ask a priest to bless a new house or a new baby. This could be taken at a superficial level, as if it were a magical charm to keep away bad luck. But there is another level, at which one is hoping for the realisation of new experiences and opportunities which will be enriching and beneficial. Such occasions make us think of our own goals and attitudes, and encourage us to reassess them so that we can commit ourselves to realising the sorts of values that are appealed to on such occasions.

What is being done, by using the word 'God', is evoking deep feelings, discernments and commitments, which lead people to assess their own hopes and fears, and find new strength to live their lives with courage and hope.

You can see this illustrated very well at funerals. The minister very rarely says things like, 'As we come to bury Joe, I have to say that he has very little chance. He was a real rotter when he was alive, he showed no signs of repentance, and it looks very much as though he is probably going straight to Hell. In fact I would assess the probability as much higher than 56 per cent, which, as you know, is my favourite probability. Let us pray.'

If you saw religion as a matter of factual beliefs, beliefs about what would probably happen to people after they were dead, you would expect to hear more of that sort of thing. But ministers who visit the bereaved very rarely have theological discussions about what happens after death. Such things are best left in a sort of reverent silence. If someone does ask, 'Will I see him again?' you do not say, 'Let me tell you about a fascinating series of lectures I heard just the other week.' If you are sensible, you say, 'Of course' – but you do not go into any details about what he might be wearing, or whether he will still be bald, or even how old he will be.

So what do ministers do at funerals? They try to comfort, console, encourage, and evoke feelings of gratitude for a life now over, acceptance of parting, and commitment to some of the values that life expressed. They do not recite facts about the afterlife. They deal with profound human feelings, and try to lead people to their own inner ways of coping with death, loss and grief.

Passionate inwardness coupled with objective uncertainty: that is exactly how many people feel at funerals, as they come to terms with the death of a friend, with their own deaths, with the fact of death as the one certainty of life. The objective is not of primary concern in such a context – the bare recital of the facts of biological processes and genetic deficiencies. It is the subjective that is the primary concern, the question of the way one encounters and reacts to such events. At that point every individual is alone, challenged to new discernments and commitments in the one life that only they experience and to some extent shape.

Religion and 'seeing-as'

Of course not everyone will take a 'religious' approach to such matters. Some will be consoled and encouraged by the religious ritual of a funeral service, while others may be alienated or simply indifferent. And that, says Wittgenstein, is just what we should expect. The difference between believers in God and non-believers is not one that either of them understands clearly, as if they both clearly see the options, but one person chooses to believe in one extra entity or in more life beyond death and the other chooses not to. Rather, believer and non-believer do not understand one another.

An example that Wittgenstein uses is those intriguing puzzles consisting of lots of dots that, seen in the right way from the right angle, make a picture. Some people will see the picture quite quickly. Others might never see it. Both see the same dots. But one sees what the other never sees. The facts are the same. But for one the dots have a meaning that they do not have for the other.

So religious disputes are not really about the facts, or at least not about facts that can be established in principle by patient observation and experiment. They are about discernments of meaning in life that we may or may not see, depending on personal factors we may be unaware of. But we should not conclude that such discernments are 'merely' subjective, that they tell us nothing about what is the case. Eternal, objective goodness is real, just as the numbers that mathematicians talk about are real. But it is not real in the way that physical objects are real. It is real in its own way, and the way to that reality is by a path of interior discernment and personal orientation, an orientation away from the temporal and towards the eternal.

These words are reminiscent of Plato, and in a sense Western philosophy has not even now entirely lost touch with the thought of the ancient Athenian. Few people would associate Wittgenstein with Platonism. For did Wittgenstein not reject the search for essences, and the thought that each word must stand for some definite conceptual reality? True, Wittgenstein directed our attention to the many different ways in which words are used, to the fact that words may have many family resemblances without standing for any common essence, and to the fact that learning and speaking a language is a public, social activity which is inextricably linked with particular forms of life and behaviour. Wittgenstein, unlike Plato, was definitely not an essentialist.

Wittgenstein also directed our attention away from the inner contents of an alleged private mind towards the social context of utterances. For him, words do not refer to essentially private experiences, and they do not take their meaning from reference to such experiences. Words, or the sentences in which they are used, have a publicly accessible context, and they take their meaning from the practices and activities of groups of human animals. Wittgenstein, unlike Plato, was definitely not a dualist.

So in what sense does a Platonic element remain? To get at that sense we need to look at the way in which Wittgenstein connects language with human activities, and the way in which some of those activities elicit talk about God. Wittgenstein emphasised the diversity of language uses, and the diverse and changing forms of life of which language is part. The word 'God' has its primary use in contexts of worship and prayer, particular forms of life which involve such acts as bowing, kneeling, putting hands together, closing the eyes, singing and sitting quietly in groups. Although they are not totally individualistic, such practices are not universal either. They are not shared by all, and may be incomprehensible to some. If you ask, 'What are these people doing?' we may say that they are praising or thanking God, confessing sin, or remembering their friends before God, or dedicating themselves to God.

Wittgenstein suggested that the best way to find out what the word 'God' means is to try to understand such activities. It is a word around which such activities are built, which gives them point. But what is it doing? Perhaps one thing it is doing is marking moments of insight, when something came to seem of great importance to human living, at least for that group. They may say, 'We met this person, and were overwhelmed by a sense of peace and love.' They may say, 'My life was changed with a glance.'

An analogy would be falling in love. I have been reluctant to indulge in analyses of what love is ever since early in my married life, and my wife asked me if I loved her. Being a professional philosopher at the time, and very aware of my philosophical responsibilities, I said, 'Well, what do you mean by love?' ... Some time later, after recovering consciousness, I resolved never to ask that question again. (The answer should obviously be an unequivocal 'Yes!')

Still, when you fall in love you see something in another person that no one else sees. But what is it? Does it make sense to say, 'I love you because you have big ears ... you have white teeth ... you have an IQ of 92'? And if so, does that mean you will fall in love with anyone who has even bigger ears or whiter teeth? When you fall in love, you see something new and different in a person, but you cannot grasp that by giving a descriptive list of the person's characteristics, and saying exactly which ones are the ones that have caused you to fall in love. Whatever it is, falling in love is just feeling an irresistible attraction to another person, and it is connected with seeing them in a new way, and committing yourself to them with total intensity.

Is believing in God rather like falling in love with the universe? Perhaps that is a rather large object to fall in love with. But you might say that something particular leads you to see the whole of your experience in a new way. It functions as a sort of key experience which gives a clue to interpreting all of your experience. And when you see it that way, you respond to it in a new way, as something awe-inspiring and wonderful, perhaps. You see a depth to experience that can only be evoked by using words like 'eternal' or 'ultimate'. 'You are the most beautiful girl in the world,' we might say, but would be taken aback if asked to justify the statement objectively. So we might see love as changeless and stronger than death, though we would not like to put that to an experimental test.

Learning to believe in God is learning to see and react to all our experiences in a way that is only made possible by rehearsing the practices within which such specialised uses of words are an important part. Wittgenstein calls this the 'dawning of an aspect', seeing, interpreting and reacting to things in a way that can only be put into words in a special way. This is the remaining Platonic element, the 'depth', the 'transcendence', the reality often unseen by others, the eternal which cannot be seen by hearts set on and bound by the temporal, the self-existing supreme value before which human existence is put in question or affirmed.

Rather than asking what the word 'God' stands for, you should ask, 'How is it used?' and then you have to observe, not theorise, and see that it is used to evoke and sustain a way of seeing the world which cannot be expressed in any other way. To understand that, you have to enter into the practice, the form of life, of which it is part, and which it makes possible. You may not be able to do that. You may find it repulsive. Or you may find yourself drawn into a way of seeing and being that you find irresistible.

The religious person – and many an irreligious person too – is one who has been drawn into a way of seeing human life which comes to seem appropriate. Great novelists, poets and playwrights have the capacity to evoke such ways of seeing. They have their devotees, whose lives are at least in part patterned by the words that have seized them with passion. We might not call the devotees of *Star Trek* religious, though their lives might be imbued with the values of heroic humanism and optimism that characterise that TV and film series. But they have entered an important part of the religious world. They have a canonical text, they tend to wear distinctive clothes, and they utter such incantations as, 'Beam me up, Scotty.'

What is as yet lacking is a ritualised practice of mental formation that is supposed to deepen the understanding of human reality. To believe in God, as opposed to dressing like Mr Spock, is to enter into a community of social practice in which minds are systematically shaped to see and react to the events of their lives in a set of ideal ways. In this process of self-formation, the word 'God' is used in many ways, but primarily to evoke various general responses to human experiences, responses of adoration, thanksgiving, penitence, and concern for the needs of others.

Spirituality without belief

These responses have a value which does not depend on prior theoretical beliefs about whether or not there is a God. Perhaps one day it will be necessary to learn the practices without the theoretical beliefs. This will clear away the lumber of much popularising talk about God. It will help to prevent the confusion of religion and science. How might prayer look if we avoided the word 'God', and concentrated on the practices that form the normal contexts of its use?

First we might be encouraged to take attention away from ourselves and our own needs, and attend to the goodness, beauty and wisdom that can be found in the world as we experience it. We might be encouraged to revere goodness in all its forms, and to overcome attachment to objects by contemplating their intrinsic goodness. This would be very like what believers in God call adoration or worship, not telling some supernatural person how marvellous he is, but rejoicing in the contemplation of goodness.

Then we might be encouraged to be mindful of the transience and sheer gratuitousness of life and consciousness, and to take time to appreciate what we experience, as if it was a precious and undeserved gift. We might be encouraged to have faith – not in the sense of believing lots of odd things on authority, but in the sense of committing ourselves to the continual possibility of goodness. This might be like what believers in God call gratitude or thanksgiving.

We might also be encouraged to examine our motives and desires, to turn from egoism towards a true concern to help and value others. We could be encouraged to experience release from the tyranny of the past, and be freed to face the future with a hope which is much more than optimism. Whereas optimism believes that everything will get better one day, hope expects nothing, and does not require a high probability of success. It commits the self to positive action for good. This is like a sort of penitence, or a turning of the mind from self to the possibility of objective goodness.

Finally we might be encouraged to develop compassion and empathy for others, and to reflect on how goodness can be increased in the world, not for ourselves, but for all sentient beings. It is not a matter of saving ourselves the trouble of doing anything practical by praying for a while in a nice warm chapel. It is, or should be, a matter of preparing ourselves to go and do something practical. We might be encouraged to have love, not in the sense of having sentimental feelings about others, but in the sense of being actively concerned for the good of others. That would be like a sort of intercession, of 'praying for others'.

So it might be possible to cultivate a sort of spirituality, a discipline of the mind and heart, without reliance on controversial doctrines and abstract theological problems. And if we do so, we might find, to our surprise, that what we are doing is to penetrate to the heart of prayer, and of what genuine belief in God really means.

Flattery, sentimentality, credulity and optimism are attitudes, and often rather superficial ones, and religion seems to some to be precisely the adoption of such superficial attitudes to some imaginary being, God. But adoration, love, faith and hope are virtues that can permeate the whole of life. They are virtues that relate your innermost self to values you hold as ultimate, and which may captivate you if you attend to them. Religious practice is, or ought to be, a practice of the formation of the self in virtue, in the proper excellence of being a truly human person.

Do you have to believe in God first, before you can undertake these practices? To think that would be to get the whole thing upside down. Believing in God *is* undertaking these practices. If God bothers you, forget God, and think of adopting a way of self-formation which sees human life in the light of values that are of eternal worth. An intellectual atheist, someone who denies that God is a supernatural person, could pray in these ways. Why should they? There is no general reason that can be given, except to say that such a practice, such a way of being in relation to the world, might come to exercise a fascination, so that it seems to show its intrinsic value as the practice itself develops.

If you were asked, 'Why should you like Shakespeare?' Inadequate answers might include the consideration that it is great art; it offers great insight; it exercises its own appeal. So it might be said that the religious attitude discloses depths of meaning and insight that exercise their own appeal. For the believer, to miss that appeal would be to miss something of great importance in life.

If an atheist entered into such a life of prayer, what they would be doing is getting to the heart of what prayer to God has always really been about, though it has been dressed up in symbols and images which some may now find off-putting. If this is so, the believer in God is not discovering a new and hitherto unknown fact or being, but is making a distinctive sort of personal commitment, and thereby discovering a new depth to or aspect of experience of the world, and of the world itself.

This is not as different from the classical view as people sometimes think. Both views regard most of what is said about God as metaphorical or symbolic. For both, God is not an explanatory hypothesis, but the object of prayer and contemplation. For both, talk of God, or prayer to God, is a way of relating to reality in its most significant aspects. What is different is that the classical view regards this world as less real, ultimately, than the self-complete reality of God. For the post-metaphysical view, the world is the only real, and God is not another reality beyond the world. Talking of God makes possible a certain attitude and response to the real world which liberates the self from despair, guilt and desire, and enables it to attain a blissful, creative and contemplative state.

Non-realism and God

The twentieth-century approach is sometimes called 'non-realism', because it does not regard God as 'real' in the sense that material or finite objects are real, and it does not regard God as a personal being who exists independently of the world and relates to it in various ways. Very few thinkers, however, would agree that this God is not real at all. There are some who do regard God as a fiction, the function of which is to evoke a certain sort of commitment. These are the real non-realists, but they are few.

Mostly, twentieth-century writers are concerned to stress that the reality of God is of a distinctive sort, and should not be confused with the reality of causes and agents in or just outside the universe. They are also keen not to confuse it with some metaphysical speculation, as though it was only accessible to high-powered intellectuals and devotees of the System.

Somehow the concept must be rooted in ordinary human life and experience. Some might speak of the reality of mathematics, or of music, or of ethics. Those who speak in such ways emphasise that there really are mathematical truths to be known, discoveries to be made. We do not just make mathematics up. Even Bertrand Russell remarked that he found in mathematics a world of clarity and intelligibility that gave him something as near to a mystical feeling as he could get.

So in music, you may feel that you are entering into a world of rich feeling, complex harmony and beautiful structure that is mediated by sound waves and neurochemical impulses in the brain, but that is more than and different in kind from all such physical data. And in ethics you may feel that there are truths to be known, obligations to be acknowledged, visions of goodness to be discerned.

Those who speak of the reality of God are saying something akin to this, but something wider and more inclusive, and also something involving more of the totality of the self. Kierkegaard spoke of three stages of life or spheres of existence: the aesthetic, the ethical and the religious. The first is dominated by the search for pleasure. It is open to contemplation of many forms of beauty, but is often untouched by moral considerations (artists are notoriously indifferent to many moral conventions). The second is concerned with universal norms and obligations, with the duties and responsibilities of profession and family. The third, Kierkegaard thought, is concerned with seeing the emptiness of the temporal concerns of life, with all their incipient anxiety and despair, when set against the background of eternity. Faith is a risk, a willed decision in objective uncertainty, a total commitment of the self to the whole of experience. It is a matter of the way you relate yourself, at the deepest level, to whatever meets you in experience. It is a way in which you see all things in face of eternity, and you believe in eternal bliss, and love, and hope, despite the agonies life brings.

Such a faith might be seen as a commitment to seeing each moment as one in which you decide for temporality (sensuality or convention) or for eternity (freedom from the past and anxious care, and freedom to give yourself to others without fear or contempt). It is not just a matter of keeping moral rules. It is a matter of how you understand your own being in the world. It sees each moment as an encounter with challenges and possibilities for deepening such understanding, in relation to what come to be seen as eternal values.

It is sometimes said of Wittgenstein that he eliminated private personal experiences from his philosophy, that he was a behaviourist. This is almost certainly not the case. What Wittgenstein held was that the way you identify and speak of your private experiences depends on the concepts, the language, you have, and that is a social affair. 'What gives the impression that we wanted to deny anything?' he asks, in the *Philosophical Investigations*, going on to explain that 'what we deny is that the picture of the inner process gives us the correct idea of the use of the word'. Wittgenstein is not denying that people have deep and sensitive experiences. Only, how can you speak of that deepness? 'If only you do not try to utter what is unutterable then nothing gets lost.' But the unutterable can be *expressed* by words, nonetheless.

So Wittgenstein says, 'If I thought of God as another being like myself, outside myself, only infinitely more powerful, then I would regard it as my duty to defy him' (Rhees, *Recollections of Wittgenstein*, p. 107). Yet 'man is a ceremonious animal', and utters the word 'God' when he feels thankful, fearful, elated or oppressed, in the context of social practices that express such feelings – feelings that are not just subjective inner events, but ways of relating to the world which have been learned and shared in social contexts.

The word 'pain', says Wittgenstein, does not refer to an inner object – yet pains exist. The word 'God' does not refer to a supernatural object – yet God may exist. I say 'may' in this case, simply because there are communities that do not use the word, or that specifically exclude it. They have their own forms of life and practices, their own ways of coping with the common situation of being human, finite, dependent and uncertain. Those ways do not focus on an 'object' of devotion, adoration, longing and sustenance, for they feel that to posit such an object would demean humanity in some way.

Believers, however, do not suffer from illusion in positing God. That is how they relate to their world, and the reality of God is established in their practices. This may make faith seem like an option, and of course it is not. When it exists, it compels, so it is not freely chosen. The only thing is not to confuse believing in God – a passionate, self-transforming, existential commitment – with believing that there are chairs in the next room.

Are believers correct, or are they mistaken? There is no neutral rationality to decide that. Human knowledge has no absolute bedrock of certainty, standing on which one can decide impartially on the truth of such ultimate questions. To believe in God is to worship, and to worship is habitually to attend to a single perfect transcendent ideal which is incorruptible and indestructible. Something of what such a thing would be like is given by the experience of contemplating works of art. As the novelist and philosopher Iris Murdoch puts it, 'Great art teaches us how real things can be looked at and loved without being seized and used.' Contemplation of beauty in art and nature checks selfishness in the interest of seeing justly and truly.

Moral commitment, too, provides an element that is involved in worship. Commitment to compassion and love in the face of numerous temptations to petty selfishness harnesses action to contemplation. Morality teaches us how goodness can be desired and realised without seeking to possess it for oneself alone. It teaches us to subordinate personal desire to social good.

The religious way reaches even more deeply into the self, seeking to root out attachment and possessiveness from its inner recesses, and centre attention on a supreme objective goodness. Centred on the good, the finite self becomes more than the aesthetic or the ethical self. It becomes a self transfigured by goodness, and it might be spoken of as taken up into the eternal, liberated from the concerns of the temporal.

Only a few can follow this way in its full rigour and intensity. Its reward is simply the companionship of the Good, that personified ideal of which the *Gita* (6, 30) speaks: 'He who sees me in everything and everything in me, him shall I never forsake, nor shall he lose me.' To look for the good in everything, to see everything embraced by goodness, is to be united to the indestructible, to be possessed by the Good. Those who are so united we call saints. Most of us follow a lower path, in which penitence and forgiveness play an essential part, and in which our hope is that we shall from time to time be touched by a goodness that we cannot of ourselves attain.

The silence of the heart

It is not accidental that I have ended by speaking of the Good rather than of God. The idea of God, with its long history of debate and dispute, has been too much overlaid with ideas of a supernatural person, arbitrarily saving us from death while around us millions drown. If we could think instead of transcendent goodness, offering nothing but itself and our transient participation in its life, we might come nearer to the heart of the classical idea of God.

The good, while indescribable, is symbolised by imagery, clothed in personifications that are both imaginative and inspired, and mediated by rituals that preserve some awareness of its reality. When such images become the object of metaphysical or historical speculation, they become both endlessly disputable and religiously irrelevant. Attention is transferred from the role they play in forming our inwardness, our inner attitude to the world, and is instead focused on some vain attempt to establish objective facts about the nature of the cosmos or the events of past history. Instead of asking whether worship gives access to profound aspects of reality, we are led to ask whether Jesus went to Jerusalem on a Friday or on a Saturday. Then we split into two different groups, one committed to keeping Fridays special and the other committed to specially remembering Saturdays, neither speaking to the other – and with no possible way of resolving the argument.

So widespread did this misdirecting of images become that for many twentieth-century European writers the images themselves had to be renounced. Especially after the two great wars of the twentieth century and the *Shoah*, commonly called the Holocaust, the thought of God as a providential parent seemed almost comically irrelevant, and the thought of God as a white-bearded Judge casting down millions of souls to endless torment seemed morally bankrupt.

What was left was silence, though not a silence in which nothing begins or ends, and there is no memory of what has ever been. It is a silence like that which follows profound music, where all has been played and any further sound, even applause, would seem demeaning. Such silence reverberates with ended sound. There is a place where words and music end. This is not just darkness; it is darkness between stars, taking its contrast from a million suns. Moses knew that darkness, in the cloud covering the mountain. Elijah knew it, after the earthquake and the fire. Thomas Aquinas knew it, when he left his great *Summa* unfinished. It is the cloud of un-knowing, which can only be pierced by love.

In the journey of European thought about God, we have travelled from an ancient world full of gods to a world where there is empty silence within, from the blaze of the Platonic sun to the darkness between stars. In a sense, having come to know much more, we realise that we know much less than we thought. But if we have made that journey, if we have followed the wrestling of these human souls with an unnamed god, or with an idea of such a god, then we might see what we had not seen, though what is seen cannot be said, and our lack of knowledge may reveal more than the sum of words in the *Shorter Oxford Dictionary*.

> Why no! I never thought other than
> That God is that great absence
> In our lives, the empty silence
> Within, the place where we go
> Seeking, not in hope to
> Arrive or find. He keeps the interstices
> In our knowledge, the darkness between stars.'
>
> From R.S. Thomas, 'Via Negativa'

Find out more . . .

A.J. Ayer, *Language, Truth and Logic* (London, Victor Gollancz, 1971 [1936]) is a clear exposition of logical positivism. Chapter 4 is about God.

Francis Bacon, *Proficience and Advancement of Learning* (London, Henrie Tomes, 1605). There are many subsequent editions.

Søren Kierkegaard, *Concluding Unscientific Postscript* (trans. Howard and Edna Hong, Princeton, Princeton University Press, 1992 [1846], especially part 2, section 2, chapter 2), is most relevant to 'truth as subjectivity'. See also *Fear and Trembling* (trans. Walter Lowrie, Princeton, Princeton University Press,

1955 [1843]). The distinction between Socrates and Jesus is in *Philosophical Fragments* (trans. Howard and Edna Hong, Princeton, Princeton University Press, 1985 [1844]).

On symbols, see Paul Tillich, *Systematic Theology* (Chicago: University of Chicago Press, 1951). The introduction to vol. 2 is most relevant.

Material from Wittgenstein is largely taken from Ludwig Wittgenstein, *Lectures and Conversations on Aesthetics, Psychology and Religious Belief* (ed. Cyril Barrett, Oxford, Basil Blackwell, 1966) and *Tractatus Logico-Philosophicus* (trans. D.F. Pears and B.F. McGuinness, London, Routledge & Kegan Paul, 1969 [1921], 6.362–7). See also *Philosophical Investigations* (trans. G.E.M. Anscombe, Oxford, Basil Blackwell, 1974).

One of the most helpful books on Wittgenstein and religion is Fergus Kerr, *Theology after Wittgenstein* (Oxford, Basil Blackwell, 1986).

Any book by D.Z. Phillips is worth reading for an exposition of a 'non-metaphysical' view of religious belief.

7

The personal ground of being

In which the reader will find that God is not a person without a body, and may wonder if God can ride a bicycle or whether God knows if humans will ever land on Mars. The reader will discover why nineteenth-century Germans became more and more depressed, and that the Trinity, though it is indeed three persons in one substance, is not three people sitting in a bowl of soup. Finally the reader will find that evolution need not be the desperate struggle for existence that some pessimistic souls suggest, but may be seen as a striving for higher life and consciousness. God may not ride a bicycle, but God knows plenty of people who can, and will ensure that in the end they will do so exceedingly well.

God as omnipotent person

This guide to God may not have delivered what was expected. Not only have I not set forth the doctrine of a supernatural person who can do absolutely anything, who knows absolutely everything, and who would never cause harm to anyone, but I have castigated that doctrine as a travesty of what the best-known philosophers of all ages have written about God.

There are certainly plenty of people who do think God is pretty straightforwardly a supernatural person. They no doubt existed in ancient Greece, and thought that Pallas Athene really would fly down to help when they were in trouble. On the other hand, the fact that she never did was not apparently of great concern to them – which may make you suspect that they were not really concerned about the literal reference of their language, whatever they might have said when asked. There are plenty of people who think God is like that today – but again, they do not seem to be seriously concerned when God never appears, or when God says 'No' to most of their prayers.

Nevertheless, is it really plausible to say that God is not to be conceived of as a person in any sense at all? The great classical writers certainly cause us to qualify the idea of 'person' to an enormous extent, but is there no place in their thought for the personhood of God? And can the idea of God as person not be defended in a sophisticated way?

Of course it can. In America there is a justly renowned school of personalist philosophers, such as Edgar Brightman and Peter Bertocci. And one of the most widely quoted definitions of God in recent philosophy is given by the Oxford philosopher Richard Swinburne. God, he writes, is something like 'a person without a body (i.e. a spirit) who is eternal, free, able to do anything, knows everything, is perfectly good, is the proper object of human worship and obedience, the creator and sustainer of the universe' (This is the second sentence of the introduction to *The Coherence of Theism*). His books provide the best exposition and defence available of his own definition, so it would be a total waste of time for me to make up what would only be a less elegant and scholarly version of it here.

It needs to be noted, however, that the idea of 'person' that is being used might be quite different from whatever applies to human persons. For Swinburne, God is eternal, perfectly free and omnipotent, which human persons certainly are not. Swinburne gives these terms a meaning which is more obviously personalistic than the classical tradition, but God still turns out to be very different from human persons.

In Swinburne's interpretation, 'eternal' does not mean, as it does for classical theologians, 'timeless'. It means without beginning or end.

'Free' does not mean that God might do any logically possible thing. On the contrary, it means God will always do something if God knows that doing it would be better than not doing it. God is totally and purely rational, and if we were just as rational, we could predict almost everything that God would or would not do. 'Omnipotent' does not mean that God can bring about any logically possible state. For instance God must do good and avoid evil. So God is not a moral agent, in the sense that God is capable of doing wrong, and is under obligation to do what is right. Put more generally, on this understanding, an omnipotent being is one who can do anything that falls within the realm of the undetermined or non-necessitated actions of that being which is the source of all actual and possible powers. As Swinburne himself puts it, 'A being who is perfectly free and omnipotent in my sense has as much control over things as it is logically possible that a being could have' – and we might not know exactly what the bounds of that 'logical possibility' are.

This is a very qualified notion of omnipotence, but (I think) is a perfectly coherent one. We simply do not know how much control over things a perfectly good and rational being would have, what undetermined things there are to be done, or what would necessarily follow from its nature. It is very easy to invent a phrase such as, 'a universe just like this, but without any suffering in it'. But how can we possibly know whether such a universe is really possible? Well, we might say, with God all things must be possible. But it is not so easy. Even if God is the source of everything other than God, and the source of all powers, so that nothing can be more powerful than God, we have not the slightest idea what powers God actually has. 'All powers, of course,' you say. But has God got the power to ride a bicycle or to run a mile in three minutes? If you are tempted to say 'Yes, of course,' remember that God does not have a bicycle, and has no legs either.

'But God can make legs.' This is not totally absurd. Some Christians believe that God did make some divine legs, namely, the legs of Jesus of Nazareth – though Jesus did not have a bicycle. Some people think that

God in fact has everybody's legs, if they believe that everything is part of God. It might even be held that a good reason for creating a universe with people and bicycles in it is precisely so that God could experience what it is like to run and ride bicycles.

The real problem, however, comes from our thinking that God must be able to do anything we can think of or imagine. Because we, ignorant as we are, can imagine lots of things which are really quite impossible. For example, we can imagine going back in time to kill our grandparents before they had any children – you can even see films in which such things happen. Yet we can see that such a thing is obviously impossible, since without our grandparents we would not exist, so we could not kill them. We think we can imagine finding a square equal in area to a given circle – but mathematicians can prove that is logically impossible. We think we can imagine the force of gravity being just a little stronger than it actually is – but physicists can tell us that, if it were, then electrons would collapse into the nuclei of atoms, there would be no atoms, and so there would be no organised universe at all.

The truth is that we are just not very good at imagining things properly and in enough detail to see whether they are possible. It does not follow that because we think we can imagine something, it must be possible. In chapter 4, we found that some people thought they could imagine a God who exists in every possible world. But other people were equally certain they could imagine a possible world without a God in it. Obviously they cannot both be right. One of them must be imagining the impossible, but there is no agreed way of telling which.

Our imaginations are a poor guide to what is really possible, because we have absolutely no idea of what sorts of things can really exist, or of what might be necessary or optional for God. So I think we just have to say that God is powerful enough to create the universe, and that no other being could be more powerful, and that is as much as we have a right to expect from omnipotence.

Discussions about the omnipotence of God usually run into abstruse discussions of whether God can make a stone that is too heavy for God to lift, or whether God could commit suicide, or make a being more powerful than God is. If God cannot make such a stone, God is not omnipotent. But if God cannot lift it, God is not omnipotent either. All these puzzles end by saying that there are some things even God cannot do, but they do not undermine his omnipotence, since omnipotence has to mean simply that no being could possibly be more powerful than God.

The problem of evil

It should be pointed out that this at once resolves the so-called problem of evil (though of course only in an intellectual sense; the existential problem of facing up to evil remains as hard as ever). The intellectual problem of evil is the problem of how an omnipotent and good God could create a universe with evil in it. All we have to say is that no universe with rational beings roughly like us in it could exist without evil, and that God, who is the most powerful being there could possibly be, has to create some such universe. Moreover, this God is good, because God is of supreme value, intends that the universe should produce good things, helps it to do so, and will ensure that it does so.

As you would expect, Plato saw this long ago, when he held that God's shaping of the universe is limited by necessity. Fully fledged theists place necessity in the divine being, instead of regarding it as something external, limiting God. And they regard God as the creator, not just the shaper, of the universe. This enables them to say that God positively wills the universe to exist, and wills it for the sake of the goods it contains and makes possible. Nevertheless, what God wills must be an expression of the divine being and the possibilities it contains. Though God affirms the divine being, and its actualised nature is perfectly good, God does not choose it; it is necessarily what it is. Many of the unactualised possibilities in it are evil, or undesirable and not rationally choosable for their own sake. God will not therefore actualise them for their own sake; God will not positively intend them to be actualised.

God does intend to actualise a universe (at least one, and maybe many). God does so because it is good to do so, and because it is in the divine nature to do so. But such actualisation may involve the actualisation of some actual evil and much possible evil (evil that can be unpreventably realised by free finite agents). Even the most powerful possible being cannot prevent that, though it can share in and sublate (or redeem) such evils, making them integral parts of a whole that is good in a unique way, and that can be recognised as such by all sentient beings which are capable of such recognition.

Of course we do not know whether all this is true or not. But it makes sense. It resolves the problem of evil. And once you admit that you cannot imagine or comprehend the nature of God, you cannot rule such a proposal out by appealing to some shaky definition of omnipotence such as 'the ability to do absolutely anything I can imagine, or that I can state without apparent contradiction'. It follows that God does not positively intend everything that exists, but only the good things. God does not intend the bad things. God has to accept them, since they (or many of them, anyway, such as the deaths of animals) are necessarily there, or they are produced by good things that have somehow gone wrong (like human beings). If you say that is not omnipotence, it may be the best you can get. Anyway, it is a perfectly good definition of omnipotence, because it says that God contains all the potentialities there are, and that all possible power comes from God. If you want more, you may be letting your imagination get out of control.

Fichte, Schelling, Schopenhauer and Nietzsche: beyond good and evil

It may be felt that making some evil necessary is a dangerous move which threatens the goodness of God. A whole line of German philosophers after Kant, who regarded themselves as either post-Christian or anti-Christian, began to reject the view that God is good. **Johann Gottlieb Fichte** (1762–1814) claimed to be completing the thought of Immanuel Kant. Kant held that all our basic concepts of thought, and even space and time, are contributed to knowledge by the knowing self, and are not features of the objective world. Fichte concluded that the whole universe is the product of a vast cosmic self, the Absolute Ego. This Ego is not personal, but realises itself gradually in history, until it results in a human society in which everyone 'joyously does what is right', and there will be no further need for religion. In this sense, Fichte's God could still be called good, despite having no personal relation with the universe. Kant, however, did not like this, complaining that Fichte's Absolute Ego was bigger than his (Kant's) Absolute Ego, and suspecting that Fichte really thought he (Fichte, not Kant) was the Absolute Ego.

But the idea of the universe realising itself through a process of self-development caught on. **Friedrich Wilhelm Joseph von Schelling** (1775–1854) decided that the Absolute Ego was largely unconscious. Out of a primordial blind necessity, which is a non-rational and unconscious Will, nature and spirit both evolve. Whereas in the thought of Hegel, Reason is ultimately in control, for Schelling the Will, the non-rational and heroic striving that transcends morality and accepts the necessity of evil as part of its development, becomes primary. Now the universe or Nature takes over from God as cause of itself, and a stress on necessity leads to advocacy of a trans-moral power of the will and of heroic striving, the 'struggle for life' which was so much to influence Charles Darwin. This is probably as near to pantheism as philosophers get.

German philosophers now became gloomier and gloomier, and the goodness of the supreme being began to disappear altogether. **Arthur Schopenhauer** (1788–1860), usually regarded as the greatest pessimist of all time, saw the whole universe as the tragic appearance of a blind striving of the will, a striving which leads inevitably to conflict, unhappiness and suffering. So the course of eighteenth-century German philosophy flows from the happy necessity of Leibniz, which accepts the universe as rational, and as the best of all possible worlds, even if it is

Nietzsche trying to be Superman. A portrait of Friedrich Nietzsche by Horst Janssen (1998).

usually unpleasant, to the unhappy necessity of Schopenhauer, which does not accept the universe but cannot get out of it. But the worst was yet to come.

Friedrich Wilhelm Nietzsche (1844–1900) looked forward to the advent of the superman, who would completely reject Christian values such as mercy and submissiveness, and incarnate in himself the pure will to power, in a life serene and pitiless, strong and free. The God who intends good but cannot avoid creating some evil has been transformed (sublated, but in the wrong direction) into the universal Will which is beyond good and evil, and for which ceaseless striving without a moral goal is the only reality.

That is what happens when the vision of transcendent Goodness is lost, and one sees only the struggle and suffering and the will to power of the universe itself as the final reality. The fact is that evil plainly exists in the universe, so if you identify the universe with God you are going to have to include actual evil in God. For all the main revealed traditions, however, God is supremely good, and so must transcend the universe in the primordial divine nature. It might just be worth repeating that most Indian traditions, which have sometimes been called 'monist' or 'pantheist', do accept the goodness of God, so even if the universe manifests God in some way, God remains beyond the universe in goodness.

The problem for the theist who accepts, perhaps on grounds of prophetic revelation, that God is good, is to account for the evil in the universe. This can be done, I have suggested, by supposing that even a good God creating a good universe for a good reason may have to create some evil, though God can never positively intend that evil either directly or as a means to some independently existing end. This in turn requires that God is in an important way transcendent to and distinct from the universe, and that God does not directly intend everything that happens in the universe, though God is the cause of everything in the universe.

Omniscience and creative freedom

Swinburne might not go as far as I have gone in ascribing internal necessities to the divine being. But he does qualify 'omnipotence' so that it has to mean 'compatibility with the necessary nature of God', so I do not think I have strayed too far from his basic insight.

He qualifies 'omniscience' in a similar way. 'God knows everything,' Swinburne says, which does not mean, as in the classical tradition, 'God knows of every possible true or false proposition that it is true or false.' It means, 'God knows everything that it is possible for any temporal being to know' – and God is a temporal being. So, for example, undetermined events in the future are not now knowable by any temporal being. The future might be open, and even God has to wait to find out what happens – unless God decides to determine the future unilaterally.

This may seem very restricting. If God does not know exactly what I am going to do next, this may have huge unforeseen consequences for the future. I may write a letter which causes a physicist to leave his job, which means that the American Space Program grinds to a halt, which means that no one ever lands on Mars. Or I may not. So God does not know whether humans will ever get to Mars. Presumably, for similar reasons God does not know whether or not the world will end with a nuclear explosion, having no idea of what will be going on a few years from now. That sounds like an odd definition of omniscience.

Of course it is not true that God has no idea of what might happen. God knows, and indeed makes possible, all the possible things that might happen in the future. God controls the alternatives between which people choose. Furthermore, God can determine choices if God so wishes, so God can control the future completely. But normally, for the libertarian anyway, God refuses to exercise such control. God permits people to be free, within limits that God lays down. God can step in to eliminate evil or help efforts to achieve goodness, but God lets agents largely decide their own exact future. In other words, if God wants people to get to Mars, God will find some way of getting them there. But God might prefer to wait and see what ideas people come up with.

There can be a real element of creative freedom in the universe, and the existence of such creative freedom might be of great value. But the universe never gets out of control. God knows and will ensure that in the end evil will destroy itself and good will be realised and conserved. God knows that finite agents will never pass beyond God's power to forgive and help them. And God knows that the divine purpose for creation, that new values should be created and enjoyed, will be realised. God is as omniscient as any being can be that wills that a universe of creative freedom should exist. And that is what omniscience is.

God: person or personal?

So it is possible to give eternity, freedom, power and knowledge an interpretation rather more restricted than that of the classical theologians, and, I think, rather more appropriate to a fully personal being. Even so, if this God is called an 'unembodied person', that does not mean, as it might ordinarily mean, a continuing spiritual substance who infers, feels, deduces, and learns to act and react to other persons. It is used in an 'analogical sense', which Swinburne defines as meaning that God is more like such persons than like other things which are not persons. God is more like a thinking thing than like a rock or a vegetable. But God might still be very different indeed from the persons we know about in ordinary experience.

In this sense, we might say that a human being is more like a frog than a star – they share DNA and, possibly, consciousness. I myself would still find it odd to say that I was a frog, even an analogical frog. But perhaps that is because I am more like other things – chimpanzees, for example – than I am like a frog. If I was the last human being in the world, I might say, by analogy, that I was a chimpanzee. I would be more like a chimpanzee than anything else around.

All the same, this might be very misleading for other non-analogical chimpanzees, were they to understand me. They might very well say, 'You don't look much like a chimpanzee to me.' 'That may be so,' I could reply, 'I admit I have loosened some of the syntactical connections of the word – so, for instance, being a chimpanzee no longer entails being hairy all over. But I assure you that I am a genuine, if analogical, chimpanzee.'

This conveys very well why many theologians have been wary of saying that God is, even analogically, a person. God might be more like persons than like anything else in the created universe. But it might still be quite misleading to say that God 'is' something which only really exists in the created universe. Why not stay with the thought that God is, in some respects, more like persons than like sub-personal entities? That is, there is something in God that resembles awareness and purpose more than it resembles unconsciousness and accident. We can truly say that God is aware of the universe, and intends it to exist.

If we did not use some terms drawn from the finite world that we know about, then we could say nothing about God at all. Even those who speak of 'the Good', and of 'the darkness between stars' are using terms drawn from the finite world. There is no escape from analogy – from speaking of God in terms of finite things. It is a question of how far you are prepared to go. Speaking personally, saying that 'God *is* a person' is a step too far for me. It does seem to make God too much like a finite entity. Swinburne, however, does suggest an alternative phrase (which in fact comes from Paul Tillich), that God is 'the personal ground of being'. I confess to feeling much happier about that, since it makes the point that the ground of being, the ultimate source of all that is, possesses something more like consciousness than like a permanent state of unconsciousness, and something more like intention than like complete accident or oversight.

It might still be true that, in some ways, God is more like non-personal things than like personal things. If you ask, 'Is God more like darkness than like persons?' the correct answer might be, 'God is a bit like both, in different respects.' Maybe we need more than one set of analogies to speak least inadequately about God.

How is God like darkness? Remember this has to be a special sort of darkness. Not sheer nullity, but, in R.S. Thomas' words, 'the place where we go seeking'. It is like an infinite depth, into which we are willingly, though often fearfully, drawn, which elicits awe and abandonment of intellectual analysis. It is the thought of the incomprehensible abyss of infinity that relativises any talk of persons – who are, after all, finite things. If you look at the Michelangelo painting on the Sistine Chapel roof, or at Blake's much reproduced picture of the *Ancient of Days*, then you may want to say, 'That is not God. God is the unpicturable, the unbounded, and by contrast with all the limited spaces we imagine, using colour to delimit their boundaries, God is the darkness, the beyond, the inexpressible.'

But there is not much you can do with the inexpressible. Religions have usually needed pictures to evoke devotion, submission, love and desire. Even Islam has pictures, not visual but verbal, of God on the throne of glory, with all-seeing eyes and all-encompassing hands.

Infinity appears, for the sake of devotees, in a multitude of names and forms. And these are usually personal names and forms.

It is hard, after all, to love the Good, when it cannot even be envisaged. To be existent goodness, more than a mere possibility, the Good must be subsistent. It must consist of an actuality of supreme value, of something supremely worthwhile. And nothing can actually be supremely worthwhile unless it involves consciousness and positive valuation of that worth. Thus the Good has to be thought of as in some sense self-conscious feeling, aware of itself and satisfied in the contemplation of its perfection. If we are to know the Good, we are called to share in the self-contemplation of perfection, in that non-dual consciousness of an object non-different from itself, and of its unchangeable perfection.

Because it involves consciousness and bliss, and just for that reason, the Good may be thought of as in some remote sense personal, if not 'a person'. Yet a good reason for not calling it a person is that it has, as such, no relationship to others, no duality, no mutuality of give and take.

Persons as relational

The darkness and the Good are different ways of envisaging God, as the final object of human contemplation and adoration. But those ways are still too abstract to catch the imagination and evoke the passion of more than a few intellectuals and mystics. What hope is there for human beings who contain passion that needs to be redirected, enmeshed in material well-being, that needs to be untangled? For them (and that is, for nearly all of us at some level), God needs to take a more personal form, a form which can be embraced and loved, pictured in words or images. It is now that God takes form as, in a sense, a person, an Other which encounters us as stern or kind, judging or forgiving, severe or compassionate.

To see God as a person is to see God as an Other who encounters us in a personal way, who has a relationship with us which is one of father (or mother) to child, or lover to beloved. This view is associated particularly with the Boston 'personalists', such as Peter Bertocci, and with a group of British theologians at the beginning of the twentieth century, including H.H. Farmer, John Oman and John and Donald Baillie. They were particularly concerned to stress the way in which God is not an impersonal force, but one who relates to us in encounter as a person, as a 'Thou' to an 'I', and evokes respect and love from us. However, they also stressed that to speak of God as person should not be taken as the only word about God. It draws attention to a condescension of the infinite God who is perfect goodness, a *kenosis* or self-emptying, a limitation of infinity to encounter the finite on its own ground. This would be what Kierkegaard called the absolute paradox, the absurd – that the infinite should be finite, and the perfect should be involved in our joys and sorrows. But the paradox is dissolved when we remember that the infinite is only so for us and for our sake.

It is not that the infinite is really a person, who thinks and feels, wonders whether to create a universe, makes moral decisions, feels lonely and would like to have some friends, and wonders whether we will love God or not. It is rather that the infinite relates to us in a personal way, contracting infinity to finite form in order to bring us and all creatures capable of it to moral and intellectual maturity and lead our finite lives into fulfilling relationship with their infinite source and goal.

Thinking of God in this way as a relational being, a personal being in relation to a universe of finite spirits, can be strengthened by taking insights from both Hegel and Whitehead, and supposing that the Supreme Spirit realises the most creative potentialities of its own being precisely by generating and relating to beings who are genuinely other than it is, who stand over against Spirit, and who have their own proper autonomy. God can create genuinely free agents, and so the process of history will not be the artistic product of a lonely genius. It will be a product of the interaction of many finite agents and the one unlimited creator of all things, who restrains the divine power so that such relational freedom can exist.

In such a universe, evil will be the product of wills that choose selfish goods, not part of the divine self-expression (this is the Whiteheadian bit), but evil will be eliminated when the historical process has run its course (this is the Hegelian bit). Its elimination will end the historical process, or at least all that process in which egoistic choice remains a possibility, so we should be careful about asking for its total elimination too soon.

History becomes an arena of real moral choice for each rational individual. Within it, God may indeed seek to persuade or encourage rather than single-handedly determine. But in the end God will ensure the triumph of goodness and the elimination of evil.

This happens already for both Hegel and Whitehead in the consequential nature of God, in the divine experience and memory. It is not clear that either philosopher believed in any personal existence after death. But there is no reason, so far as we can see, why a creator God should not be able to ensure that all agents may be given an opportunity to discern the meaning of their own lives within the completed divine pattern. That would be heaven, life fulfilled in God, and maybe that is the destined completion of the cosmic process. The completion could not exist without the process, but the process is one that has its completion outside itself.

In this grand cosmic scheme, God is the one who creates an intelligible universe containing finite agents, and who restrains divine power to give them freedom. God is the one who shapes them by love to realise new and distinctive values in time. God is the one who ensures that evil is self-destroying in the end, and who redeems suffering by sharing it and sublating it in a wider experience in which it is not forgotten. Its pain is dulled, and it is given a positive role in building up the final vision of the universe in which all contradictions are unified and reconciled. God is the one who draws all the goods of creation into a completed divine experience, in which creatures might be able to share in a way suited to their capacities.

Some religious traditions, or parts of them, take the personal form as the final form of Godhead. For them, God really is in some sense a person, an individual who encounters humans in an accessible, even recognisable way. But most traditions regard the personal form as just one part of a much richer divine reality. Thus Sankara, in the Indian tradition, takes the Supreme omnipotent Lord to be a manifestation of *nirguna Brahman*, the Absolute without qualities. And in Christianity, the person of Jesus is usually taken to be the earthly form of just one of the three aspects of the divine being that together make up the Trinity.

The idea of the Trinity

The Christian idea of the Trinity is beyond the scope of this book, which is just about the idea of God in general (I have written about it in *Christianity: A Short Introduction*). But we cannot ignore the fact that most of the writers I have mentioned have been Christians, and the largest theistic faith does think that God is, in the words of the Athanasian creed, 'three persons in one substance'. (As you might expect by now, this creed is not by the fourth-century St Athanasius. It is a Latin creed of somewhat later date, and is usually not now said in churches. One reason for this is suggested by my experience the last, and only, time I tried to get an Anglican congregation to recite it aloud in church. When they got to the phrase, 'the Father incomprehensible, the Son incomprehensible, and the Holy Ghost incomprehensible ... and yet there are not three incomprehensibles', they all burst out laughing. The whole thing was just too incomprehensible, and so the Trinity still seems to many people.)

It might seem bad enough to say that God is a person. But to say that God is three persons sounds much worse. Muslims often just think that this is polytheism, believing in three gods. Christians might be confused, but they are not polytheists. It is just unfortunate that the traditional phrase, 'three persons in one substance', tends to evoke a picture of three people sitting in a bowl of soup. Things get worse if you go on to think of these three persons having discussions with one another about how things are going. 'I think one of us should become incarnate,' says one. 'I'll go,' says another. 'What am I going to do while you are away?' says the third.

This impression could be dispelled by the additional doctrine that each of the persons is omnipotent and omniscient. This does get rid of arguments and interminable discussions over strategy, since each person already knows exactly what the others have decided or will decide, and each knows exactly what the others know. The price, however, is that life in the heavenly soup threatens to become rather boring. 'I thought I would create a universe,' says one. 'I knew you were going to say that,' says the second. 'I think I will create one as well,' says the third. 'Well it had better be the same as mine,' says number one. 'You already know that it is,' says number two. 'I knew you were going to say that,' says number three. None of these persons can ever surprise the others, or tell them anything they did not already know. 'Let me tell you what I did today,' says one. And the others reply in unison, 'Don't bother. We already know.' How frustrating! None of them can do anything that the others do not know all about, and they can never be in conflict with one another (or they would not be omnipotent). What, in short, is the point of having three persons, if they all agree completely about everything, and all know and do exactly the same as the others?

The only thing to do is give up this picture of three distinct individuals altogether. There is only one individual (that is what 'substance' means), God. But there are three 'persons' (the early Greek word was *hypostases*, which is probably better, precisely because nobody knows exactly what it means) within the being of God. One way of putting this today would be to say that there are three different aspects of the one divine being, that none of them can be collapsed without remainder into the others, and that all of them together are necessary to an adequate idea of God.

One aspect is that God is the utterly transcendent creative ground of all being, beyond human comprehension, the unlimited ocean of infinity, the abyss beyond duality from which all things issue, the ultimate cause of all.

A second aspect is that God is the supreme intelligence in which all possibilities exist as thoughts exist in the mind. Here all the archetypes of being are rooted, and ordered with perfect wisdom. Infinity takes form as mind and self-luminous awareness, and exists as the uncreated light of wisdom which gives form and intelligibility to all things.

A third aspect is that God is the dynamic energy which gives actuality to the forms conceived by the divine wisdom, which values and affirms them, and which delights in their particularity.

God as transcendent abyss, God as particular yet unbounded intelligence, and God as the immanent creative energy of being – these, it might be said, are three distinct ways of being God, all of them necessary to the divine nature, and all bound together in a uniquely perfect reality which is at once deeply personal and yet infinitely more than either one rational individual or three such individuals of the same sort. God as threefold, as Trinity, remains for ever a mystery, but it is not an absurdity. The reality of God remains beyond human comprehension, but the idea of a threefold God can be seen to be deeply rational, and to be unequivocally a form of monotheism, of belief in one God.

Of course, to most Christians all this may seem rather abstract. The Christian God is not, after all, known as threefold because of some abstruse philosophical argument. God is said to be threefold because Jesus is in some way seen as the incarnation or embodied image of God, because he referred to God as 'Father', and because the Holy Spirit is experienced as a present life-changing reality. But Christian reflection can deepen these primary beliefs by showing how they express a particular understanding of a God who relates to humans as personal, but who is infinitely more than 'a person'.

So in the Christian faith, the first aspect of the divine being is the transcendent cause of ground of being, which Christians call, in a metaphor, the 'Father' of beings. The second aspect is the wisdom or intelligence which finite things to a greater or lesser degree image or express. Christians see Jesus of Nazareth as 'the Christ', the one who is the human embodiment of divine wisdom, who expresses the divine love and is a freely obedient vehicle of that love in his own person, and who is for humans the 'image of the invisible God' (Colossians 1:15). The third aspect is the immanent creative power within the cosmos, which is felt in human lives, inspiring them to courage, heroism, insight and the creation of works of beauty and power. This is 'God within', the Spirit who works inwardly to shape all things towards their own unique fulfilment as manifold images and vehicles of the divine.

A Trinitarian idea of God means that God cannot be called a 'person', in any straightforward way. God can for some religious traditions, including the Christian, be truly expressed for us in the form of a person, but the full reality of God is far beyond anything we can think of as a person. Jews and Muslims, and other believers in God who reject the idea of the Trinity, could, in my experience, be quite sympathetic to this interpretation of the Trinity, if the qualifications required by the acceptance of analogy were kept firmly in mind – though they might still reject the idea that Jesus is the unique personal form of God. There is never going to be complete agreement about God and the way in which God relates to us. But it should be obvious by now that theists do not all agree with one another anyway, whether they belong to the same 'religion' or not. We have learned something, however, when we see that the disagreements are not simple contra-dictions, as if everybody knew exactly what they were talking about, and could draw up a clear list of what they agreed with and what they disagreed with. One of the lessons of a study of ideas about God is how very feeble the human mind is, and how very little it can understand of a reality that is supposed to be supreme in value and power.

The revelatory roots of religion

I have been talking about reflective, philosophical thought about God. But, as I have tried repeatedly to stress, most religions, if not all, depend not only on reflection, but also, and indeed primarily, on revelation.

That is, they look to some person or persons for authoritative guidance to spiritual insight. It is very natural to think that if there is a God, God will give some revelation of the divine nature and purpose, and any such revelation will necessarily have to be given at a particular time and place, and through some specific individuals. There are many claims to revelation, and it is only too obvious that they do not all agree in detail. Yet there is one important consideration which should take the sting out of many of the differences that exist.

Revelations are not, despite what some people might hope for, clear and precise sets of doctrines and commands. Taken at their deepest level, revelations are tremendously mysterious, and they are revelations of a being who remains ultimately mysterious. All genuine revelations are revelations of mystery. Like the ancient oracles of Greece, they do not give definite and unambiguous answers to our direct questions. They seem to give cryptic and very ambiguous utterances, which we have to tease out through meditation, prayer and often through a liberal use of imagination. They speak in terms of metaphor and symbol, and different religious traditions diverge partly because of their different ways of interpreting these symbols.

The root of Semitic ideas about God lies in the experience of the ancient Hebrew prophets, who discerned God primarily as ethical demand and historical purpose, giving the descendants of Abraham a special part to play in working out this purpose. This still leaves open many variant understandings of just what the demand and purpose is. How is the Torah to be kept, to the letter or in the spirit? What does God want of the Jews, should they try to make converts or not? There are many varieties of religious Judaism, all of them seeking to be responsive to the primary prophetic experience in a way that feels right for them.

One of these varieties was that of a small group of Jews who saw the nature and purpose of God disclosed in a new and vital way in the life, death and (they believed) resurrection of Jesus of Nazareth. Their new movement was soon flooded with Gentiles, and the Christian Church split off from Judaism as a movement with distinctive views about a God who could become incarnate. Still, there were always many varieties of Christianity. Some of them made the claim to be 'orthodox' – that is, holding correct beliefs as defined by some authority. But they did not agree on what that authority should be, some (Roman Catholics) preferring the Bishop of Rome, others (Eastern Orthodox) insisting on full councils of all the Bishops, and yet others (Protestants) denying that there was any human authority with the right to define correct belief for everybody else.

Islam might be seen as a faith that seeks to return to a more prophetic tradition, not being sympathetic to the idea of an incarnate God, and wishing to open the Law (*Shari'a*) to the whole world, not just the Jews. Traditions within Islam range from sorts of Sufism which almost seem to identify the world with God to forms of Sunni Islam which see God as wholly other than creation. When the thought of Aristotle was used to expound an idea of God, Muslim philosophers were the first to apply it, and established very independent schools of philosophical thought which, unfortunately, have not on the whole endured. Thus the Semitic traditions of religion have much in common, though they differ both among themselves and with one another about the precise interpretation to be given to their revelatory origin. Revelation, it is very clear, must be very unclear, if so much genuine and conscientious diversity can exist among those who seek to adhere to it.

There is another main set of traditions in which revelation from God is claimed, that of India. There the Vedas and Upanishads are traditionally said to have been revealed to ancient sages by the gods. They form the basis of traditions that tend to see the personal God (or the gods) as manifestations of *Brahman,* Absolute Reality, and the universe as in some sophisticated sense one with the Absolute. The variety of traditions ranges from an intensely personal theism, in Vaishnava schools, to the non-dualistic philosophy of Sankara.

In all these traditions, there are prophets or religious teachers who are taken to be the primary source of revelation, and then there are many different schools of interpreting or developing that revelation. Since cultures and peoples are so different, it is not surprising that there are many different ideas of God, and many different paths towards knowledge of God. Yet the situation is not that the main religious traditions are simply in total conflict and opposition. There is in all this variety of tradition and interpretation a great amount of convergence in thinking about God, as writers puzzle out what is meant by a being of supreme power and value. It can fairly be said that the differing strands of thought in this book are all found, in some form, in each major religious tradition.

It is important to remember, and I have tried to stress, that thinking about God is not just an intellectual exercise. It is thinking about the best way to live as a human being, and about the deepest understanding of the world in which we live. For some people, God does not help at all, and is even an obstacle to an honest understanding of the universe and the adoption of a free and mature way of life. For other people, thinking about God remains at an oversimplified level, the level of a supernatural person in the sky. But in a world where we can all cope, more or less, with computers and air travel, it is not hard to be more aware of the centuries of reflection that have gone into thinking about God, and also of new possibilities of thinking about God in our really quite recent scientific understanding of nature.

When we start to think about God, we will all start from some particular viewpoint. What we have learned as children, what we have read and experienced, what our own society teaches us about natural ways of feeling and acting, all these things will provide us with a viewpoint from which to start. It is then possible, in our world, to come to a fuller knowledge of the viewpoints of others, and thereby to broaden and deepen our own perspective. It will never be possible, or desirable, to see from every point of view at once. But it is possible to expand our knowledge and experience so as to have the widest view that is available to us. Reflecting on the history of ideas about God, seeing how such ideas have developed and interacted, noticing how they have emphasised different aspects of human experience and expressed different fundamental human commitments, our own initial ideas are bound to change. Such change is not to be feared, for it can hardly fail to be a growth in knowledge and understanding.

Conclusion: seven ways of thinking about God

It is time to take stock of the ground that has been covered in this book. It might be tempting to think that, after looking at all these views of God, we can at last come up with the truth. The temptation should, however, be resisted. What we can realistically hope for is to avoid the crudest misunderstandings of the beliefs of others, and to see the uncertainties and unclarities of many of our own beliefs. We might also hope to obtain more clarity about the beliefs to which we are most fundamentally committed. While any reflective human belief must be to some extent exploratory and provisional, there will nevertheless be some beliefs we cannot renounce without renouncing our own integrity. To discover what these are, and to formulate them more sensitively and judiciously, is one goal of philosophical reflection.

With this in mind, if you ask what the most fundamental thing is about believing in God, I would say that it is believing that there is a personal ground of being, that the universe is in some sense grounded in a personal reality. The universe is not the product of blind unconscious will, law or accident. It is the product of a reality which we may rightly call conscious, purposive, wise and good. Moreover, a form of relationship is possible to that transcendent personal reality which leads towards an overcoming of egoism and a life of compassion, wisdom and bliss. It becomes appropriate to approach all our experiences as encounters with that personal reality, embedded in and mediated through the extremely complex network of physical laws and finite free acts that go to form the world in which we exist.

If the universe is in some sense founded on a personal reality, the nature of this reality has been construed in a number of different ways.

We may at last have reached an age in which each of us can be spiritual heir to the whole religious history of humanity.

I have tried to pick out seven main sorts of interpretation, and present them in a sympathetic yet critical way. Overall, my view is that they all express aspects of the reality of the divine which need to be considered in any attempt to achieve an adequate idea for oneself.

The powers of being

In those religious traditions that have many gods, the personal character of the world is split into many varying facets, generated by a combination of visionary imagination and revelatory disclosure in a particular environment and history. Each divine symbol discloses some creative or destructive energy or power of reality, as it has become known in history, in nature, and in the minds of men and women. These powers evoke mystery and dread, terror and ecstasy, and all point to moments of meeting at which finite things and events seem to become transparent to a depth beyond them. We can cultivate that sense, in the solitude of the natural world, in the experience of great works of art, in the warmth of friendship. Feeling the presences of the gods, we know that we are not imprisoned in an alien mechanical machine, but are integral parts of an interconnected web of energies which have their own 'feeling' or atmosphere. The gods have not fled from the world. They are its moods and forms of being. Though nature is not itself divine, if we do not feel and respect its multitudinous forms of inwardness, which is what the gods imaginatively represent, we neglect an important element of human knowledge of being.

The one beyond speech

Nevertheless, in both Indian and Semitic traditions, major prophets and saints arose who taught that eventually one must go beyond the gods to a reality in the face of which all words fail, where there is being devoid of form, a darkness not by lack of light, but by an excess of light which dazzles and blinds. There, all that is possible is a 'dark gazing', a simple contemplation which discerns no duality of self and other, of diversity and division. The path of contemplative prayer is a journey towards an ideal which is never fully attained. It is a journey from particular attachments towards that dispassionateness – which the Greeks called *apatheia,* though the English word 'apathy' hardly seems appropriate – which has set aside all selfish desire, even for a friendly personal God. The journey could involve, at its beginning, passionate attachment to a personal form of the divine. It will involve, along the way, love of and unselfish desire for many varied forms of goodness and beauty. But as it progresses, it enters into silence, beyond change and decay, beyond beauty and goodness, beyond intelligence and mind. And then there is nothing further to be said. As the *Tao te Ching* puts it, those who speak do not know; those who know do not speak.

This is a hidden and inward journey, and it is a journey from which there is a return, and that is part of the journey too. Then, knowledge of beauty, truth and friendship are given back to those who have renounced them, who are not bound by them, who do not fear their loss. For the reality beyond the gods is the origin of all things, and is so through what we must think of as consciousness and intention, in order that we might avoid thinking of it merely as some sort of blind energy or force. Thus, the prophets tell us, we must think of God as the one creator of all things, transcending but not less than all we think of as perfections, beyond all thought and yet descending to make itself known in the finite forms, whether words or images, by which we can learn each day to participate in eternity.

So religion moves between imagery and iconoclasm, from the multitude of embodied gods in ancient Greece to the imageless assemblies of Islam. Yet in each tradition images, whether verbal or visual, are both essential and ephemeral. And in each, for the discerning, what is offered, in the presentation of images and their sublation, is a training in virtue, the formation of individual life in the pattern of human excellence, in relation to that which is conceived to be supreme objective self-existent value.

The perfect good

The notion of value is essential to the idea of God. For though God is much more than we can conceive, God is certainly not less than the best we can conceive. Supreme value must be conceived as existent, as entertained in consciousness, and as valued or enjoyed, since otherwise it would not be actualised value, but a mere potentiality for evaluation. In the Indian traditions this actualised value is characterised as *sat–cit–ananda* (being, consciousness and bliss). In the Christian tradition it may in a not dissimilar way be seen as the self-affirming power of being (the cause or 'father' of all being), the consciousness of being (the divine *Logos* or Wisdom), and the love of being (the Spirit of joy and delight). Some traditions are content to speak of God as unrestricted being which is pure goodness, and is blissful in the contemplation of that goodness. It is not hard to see the common theme, in most of the world's traditions about God, that the Supreme Good is existent, and has the nature of consciousness and bliss. It is not enough to speak of darkness and silence alone, without some intuition of its supreme goodness which transforms our lives as we contemplate it.

The Good, which is beatitude in contemplation of the highest perfection, is still unimaginable by us. We can only think of the sort of finite goods, always mixed with imperfection, essentially temporal and transient, that we experience. We can only form the vaguest idea of a supreme perfection which is unchangeable and unmixed with imperfection. But to believe in God is to believe that the whole universe descends from, or is generated by, such a perfection. From this perspective, the moral life is one of seeking to apprehend and respond to the Good and, so far as it is possible, to reflect its perfection in the unique particularities of our own lives.

In most of the religions of the world, sacrifice has been seen as the right way to approach the gods, and sacrifice is seen by the major prophets not as an offering of an animal's life to obtain favours for ourselves, but as the offering of the self to God to be used for the sake of others. Through this offering, God is able to realise, at least to some extent, the divine creativity, compassion and love through human lives. To believe in God is to give yourself to goodness, to affirm, in a leap of faith, that the claim of goodness is absolute, and to commit yourself without reserve to the power of its presence and the possibility of its actualisation in the world. That commitment to the absoluteness of the moral demand and to the realisation of goodness in the face of injustice and selfish pleasure alike, is at the heart of believing in God.

The self-existent creator

Believing in God is primarily a practical commitment, not a matter of adopting a speculative hypothesis. Nevertheless, it does involve some theoretical commitments, too, and it is natural to try to make these as coherent as possible with all that we know about the nature of the universe. If God is perfection, consciousness and bliss then it is necessary to ask how this God is related to the universe as we know it to be. For Plato the universe was shaped by an architect who used the Good as his pattern. For Aristotle the perfect Good does not change, but the universe tends to be attracted to imitate it. For the Hebrew prophets, however, God is the absolute creator of the universe, and it is that idea of creation that has come to be generally definitive of God in subsequent thought.

There is a common tradition of thought about creation in Jewish, Christian and Muslim thought, partly because all depend on Plato and Aristotle to a great extent for the ideas they use. God is the necessarily existent and supremely perfect ground of all beings, and the universe is actual because God consciously and intentionally chooses to actualise it out of all the possible worlds God envisages, for the sake of the distinctive goods it contains, which would not otherwise exist. God is timeless, changeless and untouched by suffering or evil, and the whole universe proceeds from the sovereign will of God by an eternal decision which cannot be affected by anything creatures do or think. The best human life is one that seeks to turn towards the divine perfection in loving submission to the omnipotent will of God, and to hope for a fuller vision of God in the life hereafter. Prayer is the orientation of the changing and imperfect to the changelessly perfect, a quest for the vision of eternity amidst the things of time, and for union with a love that cannot be changed, injured or defeated by anything in heaven or on earth.

Since such a view has to be worked out philosophically, there is a danger that we may be distracted by the System, and become obsessed with defending particular philosophical theses against allegedly incorrect or 'heretical' alternatives. But if we remember that all systems are provisional, subject to change in the light of new knowledge, and imperfect in understanding, then there is a point in seeking to construct an elegant, coherent and plausible vision of the universe as the creation of one self-existent ground of being. The Augustinian–Thomist synthesis is able to present religion as a rational enterprise, which can thus fulfil the human desire for intelligibility as well as for moral and spiritual insight. In so far as we can see all things in the universe as dependent on a self-existent reality beyond them, as rationally ordered by an ultimate wisdom and truth and as participating in a changeless perfection which is the source of their being, we share in this religious vision.

The self-realising spirit

The price to pay for constructing a System is that it will have to change if and in so far as human knowledge changes. From the seventeenth century in Europe the Platonic axiom that the perfect is changeless and the world is poised between the real and the unreal began to be undermined by the thought that all perfections must exist in time, and that the Platonic Forms or Ideas are only abstractions. So, in the thought of Hegel, the universe is seen as the self-realisation of Absolute Spirit, in which the divine potential can be actualised in historical forms, and those actualisations can then be integrated into the divine experience. Time and change, development and struggle, become essential to God.

For such a scheme, human life is a participation in the divine self-realisation, and true prayer is the creation and contemplation of many finite forms of value in the historical process. Process philosophy is a variant on the Hegelian system, produced by mixing it with elements drawn from Leibniz and from radical libertarianism, which gives the decisions of finite agents a more prominent place in the scheme of things. In the end, the experience of God is shaped by the processes of history, and gives those processes everlasting meaning and significance, as they are integrated into the divine experience of the world. To see history as the realisation of the divine potentiality, human lives as called to play a part in this actualisation of new possibilities, and every good as conserved in God for ever, is to give to human history and to human actions a truly transcendent significance.

The ultimate goodness of being

Nineteenth-century ideas of an evolutionary universe long predate Charles Darwin's theory of evolution, and undoubtedly influenced his exposition of it. Nevertheless, Darwin's account expresses a general change in the perception of the universe which accelerated in the nineteenth century. This is a change from seeing the universe as wholly rational and intelligible, the stage on which a positive evolutionary goal could gradually be realised, to seeing it as a product of blind impersonal laws, operating without consciousness or purpose, and blundering by chance from one temporary and makeshift survival mechanism to the next. Evolution began as a product of spiritual Romanticism, but was taken over by the forces of pessimistic materialism.

In the twentieth century, philosophers were so impressed by the achievements of the natural sciences, and so depressed by the endless quarrels and trivial pursuits of the philosophers and theologians, that they tended to separate faith in God completely from an understanding of the natural world. A materialistic interpretation of nature, of the objective world, was accepted, and religion became a matter of subjectivity and personal life choices.

There is here the important point that believing in God is an intensely practical matter. Prompted by the thought of Kierkegaard, we might say that believing in God is passionate commitment to the ultimate goodness of being. It is not primarily the acceptance of a grand metaphysical scheme, or the acceptance of some historical truths as certain. It is committing yourself in response to a discernment of goodness, in faith that moral effort will not be in vain, and that goodness will be conserved and vindicated in the face of evil and failure.

Yet such a commitment cannot be divorced from an assessment of what the universe is really like. You could commit yourself to the goodness of being in an impersonal, non-purposive, accidental universe. That might be, as for the French novelist Albert Camus, a choice for absurdity which carries a certain moral grandeur. But if it is *being* that is affirmed as good, and if the universe is part of being, as it most certainly is, then those who believe in God have to do something to try to show that the universe is good, or at least is a condition of the possibility of some ultimate good. That is where both historical and metaphysical claims, however objectively uncertain, have a place.

The personal ground of being

Hegelian and process thinkers may sometimes seem to have been caught up in the cogs of their own elaborate metaphysical machine. But it is surely right to make some effort, however tentative, to square scientific knowledge with belief in God. It is slightly odd to commit yourself unreservedly to the goodness of being if the whole thing is so accidental and random that it might, at any moment, for all you know, wipe out every living being for ever.

In fact the scientific world-picture is not one of a succession of random accidents. The astounding progress of modern physics shows a structure of laws of intricacy and elegance, in which hardly anything is left to pure chance. This is a law-governed universe, and even if there is an important degree of indeterminacy and probability at many levels of nature, the process as a whole can be well predicted from a knowledge of the basic laws and constants of nature. There seem to be deep necessities in the nature of things, so it does not fit the facts very well to see the cosmos as just a product of sheer chance.

The question of purpose is more difficult. Sciences like physics attempt to disregard questions of purpose. A purpose is a state which is valued or desired by a rational agent, and which that agent intends to bring about by some appropriate process. Physics does not deal with desires, agents or intentions, and so it simply has no view on whether there are purposes in nature. The theist will say that God is a reality analogous to an agent with desires and intentions, who brings the universe about in order to achieve some state that God values.

We cannot check whether such a God exists. But we can ask if the universe looks as if it is well ordered to achieve some states of value. If it is, then at least God is a going hypothesis – and remember, God is not posited primarily as a hypothesis. The hypothesis just seems to follow from the passionate commitment to the goodness of being.

Physics shows that the universe is well ordered. The relation of the basic physical forces which allows atoms to form in increasingly complex configurations, the apparent propensity of self-replicating molecules to form and build organic substances, and the formation of central nervous systems from which consciousness and intention originate in finite organisms, all display a degree of complex and stable organisation which is breathtaking. Since states of value involve the existence of states of conscious enjoyment, the formation of brains does make possible the existence of states of value (conscious beings enjoying things), when previously, throughout the long history of the universe, there were none. Naturally, since God always experiences the processes of the cosmos, there were values before the existence of finite sentient beings, the values existing in God as a result of creating and experiencing the cosmos. But the values experienced by finite beings will nevertheless be quite new and distinctive. It looks as though the processes of the universe are ordered to the production of new values.

So the universe can plausibly be seen as purposive, as realising the purpose of a personal God. Science does not compel us to see it as random and purposeless. What we might see is a simple set of intelligible laws leading by probabilistic processes to worthwhile goals. It goes without saying that you do not have to agree with this view either. You could say that the goals are not good enough; they do not counterbalance the cruelty of evolution and all the suffering it involves. That does not deny purpose, but it questions the goodness of the process. The theist's response may be to say that nature progresses through trial and error and struggle towards realised value, and that will involve blind alleys and defeats, as well as new breakthroughs and successes. Such a process is necessary for the existence of the sorts of conscious agents humans are; God shares in the suffering and can help to bring good out of it; and God integrates all realised good into the divine experience, which can then be shared by finite sentient beings.

Some people think of evolution as a desperate struggle for existence against all odds, so that life only exists at all by temporary good luck. But you can also think of it as a creative striving for higher life, whose eventual success, despite many setbacks, is assured by the fundamental principles of the natural order itself. Charles Darwin himself could not make his mind up between these two views. Science cannot resolve that difference of vision, which indeed marks a deep difference between atheism and belief in God.

In short, this cosmos could be a product of blind necessity, in which human lives are a mere flicker in a process which is bound to end in oblivion, as energy inevitably drains away over billions of years. But the cosmos could also be an arena intended for the realisation of created powers which will generate consciousness, desire, intention, purpose and value, perhaps on countless planetary systems over countless aeons. As the physical cosmos dies, its creator can take all the values the cosmos has realised, and ensure that they are conserved for ever in the divine consciousness. God may even make it possible for finite agents to experience those values in their fuller, eternal, context. That is what it may be like if there is indeed a personal ground of being, and those who are passionately committed to the ultimate goodness of being will at least find it natural to hope or believe or affirm that there is.

We might be very unsure of the details of any grand system which we devise. Both Kierkegaard and Wittgenstein warn us against metaphysical inflation. But a passionate commitment to goodness, and to the goodness of being, is connected to an assessment of what the being we experience and come to know better through scientific analysis is like. To this extent the believer in God will be committed, with varying degrees of assurance and hope, to the view that the cosmos results from consciousness and intention, that its evil can be sublated or redeemed and its good conserved, and that we who are its children might be able to experience, in some manner, the completion of the cosmic process in the divine consciousness. That is the essence of believing in God.

This commitment and this hope spring from deep natural impulses of the heart. They are expressed in symbols and images which are richly imaginative and varied, taking on the colouring of the many cultures in which they are formed. But in the end they do not arise simply from human speculation. They arise as responses to revelation – not perhaps to a set of clear and unambiguous propositions from on high, but to a discernment of a unique reality which discloses itself as both darkness and light, multiple and one, terrible and fascinating, intelligible and incomprehensible, changeless and endlessly creative, having the form of the personal and yet infinite and unbounded. That discernment may be, it usually will be, dependent on originative insights given in moments of vision, inspiration and divine empowerment to the prophets and saints of faith, which we can use to guide us on our way. For the most part, we must be content to catch partial reflections of those insights. Our own discernments, though they may be real enough, will be mostly fleeting and inconstant, nostalgically remembered or passionately sought.

Nevertheless, even for us the commitment of faith is a response to a vision of goodness whose attraction, once seen, is irresistible. The religious quest, the search for God, is a quest for the fuller dawning of a light once dimly seen, of creative powers obscurely felt, of haunting intimations of a personal ground of being, a hope for a time when we might no longer see transcendence as in a glass darkly, but finally meet face to face.

The seventeenth-century poet George Herbert expressed, in his own Christian context, that final vision perhaps as well as anyone can:

> Love bade me welcome: yet my soul drew back,
> Guiltie of dust and sinne.
> But quick-ey'd Love, observing me grow slack
> From my first entrance in,
> Drew nearer to me, sweetly questioning,
> If I lack'd any thing.
> A guest, I answer'd, worthy to be here:
> Love said, You shall be he.
> I the unkinde, ungratefull? Ah my deare,
> I cannot look on thee.
> Love took my hand, and smiling did reply,
> Who made the eyes but I?
> Truth Lord, but I have marr'd them: let my shame
> Go where it doth deserve.
> And know you not, sayes Love, who bore the blame?
> My deare, then I will serve.
> You must sit down, sayes Love, and taste my meat:
> So I did sit and eat.

GEORGE HERBERT (1593–1633), 'Love',
Penguin Book of English Verse, p. 113

Find out more . . .

Richard Swinburne's tetralogy on God, beginning with *The Existence of God* (Oxford, Oxford University Press, 1979), is beautifully clear but very difficult. He has written *Is There a God?* (Oxford, Oxford University Press, 2001) as a simpler introduction to his thinking.

Paul Tillich's major work is his *Systematic Theology*, and chapters 9–11 are about God. *The Courage to Be* (London, Nisbet, 1952; London, Collins, 1962) is a good shorter introduction to his thought.

John Oman's book *Grace and Personality* (New York, Association Press, 1961) gives a good, readable exposition of Christian personalism, as does Peter Bertocci's *The Person God Is* (London, Allen & Unwin, 1970), from a different perspective.

On science and religious belief, Arthur Peacocke's *Paths from Science towards God* (Oxford, Oneworld, 2001) is an excellent introduction by an organic chemist and theologian.

My book *Religion and Creation* (Oxford, Oxford University Press, 1996) might be seen as complementary to this book, treating similar themes from a different angle.

Bibliography

Al-Ghazali, *The Niche for Lights*, trans. W.H.T. Gairdner (London, The Royal Asiatic Society, 1952).

The Cloud of Unknowing, ed. James Walsh (New York, Paulist Press, 1981).

Egan, Harvey, *An Anthology of Christian Mysticism* (Collegeville, MN, Liturgical Press, 1991).

Frazer, James, *The Golden Bough* (Harmondsworth, Penguin, 1966 [1922]).

Hume, David, *An Inquiry Concerning Human Understanding* (Indianapolis, BobbsMerrill, 1955 [1748]).

Maimonides, Moses, *The Guide for the Perplexed*, trans. M. Friedländer (London, Routledge & Kegan Paul, 1904).

Nietzsche, Friedrich, *The Anti-Christ*, trans. R.J. Hollingdale (Harmondsworth, Penguin, 1969 [1888]).

Pascal, Blaise, *Pensées*, trans. A.J. Krailsheimer (Harmondsworth, Penguin, 1966).

The Penguin Book of English Christian Verse, ed. Peter Levi (Harmondsworth, Penguin, 1984).

The Penguin Book of English Verse, ed. John Hayward (Harmondsworth, Penguin, 1956).

Plato, *Symposium*, trans. Walter Hamilton (Harmondsworth, Penguin, 1951).

Rhees, Rush (ed.) *Recollections of Wittgenstein* (Oxford, Oxford University Press, 1984).

St John of the Cross, *Collected Words of St John of the Cross*, trans. Kieran Kavanaugh, OCD and Otilio Rodriguez, OCD (Vienna, ICS Publications, 1991).

Schleiermacher, Friedrich, *On Religion: Speeches to its Cultured Despisers*, trans. Richard Crouter (Cambridge, Cambridge University Press, 1988 [1799]).

Swinburne, Richard, *The Coherence of Theism* (Oxford, Oxford University Press, 1977).

Thomas, R.S., 'Via Negativa', in *Collected Poems 1945–1990* (London, J.M. Dent, 1993).

The Vedanta Sutras, trans. George Thibaut in *Sacred Books of the East* (Delhi, Motilal Banarsidass, 1962).

Ward, Keith, *Christianity: A Short Introduction* (Oxford, Oneworld, 2000).

Wittgenstein, Ludwig, *Lectures and Conversations on Aesthetics, Psychology and Religious Belief*, ed. Cyril Barrett (Oxford, Basil Blackwell, 1966).

Acknowledgements

The author and publisher wish to thank the following individuals and organisations for supplying the illustrations reproduced in this book.

Page 6, The Dance of Apollo with the Muses by Baldassarre Peruzzi (1481–1536) Palazzo Pitti, Florence, Italy/Bridgeman Art Library; page 48 © Carlos Reyes-Manzo/Andes Press Agency; page 64, St. John of the Cross and St. Theresa of Avila (engraving) by French School (16th century) Bibliotheque Nationale, Paris, France/Bridgeman Art Library; page 77, Mural in the church at Samakov, Bulgaria © Sonia Halliday Photographs; page 91, Immanuel Kant by Hagemann © Mary Evans Picture Library; page 104, Luna Marble Head of Plato, Roman, 1st century AD Fitzwilliam Museum, University of Cambridge, UK/Bridgeman Art Library; page 121, School of Athens, 1510–11 (fresco) by Raphael (Raffaello Sanzio of Urbino) (1483–1520) Vatican Museums and Galleries, Vatican City, Italy/Bridgeman Art Library; page 130, Satan and Beelzebub, from the first book of 'Paradise Lost' by John Milton (1608–74) engraved by Charles Laplante (d.1903) c.1868 (engraving) by Gustave Dore (1832–83) (after) private collection/Bridgeman Art Library; page 155 © Topham Picturepoint; page 160, by permission of Shri Kanchi Kamakoti Peetham; page 180 © Anglo-Australian Observatory/Royal Observatory, Edinburgh. Photograph from UK Schmidt plates by David Malin; page 200, photo: AKG London, Moritz Naehr; page 226, Friedrich Wilhelm Nietzsche (1844–1900) 8 December 1988 (w/c on paper) by Horst Janssen (contemporary artist) Private collection/Bridgeman Art Library.

Index

Page numbers in *italic* refer to pictures. Some subheadings are listed in age order to aid coherence.

Index

and religious practice 207–12, 249
  'non-realism' and expression 212–15
and truth as subjectivity 190–1
studies on 218
see also faith
Bertocci, Peter 220, 232
Bhagavad Gita 27–8, 188, 215
The Bible, New Testament:
  and Judaic law 78–9
  Jesus, the perfect image 113
  see also Hebrew Bible
Blake, William 11–14, 18
Book of Common Prayer 31–2
Brahman 59, 160, 161
Braithwaite, Richard 202–3
Brightman, Edgar 220
Buber, Martin 31–3

Calvin, John:
  and God's commandments 80–3
  and justification through faith 83–4
Calvinists 18–19
categorical imperative 90–6
causal powers:
  and free-will 131–3
  Hegel's and Whitehead's theories 172–6
  Tillich's theory 197
  see also evolution, theory of
Christianity:
  and Aristotelian thought 120
  Calvin and the Commandments 80–4
  and Jewish and Muslim thought 246–7
  and Judaic law 73–5, 78–80
  and Platonic thought 113–14
  see also God of the Christians; God of the
    philosophers
Cloud of Unknowing, The 63
compatibilism 132–3, 171
contemplation 63, 244
cosmos:
  in relation to personal being 246–52
  omniscience and creative freedom 227–8
  place of humanity in 111–12, 146–8, 167–71
creation:
  as self-expression of Spirit 148–52
  common tradition of thought 246–7
  ex nihilo (out of nothing) 114–17, 121–2
  Platonic view 108–9, 112–13
  as timeless act 133–6
    and faith and understanding 136–8
  by a God of intrinsic value 117–19
creative spirit 4–6
creed:
  as expression of the unutterable 202–3
  Athanasian 234
Critique of Pure Reason 89, 94, 100

damnation 83–4
Dante 99–100
Darwin, Charles 152, 186, 225, 248
death 28, 187–8, 204
Demiurge (world-shaper) 108, 112–13:
  Aristotelian thought and 119
  Augustinian thought and 114–18, 124
demons 27
demonstrations for God's existence:
  and absolute faith 189
  as intrinsic value 118
  Kant's reasoning 94–5
  necessity theory 127–8
  the 'five ways,' 53–7
Descartes, Rene 7–9, 35, 101
determinism *see* necessity, theory of
Deutero-Isaiah 40–1
dialectic of history:
  as divine self-expression 148–52
  communism and fascism and 152–7
  human suffering and 165–6
  towards divine self-realisation 167–71,
    247–8
  ideologically challenged 171–7
  and personal, relational God 232–3
Dialogues Concerning Natural Religion 13
dietary prohibitions 69–70, 71
Dionysius 57–8
Divine Comedy, The 99–100
divine grace 93–4, 98
divine purpose 227–8
divine self-realisation 167–71
diviners and seers 26
doctrine:
  of analogy 60–2
  of creation *ex nihilo* 114–17
  of marriage 95
  of the Trinity 234–8
dogma and creed 202–3
'Dover Beach' 177, 186
dualism 108–9

Eastern Orthodoxy 44–5
Egyptian monotheism 42
Elijah 40
Enlightenment 181–2
essence and energy of God 44–5
evil:
  as human disposition 93
  Devil as symbol of 198
  and necessity theory 123–9
    free-will defence 129–33
  and omnipotent God 223–4
  without belief in goodness 224–7
  elimination of 233
  see also suffering

Index

Index